Eating to Excess

**Recent Titles in the
Praeger Series on the Ancient World**

Eating to Excess

The Meaning of Gluttony and the Fat Body in the Ancient World

Susan E. Hill

Praeger Series on the Ancient World
Bella Vivante, Series Editor

PRAEGER

AN IMPRINT OF ABC-CLIO, LLC
Santa Barbara, California • Denver, Colorado • Oxford, England

Library of Congress Cataloging-in-Publication Data

Hill, Susan E.
  Eating to excess : the meaning of gluttony and the fat body in the ancient world / Susan E. Hill.
    p. cm. — (Praeger series on the ancient world)
  Includes bibliographical references and index.
  ISBN 978-0-313-38506-3 (hardback) — ISBN 978-0-313-38507-0 (ebook)
1. Food habits—History.   2. Gluttony—History.   3. Human body—History.   4. Obesity—History.   5. Excess (Philosophy).
6. Civilization, Ancient.   7. History, Ancient.   I. Title.
  GT2850H49   2011
  394.1'2—dc23   2011021511

ISBN: 978-0-313-38506-3
EISBN: 978-0-313-38507-0

15   14   13   12   11   1   2   3   4   5

This book is also available on the World Wide Web as an eBook.
Visit www.abc-clio.com for details.

Praeger
An Imprint of ABC-CLIO, LLC

ABC-CLIO, LLC
130 Cremona Drive, P.O. Box 1911
Santa Barbara, California 93116-1911

This book is printed on acid-free paper ∞

Manufactured in the United States of America

Copyright Acknowledgments

Portions of Chapter 3 were first published in Hill, Susan. "Gluttony, Corpulence, and the Good Life in Plato's *Timaeus*." *Soundings* 91.1–2 (2008): 89–108. Permission to reprint given by Soundings, The University of Tennessee Press.

Contents

Illustrations

Series Foreword

The lives of ancient peoples may seem far removed, socially, linguistically, and especially technologically, from the concerns of the modern world. Yet the popularity of historical subjects on both the big and little screens—*Troy, Alexander, 300;* HBO's *Rome,* the many History Channel programs—demonstrates the abiding fascination the ancient world continues to exert. Some people are drawn to the dramatic differences between the ancient and modern; others seek to find the origins for contemporary cultural features or the sources to provide meaning to our modern lives. Regardless of approach, the past holds something valuable for all of us. It is literally the root of who we are, physically through our actual ancestors, and culturally in establishing the foundations for our current beliefs and practices in religious, social, domestic and political arenas. The same ancients that we study were themselves drawn to their own pasts, often asking questions similar to the ones we pose today about our past.

The books in Praeger's series on the Ancient World address different topics from various perspectives. The ones on myth, sports, technology, warfare, and women explore these subjects cross-culturally, both within the ancient Mediterranean context—Egypt, Mesopotamia, Greece, Rome, and others—and between the ancient Mediterranean cultures and those of the Americas, Africa and Asia. Others, including the volumes on literature, men, sexuality, and on politics and society, examine their topic more specifically within a Greek or Greek and Roman cultural framework.

All renowned scholars committed to bringing the fruits of their research to wider audiences, each author brings a distinctive new approach to their topic that differentiates them from the many books that exist on the ancient world. A major strength of the first group is their multi-cultural breadth, which is both informative in its comprehensive embrace and provides numerous opportunities for comparative insights. Likewise, the books in the second group explore their topics in dramatically new ways: the inner life of male identity; the contributions of both women and men to the social polity; the ancient constructions of concepts of sexuality and eroticism.

Each volume offers amazing windows into aspects of ancient life. To-gether, the series provides an invaluable overview of how ancient peoples thought about themselves and the world, how they conducted their lives, and how they expressed their views in creative terms. Enjoy the journey into the past that each one provides.

Bella Vivante
Series Editor, Praeger Series on the Ancient World

Acknowledgments

No book is written without much assistance from others. I'd like to thank the National Endowment for the Humanities for support of my participation in a Summer Seminar for College and University Teachers, "The Seven Deadly Sins as Cultural Constructions in the Middle Ages," in 2006, at Darwin College in Cambridge, England. I have much gratitude for my colleagues in that seminar, and especially for Richard Newhauser, who was our excellent leader. My knowledge of the seven deadly sins, and the Middle Ages in general, was much enhanced by the work of that seminar, including memorable conversations with colleagues. Much gratitude goes to the Graduate College at the University of Northern Iowa for financial assistance during a semester-long Professional Development Assignment in Spring 2006, and a Summer Fellowship in 2007.

Many individuals offered their assistance during the writing of the manuscript. My colleagues in the Department of Philosophy and World Religions at the University of Northern Iowa helped in numerous ways. Bill Clohesy and Ed Boedeker assisted with translations of philosophical Greek. Margaret Holland and Martie Reineke read chapter drafts and gave excellent suggestions for improvements. Martie, especially, was always willing to give me a pep talk when I needed one, along with excellent practical suggestions for getting the writing done. Jerry Soneson encouraged me to teach a course on the seven deadly sins and on religion and food, so that I could try out my ideas in the classroom. Other colleagues and friends—Teresa Hornsby and Pat Geadelmann—along with my father, Ed Hill, also read chapter drafts and offered important ideas for making the work better and more readable. Any errors, needless to say, are my own.

My graduate assistant, Johnanna Ganz, meticulously read chapter drafts, found many of the art images, and performed many other textual duties, always competently and with a smile. Leah DeVries created all of the illustrations that appear here. This book could not have been written without the diligent work of the Interlibrary Loan folks at the Rod Library, University of Northern Iowa, especially Rosemary Meany. They acquired every book I requested, quickly and efficiently.

To the Fat Studies scholars at the Popular Culture Association, I owe a particular debt. Not only did they listen to my presentations on the topics in this book for a number of years, they helped me think about what it means to do work in Fat Studies. I am grateful for their support and collegiality.

I'd also like to thank Brian Romer, from the Romer Group, for putting me in touch with ABC-CLIO/Praeger Publishers and helping me to craft a successful book proposal. Michael Millman at Praeger offered much help at the beginning of this project, and Mariah Gumpert has seen it through with grace and diligence. Praeger Series on the Ancient World editor Bella Vivante has been as careful a manuscript reader as an author could possibly want.

Finally, life goes on during the process of writing a manuscript, and there are times when sympathetic ears and diversions are needed. Thanks to my parents, Ed and Aleta Hill, and my sister, Jeanne Dill, for familial support. For Friday lunches, weekend game-playing, and unending encouragement and friendship, I thank Elizabeth Wilson. Jen Heckmann, Linda McLaury, and Elizabeth have reminded me, on almost a weekly basis, that my life is much enhanced by meals at Rudy's Tacos, stories, and a lot of laughter. Faraway friends Jo Carter and Marilyn Sue Warren are two of my best cheerleaders. Colton Questra, our son, has grown up with this book and is always willing to offer much necessary distraction from the seriousness of it all. For that, I am deeply grateful. And to Brittany Flokstra—friend, partner, beloved—I dedicate this book to you. Your steadfast support, easy laughter, and tenacious love have made this—and all of my life's journeys—more meaningful.

Chronology of Important Dates

40,000–8000 BCE	Upper Paleolithic/Late Stone Age. Earliest examples of fat female statuettes found in Eurasia and across the Mediterranean.
3500–2500 BCE	Stone temples in Malta, which contain numerous fat figurines and statues, built during this time.
ca. 750 BCE	Homer's epics written.
600–500 BCE	Hebrew Bible book of Leviticus compiled.
ca. 446–386 BCE	Comedic playwright Aristophanes lives; composes works including "The Birds" and "The Frogs."
427–347 BCE	Plato, philosopher; author of the *Timaeus* and numerous other philosophical dialogues.
420–370 BCE	Hippocratic medical texts written; they are compiled in Alexandria as the Hippocratic Corpus around 280 BCE.
384–322 BCE	Aristotle, philosopher; author of the *Nichomachean Ethics* and other important philosophical works.
15 BCE**–50** CE	Philo of Alexandria blends Greek philosophical ideas with Jewish interpretations of the Hebrew scriptures in his numerous works.
4 BCE**–33** CE	Jesus's life.
27–66 CE	Petronius Arbiter, author of *The Satyricon* and friend of Roman Emperor Nero.
50–60	Paul writes his letters to the early Christian communities.
70	Final destruction of the Jewish Temple in Jerusalem.
80–90	The gospels of Matthew and Luke are written.
ca. 150–215	Clement of Alexandria, early Christian writer and moralist.
Late second–early third century	Egyptian-born writer, Athenaeus, lives in Athens and writes his 15–volume *Deipnosophistae* or *The Learned Banqueters,* an important compendium of Greek and Roman food, drink, and eating habits.

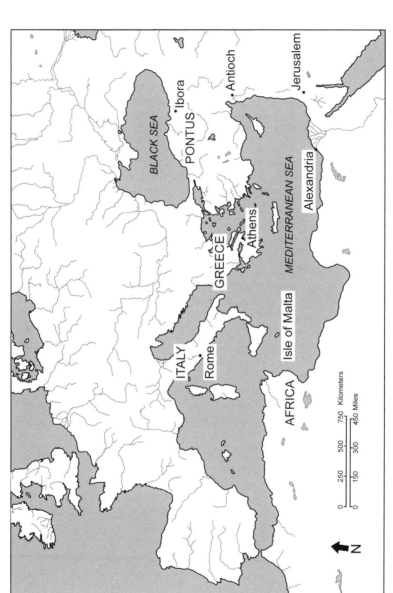

Mediterranean world around first century BCE

Introduction

The Glutton and the Fat Body
in the Ancient World

It's no sin to be fat, but it might as well be.[1]

—Jeremy Iggers

We antigluttonous moralists are never quite willing to pardon
fat. The burden of proof, we think, is upon fat people to adduce
evidence that they are not gluttons, for fat makes out a prima
facie case that they are guilty and thus owe the rest of us an
apology or an explanation for having offended.[2]

—William Ian Miller

This book began with a simple question: why is being fat considered to be a
moral failure? In the contemporary West, we are bombarded daily with a bar-
rage of messages from the media, the government, and the medical estab-
lishment that warn of the health dangers of obesity. It has been determined
that obesity should be identified as "a 'disease' " that has "a stipulated cure
(dieting) and an acknowledged etiology (gluttony)."[3] Gluttony makes you fat,
and, more often than not, being fat is not only perceived to be "unhealthy,"
it reveals undesirable moral dispositions: a lack of self-discipline, laziness
and a love of overindulgence. But why is this the case? How does the fat body
come to signify immoral behavior?

The purpose of this book is to explore the historical roots of the symbolic
relationship between fatness, gluttony, and immorality, beginning with biblical times and ending with Pope Gregory the Great's articulation of the seven
deadly sins in the sixth century CE. Many ancient texts, like the Bible, Plato's
Timaeus, Aristotle's *Nichomachean Ethics*, Athenaeus's *Deipnosophistae* or
The Learned Banqueters, Philo's *Laws*, and John Cassian's *Institutes*, along
with many others, explore ideas about fatness and gluttony, but these topics
have, until now, not been of primary interest to many scholars. Today, with
the continuing focus on, and interest in, the "obesity epidemic," ancient texts
can become important touchstones for gaining new perspectives on the contemporary world, because they can broaden the conceptual tools we have

when we examine current assumptions about what it means to be fat and to be gluttonous in the world today, as well as enhance our understanding of the past. Examining the ancient world complicates and enlarges our understanding of the moral meaning of both fat and gluttonous bodies by placing them in their historical, theological, philosophical, and medical contexts.

Indeed, looking to the past can help us gain perspective on the present because we discover that historical ideas about fat bodies and gluttons both confirm and challenge our own perceptions and assumptions. Ancient ideas about gluttons often corroborate contemporary Western views, where excessive behavior around food and drink is judged to be gluttonous; such conduct is often described in language that evokes death and disease as a result of immoderation. Consequently, when we examine historical ideas about gluttony, we find a pervasive and continuing strand of cultural thinking in the West that disparages overindulgence and privileges moderation and self-control.

At the same time, ancient ideas about the fat body challenge current assumptions about what it means to be fat. Contemporary Western culture, for instance, often makes an unquestioned assumption that being fat is the result of gluttony and therefore represents a lack of moral fortitude. Google images for "gluttony," and almost every picture shows fat people, many of them eating. And, it is hard to imagine that it has not always been the case that being a glutton means being fat and lazy. Yet, an exploration of what fat bodies mean in the ancient world suggests a complex and multilayered understanding of fatness and gluttony that, on most occasions, makes a clear distinction between being fat and being a glutton. Food scholars note that the equation of gluttony with fatness is rarely made in the ancient world, and not simply because ancient people did not have an understanding of calories, body metabolism, and the nutritional content of various foods. Rather, people in the ancient world usually distinguish being fat from being a glutton because anyone can behave gluttonously, and fat people are not inevitably gluttonous. Indeed, a fat body in the ancient world often positively represents wealth, abundance, and luxury. Recognizing the distinction between being fat and being a glutton suggests that contemporary assumptions about the unquestioned connection between fatness and gluttony are, indeed, assumptions, and that the meaning of body size and eating practices has changed over time. Moreover, the distinction between being fat and being a glutton is dependent on specific historical circumstances and ideas. This suggests that the current moral discourse about fatness does not reflect an unavoidable truth about fat bodies or their behaviors. To examine fat bodies and gluttons from a historical perspective can thus offer alternative ways of thinking about the meaning of body size and food behavior over time.

Ancient texts also challenge contemporary ideas about fat, gluttony, and gender. Although there is much contemporary research that suggests that both fat men and fat women experience weight-based prejudice and discrimination, fat women in Western society especially fat, white women are subject to more intense cultural scrutiny than men: Western standards of female beauty demand a slim body. Susan Bordo points out that, in the contemporary West, women are far more likely to diet than men and are more vulnerable to eating disorders than men. She also argues that within Western "religious and philosophical traditions, the capacity for self-management is decisively coded as male," while bodily desires requiring control are seen as female.[4] The texts examined in this book support these ideas: as we will see, ancient writers associate the social disruption of gluttonous activity with femininity, among other things. It is also the case, however, that the texts that discuss gluttony and its damaging effects are directed primarily to men, who clearly need to be persuaded to engage their capacity for self-discipline, perhaps under threat of effeminacy. While the threat of becoming "like a woman" if one indulges one's bodily desires too much does confirm the persistent association in Western culture of women with irrationality, excess, and overindulgence, the texts' focus on men's continuing need for self-control suggests that, historically, it is not only women who have been challenged to adhere to standards of bodily control, or who have been unable to overcome the insistence of bodily desires.

Examining the ancient meanings of fat bodies and gluttons gives us insight into the ways that Western culture has constructed ideas about self-control and moderation, how fat bodies and gluttons are distinguished and defined, and how bodily behavior both shapes and reflects gendered assumptions about the body. Recognizing both the similarities and differences between historical and contemporary ways of understanding the fat body and the gluttonous body reveals intriguing insights into the moral judgments often unquestioningly associated with the fat body in the contemporary world.

WHAT IS A FAT BODY?

Throughout this book, the word "fat" is used as a descriptor for body size. This is a more neutral adjective than the sometimes preferred "overweight" and "obese," which reflect a medical discourse not available in the ancient world. The word "fat" reminds us of the difficulty of determining how "fat" is defined, which further confirms the historical mutability of the meaning of body size. Attention to visual images and the language used to describe fat bodies in the ancient world exposes the difficulties in interpreting the meaning of those bodies. Although it is easy to look at an image or a statue and see that it is fat, it is quite another task to interpret the meaning and relevance of its fatness. In written contexts, words used to describe the fat body in the ancient world may not translate easily into contemporary English, or may express nuances that are no longer relevant to us. Moreover, it is difficult to ascertain exactly what being fat means in the ancient world. Examining images of fat bodies, as well as the words used to describe fat bodies in the ancient world, not only highlights the challenges of understanding the definition and meaning of the fat body historically, it underscores difficulties of those same issues in the contemporary world, as well.

The Fat Body and Female Fertility: Visual Images

There have always been fat people and representations of them. Perhaps most recognizable from the ancient world are images like the Venus of Willendorf (Figure 0.1). Fat female figurines like these, with large breasts, bellies, buttocks, and hips, have been found across Eurasia and the Mediterranean at more than 25 different archaeological sites.

There is much dispute among anthropologists and archaeologists regarding the meaning and function of such figurines. In her book *The Language of the Goddess,* Marija Gimbutas interprets statuettes such as these as goddess images that offer evidence of a prehistoric goddess worship that valued fertility, femininity, and motherhood. More recent investigations have questioned Gimbutas's assumptions about such images and have offered alternative interpretations that underscore the lack of information that we have about these figurines. For instance, such images could be toys or dolls, indicators of social or economic status, tokens used in ritual, sexual images, representations of actual women, or examples of a desired body type.

Whatever these kinds of statuettes represent, their size and shape appear to be significant. Many of these fat female statuettes have been dated to the

Figure 0.1 Venus of Willendorf. Limestone. Stone Age, Aurignacien, 25th millennium BCE

Upper Paleolithic or Late Stone Age (40,000–8000 BCE), when early humans survived by hunting and gathering their food supplies. Food was seasonally available, so there were times of plenty, and times of scarcity. Maintaining body weight when there is an irregular food supply is a challenge that correlates directly with female fertility: women must have at least 20 percent body fat in order to menstruate. People in ancient cultures may very well have recognized that women who were too thin were less likely to procreate than women who were fatter, and from both a biological and societal perspective, the female who was able to attain enough body fat to procreate would be desirable. In addition to any other meanings they might have, these statuettes may reveal the ancient recognition of the link between fat and fertility. If they are fertility images, these figurines could be used in a variety of different contexts, as ritual objects, as children's toys, or as sexual images, all of which would acknowledge the importance of fertility and childbearing in the continuing life of the group.

If these statuettes have to do with ideas of fertility, which seems likely, it is nonetheless difficult to say for certain whether these images represent goddesses or reveal a glorification of motherhood or femininity, as Gimbutas surmised. Indeed, many feminist anthropologists criticize the femininity and fecundity interpretation of these statuettes, arguing that such an interpretation reinforces the idea that gender roles, as well as attitudes about sex and reproduction, are unchanging and fixed over time. But such criticisms do not take into consideration the fatness of these figurines, which, when linked with fertility and sexuality, offers an unexpectedly positive valuation of the fat female body in the ancient world. Such an assessment runs counter to ideals of desirability and fertility in the contemporary West, where the vast majority of female images proffered by the mass media that fit those standards are thin. If we pay attention to the fatness of these figurines, we are confronted with the possibility that sexual attractiveness, fertility, and procreation were, in the past, affirmatively linked with fatness, as they are today in some cultures.

Support for the idea that fat and fertility are connected also comes from ancient Egypt. The Egyptian god Hapy is the divine representation of the annual flooding of the Nile river, which brought fertile soil to Egypt. Hapy is known for his sagging breasts and large belly, which are meant to represent his fecundity. Some representations of the pharaoh Akhenaten, who was associated with Hapy because he, too, brought prosperity to the land, also show him with a belly that hangs over the traditional kilt worn by Egyptian men.

A later, Hellenistic (first century BCE) figurine also supports the positive connection between fatness, fertility, and perhaps even divinity. A terracotta figurine of a woman with an object, possibly a basket, on her head, holding a shrine, riding a pig side-saddle, is probably a *calathus,* an object used to measure corn (Figure 0.2).

The shrine this figure holds implies that this object is religious in character, which further suggests that this statue may be associated with Demeter, the Greek goddess of corn and fertility. The plump pig, the figure's fat body,

Figure 0.2 Terracotta figurine of a woman riding on a pig. Hellenistic; made in Egypt, ca. first c. BCE

and the successful harvest make a connection to natural fecundity, which again supports a connection between fatness and fertility. Despite the significant historical and cultural distance between them, the fatness and fertility connection seen in the terracotta figurine supports an interpretation of statuettes like the Venus of Willendorf as fertility figures, as well.

Another set of fat figurines poses even greater questions about the meaning of the fat body in the ancient world. South of Sicily in the Mediterranean Sea lie the Maltese islands, which are famous for their numerous huge stone temples, built between 3500 and 2500 BCE. One of the most interesting features of these temples and the burial chambers beneath them are the many statues and figurines of fat humans that have been found. These images range in size from three centimeters to two meters, and because they have been found both at altar sites and in burial chambers, archaeologists speculate that they play a role in ancient Maltese rituals of life and death. Here we have examples of fat figurines that not only represent fertility, but may also give insight into ancient Maltese ideas of life after death.

Unlike the explicitly female images found in Eurasia, many of the images found in Malta have no obvious sexual features. There are a few statues that are clearly female, like the "Venus of Malta" found in the temple complex, Hagar Qim, or the Sleeping Lady of the Hypogeum (Figure 0.3). There are a number of unambiguously phallic carvings, too, but the majority of them are androgynous and exhibit no details, like genitalia or breasts, that would unequivocally mark them as female.

The fatness of these figures, especially their large thighs and buttocks, and their skirtlike clothes, has led to the assumption that they are female, and they have been labeled the "fat ladies of Malta."

Yet, the androgyny of these figures makes it difficult to associate them solely with goddess worship or fertility, though it is clear by the number of fat figurines unearthed that ancient Maltese culture found them to be symbolically important in some way. Excavations at the Brochtorff Circle site in the northern Maltese island of Goro have found numerous fat figurines buried with the dead, like the stunning sculpture of two fat figures sitting on a carved bed (Figure 0.4). Dressed in the skirtlike clothes common on this type of Maltese statuette, neither figure is explicitly male or female. One of the figures has a haircut with a pigtail, and both hold objects on their laps. One of these objects appears to be a tiny person; the other is a cup. Although

Figure 0.3 Sleeping Lady of the Hypogeum or burial chamber found at the Hal Saflieni site on the island of Malta

Figure 0.4 Brochtorff Circle pair found on the island of Gozo, Malta

the meaning of this figure is unclear, other sculptures in the central shrine appear to be more focused on animal and phallic imagery, suggesting a complex religious worldview that included more than a focus on female fertility.

The quantity of images found, along with their artistic sophistication, has suggested to anthropologists that Maltese culture around this time became intensely focused on itself, spending much time on building burial chambers and temples and showing little interest in developing new farming methods or building new villages. Malta was more isolated than other Mediterranean societies at this time, and, around 2500 BCE, it seems to have suffered from ecological degradation and overpopulation. The burial of these fat figurines with the dead may symbolize "an ideal afterlife in the face of population, ecological or religious stress."[5] If this is the case, it suggests that the fat, abundant body—especially in contrast with the wasted bodies of the dead—is a desired bodily form, associated with a perfect afterlife.

Although it is difficult to make unequivocal comments about the meaning of the ancient representations of fat bodies found in Eurasia, Egypt, and the Mediterranean, it is likely that they are connected to ideas of fertility and natural fecundity. Moreover, the quantity and locations of these images in temples and burial sites, especially in Malta, suggests that these images had positive and significant meaning for the people who created them. Whether they represented fertility or divinity, wealth or prestige, sexual appeal or a desired body type, these fat images offer a glimpse into a past where the fat body stood for pleasing, even enviable qualities in the human and the divine.

Defining the Fat Body: Fat Words

In addition to artistic representations of the fat body, ancient cultures also described fat bodies in writing, though the words used in those descriptions pose challenges for contemporary understanding. Much of the language we use today to talk about bodies—whether they are fat or not—is medical. The fat body today, in particular, is often framed within the medical discourse of obesity. Ancient texts that define or discuss the fat body do not define it in a way that aligns with the contemporary medical discourse of obesity, even though there are ancient medical texts that discuss fat bodies. Nor are there numerous texts devoted to defining and delineating fatness, unlike today, when attention to fatness is frequently a part of daily life. Such a difference could mean a number of things: a perception that the fat body is not a worthy or interesting subject for commentary, a lack of understanding—and consequent lack of attention—to what today are perceived as the deleterious effects of being fat, or a distinctly different way of perceiving the body where being fat is no different than any other kind of body type so that it does not deserve special consideration. Whatever the reasons are, when we recognize that the ancient world paid less attention to the fat body, and that it is difficult to know whether the ancient fat body aligns with contemporary ideas about the fat body, we are confronted with the notion that determining what fatness is, or who is fat and why, is a complicated and difficult task. Moreover, the complexities of defining the fat body highlight the idea that what it means to be fat not only changes over time, the meaning of fatness depends on the context in which it is discussed.

As an illustration of the challenge of the ancient fat body—and concomitantly the contemporary fat body—let us take a look at how the ancient fat body can be defined. Both conceptually and linguistically, the ancient fat body eludes clear classification. For instance, the most common ancient Greek word for fat (adj.) is *pachus,* a word that best translates as "thick" or "stout." It can refer to tree trunks, or thick or curdled liquids, as well as monetary wealth or rich, fertile soil. Another word frequently used to describe what may be the fat body is *sarkinos,* which means "of or like flesh," "fleshy." This word can refer to fleshy parts of the body, like the gums or gut, and can imply "substantial." *Pieira* means "fat" or "rich" and is usually used to describe land, or a rich meal, but is sometimes translated as "plump." These definitions carry multiple meanings that shift and change, depending on the context in which they are used. Given such classificatory difficulties, it seems erroneous to suggest, for example, that, "although there are no hints of the way by which human weight was measured" in ancient Hippocratic medical texts, we can nonetheless assume that Hippocrates does describe "what we call a morbidly obese individual."[6] Assuming that Hippocrates classifies bodies in the same way that we do even though there is no evidence that this is the case seems problematic, at best. It does suggest, however, that we should examine more closely what Hippocrates does say about the fat body, which we will do in Chapter 3.

Realizing that understanding the ancient fat body poses difficulties does, however, allow us to gain perspective on the challenges that contemporary definitions pose. Currently in the United States, definitions of obesity are determined by the federal government, based on reports of the National Institutes of Health (NIH). The most common way to define overweight and obesity is the Body Mass Index, or BMI, which measures weight in relation to height—a measurement that is ostensibly related to body fat—using the following formula: $\dfrac{\text{Weight} \times 703}{\text{height}^2}$. Before 1998, overweight had been defined by a BMI of 27.8 for men and 27.3 for women. Under this definition, a 5'7" man or woman weighing 165 pounds had a BMI of 25.8 $\left(\dfrac{115995}{4489} \equiv 25.8\right)$, which was not considered overweight. In September 1998, two NIH organizations, the National Heart, Blood, and Lung Institute (NHLBI) and the National Institute of Diabetes and Digestive and Kidney Diseases (NIDDK), redefined the overweight body—male or female—as greater than or equal to ($\geq$) 25–29, while the obese body was $\geq$30.[7] Overnight, the 5'7", 165-pound man or woman became overweight, along with 30 million others who had not been defined as overweight before. With so many more people now being defined as overweight, obesity quickly became a public health problem, even though actual bodies were the same size as they were before. In October 1999, the *Journal of the American Medical Association* published a theme issue on "Obesity Research," which used the phrase "obesity epidemic," thereby encouraging a model of disease to be attached to overweight bodies. Currently, there is dispute among scholars over the use of the term "epidemic" to describe shifts in body size, as well as the connection between fatness and disease, even though popular media rarely report on such disputes. Paul Campos and J. Eric Oliver, among others, continue to examine the medical evidence associated with the "obesity epidemic," and their work points out the ways in which medical information is misread or misunderstood. When placed alongside the difficulties of defining what is fat in the ancient world, these shifting contemporary definitions of, and disputes about, fatness underscore the precarious and ambivalent status of the fat body and emphasize the importance of examining not only what the fat body is, but what it means.

WHO IS A GLUTTON?

If, in the ancient world, the fat body is not necessarily gluttonous, then who is a glutton? In the ancient world, the gluttonous body is consistently associated with moral disapproval. Being a glutton reflects behaviors associated with the way a person eats and drinks that are always, inevitably, threatening to the well-being of society. Acting gluttonously consistently comes under moral censure, for it undermines social values of moderation, rationality, and appropriate gender behavior, even subverting the very definition of what it means to be human. Moreover, if one is perceived to be undermining social norms and values, it is possible to be accused of gluttony, whether one is actually a glutton or not. Indeed, many accusations of gluttony are just that: allegations of behavior that threaten social stability irrelevant of actual gluttonous behavior. Being accused of gluttony is one way of emphasizing that the person accused is undermining social boundaries and norms. From this perspective, gluttonous actions can be performed by anyone, whether a person is fat or not. Rarely is the assumption made that the glutton can be identified by his or her body size, for gluttony is defined by behavior, not appearance, and it is certainly not only fat people who may be responsible for destabilizing social ideals.

To give just one example of how gluttony in the ancient world is distinct from fatness, and how accusations of gluttony reflect social norms and values, let us think about how some early Christian theologians understood the first human sin in the Garden of Eden. Tempted by the snake, Eve and Adam eat the forbidden fruit and are forever banished from the utopian garden. Writing for his monastic community, fourth-century theologian John Cassian (360–430) argued that the sin in the Garden of Eden was gluttony, because it was an abuse of food that resulted in human "ruin and death."[8] Cassian writes that Adam "would not have been able to be deceived by gluttony had he not had something to eat and immediately and lawlessly misused it," though it is clear that "it was by gluttony that he took the food from the forbidden tree."[9] St. Aldhelm (639–709), founder and abbot of the monastery at Malmesbury in England, blamed Adam and Eve, "the inhabitant[s] of the newly made Paradise and the inexperienced owner[s] of earthly creation" for "tasting the forbidden nourishment with stuffed cheeks and smacking lips," and thereby falling "cruelly into the chasm of gluttony."[10] If a bite of a piece of fruit can be considered gluttony—an act that certainly did not result in a significant weight gain for Adam and Eve—then surely gluttony is being associated with the improper or disobedient use of food regardless of the quantity of food being eaten. This early Christian view of gluttony reveals a worldview in which the inappropriate use of food is not defined necessarily as excess, and fatness is not the primary mark of the misuse of food. Such a worldview is quite different from that of the contemporary West, where eating too much, being fat, and being gluttonous are viewed as much the same. Understanding the meaning of gluttony in the ancient world thus requires us to expand our definition of gluttonous behavior and think beyond the fat body as its only example.

THEORETICAL PERSPECTIVES

This book examines the meaning of the fat body and the glutton in the ancient Western world, using a variety of source materials written over a time period of more than a thousand years. Because of its focus on fatness and gluttony, this book can be situated in the field of Fat Studies, a growing interdisciplinary academic field that broadly explores historical, contemporary, and cross-cultural meanings and perceptions of the fat body, that examines the forms and effects of weight bias, prejudice and privilege, and that engages all topics and fields where human weight is an issue.[11] It is the intent of this book to broaden our understanding of how fat bodies and gluttony are imbued with cultural meaning, and to recognize that medical and moral proclamations that being fat is unhealthy, expensive, and detrimental to contemporary society are always enmeshed in symbolic systems of meaning that privilege some perspectives over others. This book looks to history to identify patterns of thinking that shape and challenge contemporary views of the fat body and the glutton.

To understand those sources in their distinct historical contexts, as well as demonstrate how ideas about fat bodies and gluttons reveal both continuity with the present and change over time, this book employs an analytical framework that uses structuralism as its starting point. Briefly stated, structuralism is a method that attempts to explain individual events or ideas by discovering the underlying, often implicit, patterns of thought that give those events and ideas meaning. It is based on the linguistics of Ferdinand de Saussure, who argued that language is best understood, not by what it refers to—the content—but rather, by the internal grammatical structures that make language work.[12] Those underlying structures determine the meaning of any act of language: basic relationships between grammar and parts of speech determine whether any given sentence makes sense to speakers of that language. This linguistic idea was then applied to broader cultural systems by structural anthropologists like Claude Lévi-Strauss and Mary Douglas, and in an even more eclectic and multidisciplinary manner by Michel Foucault.[13]

From an anthropological perspective, structuralism seeks to identify, analyze, or uncover cultural structures or patterns that create cultural meaning. Structuralism understands cultures as systems or structures where every individual part is defined by, and given meaning through, its relationship to the other parts. This suggests that the meaning of any given cultural idea or phenomenon is dependent on, and defines, other ideas: what is defined as male, for example, is defined and understood in relationship to what is defined as female. As an analysis of ancient texts shows, fat bodies are defined and understood in relationship to other bodies that are thin, or average, and how a culture defines its ideal body will determine how bodies that do not fit the ideal are perceived. The gluttonous body is perceived as the body whose behavior is excessive in relation to the body whose behavior is considered moderate and self-controlled.

In addition, the patterns that create cultural meaning are often found in binary oppositions that are mediated by a third term. This idea is formulated most clearly by Claude Lévi-Strauss, whose anthropological studies suggested to him that cultural meaning is created by negotiating and mediating conceptual oppositions, like nature vs. culture or life vs. death. All cultures deal with these kinds of underlying—and sometimes obvious—oppositional patterns by figuring out how to negotiate, understand, and manage them through the creation of stories, rituals, social structures, and any number of other cultural forms. According to Lévi-Strauss, cultural negotiations of binary oppositions are often found in mythological trickster figures. Tricksters are found in many different cultures, are often humorous, frequently cause trouble for humans, or do things that go against all social norms. These figures inevitably straddle the boundaries between oppositions like divine and human, life and death, and nature and culture, remaining anomalous and ambiguous. Because of their indeterminate status, they can express, mediate, and explain cultural tensions. As Lévi-Strauss maintains, figures such as these often allow cultures to articulate deep-seated fears and anxieties about paradoxical and difficult realities of human life and death.[14] As we shall see throughout this book, the fat body often functions as a cultural trickster: associated with both life and death, the fat body articulates a cultural tension between desired abundance that celebrates life and unwanted excess that overwhelms and leads to death.

Structuralism has been criticized as too binary, too Western, and too universalizing in that it can ignore the specificities of cultural context.[15] Even while recognizing its shortcomings, however, a structuralist approach can be beneficial, because noticing or discovering patterns of binary opposition in cultural expressions can give insight into the tacit ways that a culture makes meaning and negotiates cultural tensions. At the same time, noticing or discovering where ideas do not fit into binary oppositions, or where opposing terms appear to be incongruous or unexpected, can also reveal ambivalence and confusion in cultural patterns of thought. Attempting to understand how fat bodies and gluttons fit—or do not fit—into symbolic systems of thought in the West can help to clarify why these bodies embody the moral meanings that they do.

The Ambivalent Fat Body

To explore symbolic oppositions relating to the fat body reveals that fatness—perhaps appropriately—spills over conceptual binary boundaries and functions much like a cultural trickster, connecting with both life and death. Human fatness, for instance, is often a mark of luxury and wealth, which can be perceived to be either beneficial to society, harmful to social norms, or morally neutral, depending on the perception of the interpreter. Moreover, how the fat body is read depends on the context within which the fat body is found: the fat body in Greek comedy may humorously signify all kinds of social excess, while the fat human body in the Hebrew Bible can be an undesirable body that reveals what happens when humans rely on worldly things and forget God. Some authors, like Plato and Aristotle, for instance, have much to say about gluttony and little to say about what it means to be fat, which may indicate that the fat body was not perceived to be philosophically significant.

There are occasions when the idea of fat or fatness is portrayed in a positive, life-affirming way. In the Hebrew Bible (Christian Old Testament), for example, "the fat of the land" embodies prosperity and plenty, which are gifts from God. Genesis 37–50, for instance, tells the story of how a young Joseph becomes a powerful leader in the land of Egypt. Jealous of their father's love for him, Joseph's brothers conspire to kill him by leaving him in a pit to die. He is discovered by a group of traders and sold into slavery, though he eventually ends up in prison in Egypt. In prison, Joseph interprets the dreams of the Pharaoh's butler and baker and eventually ends up interpreting the Pharaoh's dream of the seven fat cows who are devoured by the seven thin cows, and the seven fat ears of grain swallowed up by the seven thin ears. Joseph interprets this dream as a sign from God that there will be seven years of "great plenty throughout the land of Egypt" (Genesis 41:29), followed by seven years of famine. The Egyptians create a great storehouse of food to carry them through the famine, saving Egypt from the unfortunate fate of the other lands. And when Joseph finally reunites with his family, the Pharaoh has Joseph bring his family from Canaan to Egypt where they are given "the best of the land of Egypt," the place where they can "eat the fat of the land" (Genesis 45:18). Here, fat animals and fat land are a sign of God's support and favor. Stories like these present a positive spin on fat that reminds us that fat—as an idea, at least—is not always or inevitably a sign of moral failure; indeed, it can be a positive marker of wealth and plenty and is a far cry from the contemporary bodily and class ideal that "you can never be too rich or too thin." Because it can imply a range of positive and negative meanings, fatness is an ambivalent symbol in the ancient world, dependent on its context for meaning.

Indeed, the idea of fatness and the fat body are, in ancient texts, symbolically associated with both life and death: when associated with life, they are connected to abundance, wealth, and prosperity; when associated with death, they are connected to excess, to abundance out of control. When abundance moves toward excess, it overwhelms and consumes, leading to death. The binary opposition of excessive abundance and excessive deficiency comes into play here, for just as excessive lack—starvation—is very literally linked to death, so, too is excessive fat that overwhelms: all excess, whether it is excessive abundance or excessive lack, is symbolically associated with death. When fatness exemplifies excess, it stands as a symbolic link between life and death that exposes their mutual interdependence, for it, too, signifies both life and death. In this way, fatness plays the role of a cultural trickster, positioned as a mutable symbol that evokes, explains, and mediates the opposition of life and death, identifying excess as both life-giving and lethal. When the fat body is associated with excess, the moderate body becomes the ideal, for it is neither too fat, nor too thin; it stands as the desired middle way between excessive abundance and excessive lack with regard to body size (Figure 0.5).

Foucault and the Glutton

The idea of gluttony also lends itself to a structuralist reading, because what it means to eat too much is defined in relation to what it means to eat

Figure 0.5 Excessive abundance and excessive deficiency

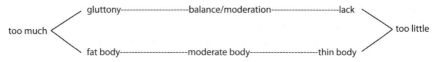

Figure 0.6 Parallels between the gluttonous and the fat body

too little, and to eat enough. From this perspective, the glutton—the person too interested in food—would, hypothetically, participate in a conceptual schema where his or her opposite lacks interest in food, and the privileged position would be someone who has a moderate interest in food. Another obvious set of oppositions and mediations would find fat on one end of the spectrum, thin on the other end, and "just right" in the middle. What the "just right" body looks or acts like may vary from culture to culture and over time, but whatever body is considered to be the moderate body should be located between the too fat and too thin body. And these two sets of oppositions also create a parallel between the gluttonous and fat body, for they are both aligned on the side of excess, as seen in Figure 0.6.

Yet, as we will notice throughout this book, the ways that people in the ancient West describe bodies and their proclivities do not conform to these hypothetical oppositions, for the moderate body does not find its balance between two extremes. Rather, the moderate body is defined as moderate only because it controls excess; there is little attention paid to the thin body or a lack of desire for food. Attempting to locate a structuralist pattern of opposition reveals an unexpected opposition of moderation and excess, where lack has no place. Discovering this unexpected opposition helps to elucidate the cultural problem with excessive eating and drinking.

It is Michel Foucault's "archaeological" project on the history of sexuality that can help explain the significance of an opposition between moderation and excess. In his investigations into the history of sexuality, Foucault attempts to peel back the historical layers of sexual sediment to understand the shift in sexual mores from the ancient Greek to the early Christian world. In the course of this project, Foucault also offers important insight into the cultural meaning of gluttony, in particular, for the patterns Foucault discovers regarding sexuality also include ideas about eating behaviors. Foucault begins his project by asking why it is that sexual conduct, more than other important aspects of life, like civic duty, for instance, becomes such an important object of moral concern.[16] He identifies four themes, found in both Greco-Roman/ pagan and Christian culture, that point to ethical attitudes regarding sexual behavior: fear of sexual expenditure, regard for monogamy, disapproval of effeminate men, and praise for mastery over one's appetite for pleasure. It is in this fourth theme that Foucault addresses the relationship between sexual pleasure and other pleasures—including the pleasure of food—with a focus on physical regimen, and it is here where the conceptual challenge of the glutton reveals itself.

Foucault's reading of ancient texts suggests that the idea of the physical regimen involves practices that have to do with every aspect of bodily existence, with the ultimate goal of creating equilibrium between body and soul. Foucault notes that the idea of the regimen includes suggestions for what kinds of exercise should be practiced at particular times of the day or during particular seasons, what and how much a person should eat, based on body type, climate, and level of physical activity, and how much sexual activity one should engage in, depending on the season and the individual's constitution. With regard to all aspects of the regimen, Foucault sees the primary concern as the relationship of a given activity with the person's individual requirements for health: if sexual activity affects the balance of the body's various elements in relation to the weather and season, it is important to limit or increase sexual activity based on such factors.

Yet, despite the apparent focus on developing a regimen that will create balance and harmony between too much or too little of any given bodily pleasure, Foucault argues that the primary goal of the regimen is to control the human proclivity for excessive behavior in all aspects of life. So, for instance, while many ancient Greek writers show little interest in making moral claims about appropriate sexual preferences or sexual practices, they are very focused on the "intensity" of an individual's sexual practice.[17] What makes sexual activity moral or immoral is based, not on what a person does, or with whom he does it, but rather, on a "division between lesser and greater: moderation or excess."[18] Immorality in the pleasures of sex— or food—is "always connected with exaggeration, surplus, and excess."[19] Though Foucault understands the idea of regimen to be ostensibly about finding balance between two extremes—excess and deficiency—he argues that it is primarily focused on curbing excess, on maintaining control. In contrast to ideas about the fat body, where excessive abundance and excessive deficiency come into play, gluttony is all about restricting excessive behavior in relation to abundance.

Moreover, as Foucault points out, the extent to which excessive sexual behavior is considered dangerous can be seen in the fact that, at least with regard to men, there is little mention in Greek medical or philosophical texts about "the troubles that might be caused by total abstinence."[20] Foucault does note that Hippocrates suggests that women's bodies are more healthy if they have sex, for "penetration by the man and absorption of sperm are the primary source of the equilibrium of its qualities."[21] For men, however, sexual abstinence may even be beneficial, especially for athletes and soldiers.[22] Too little or no sex causes little damage to the equilibrium between men's body and soul, while excessive sexual activity can lead to an imbalance that causes physical or mental illness.

There is a conceptual parallel here with the dietary regimen, as well. While total abstinence from food would eventually lead to death—a much more damaging result than sexual abstinence—the dangers of undernourishment are rarely, if ever, addressed. This ancient focus on curbing excessive behavior with regard to eating explains, perhaps, the lack of information in ancient texts about modern diseases like *anorexia nervosa*. While there is much historical evidence for intense fasting, particularly for religious purposes, I have found no evidence that ancient authors addressed the question of what it means for a person regularly to eat an insufficient amount of food. This lack of interest in what happens when a person eats too little further emphasizes the importance of curbing the desire to eat too much.

Thus, even though the balance between excess and deficiency may be expressed as the primary bodily and moral value in the texts Foucault examines, moderation always requires a greater focus on taming one's desire for excess. As Foucault puts it, "in this dietetics, whose business it was to determine when it was beneficial and when it was harmful to practice the pleasures, one perceives the emergence of a general tendency toward a restrictive economy."[23] Intense focus on ideals of self-mastery, restraint, moderation, and continence suggest the fear of excess in a conceptual system where there is no significant perceived harm in abstinence. In other words, although the hypothetical opposition is articulated as gluttony——balance/moderation——lack, in actuality, the opposition is gluttony——moderation, where the problem of deficiency or lack plays only a shadowy role in the conceptual schema. We can see this kind of opposition in some contemporary thesauruses, where the antonym for "excessive" is listed as "moderate, modest, reasonable, temperate" as opposed to deficient. In the case of the glutton, at least, examining the structuralist possibilities in dichotomous thinking reveals an unexpected opposition that suggests a powerful and pervasive cultural interest in curbing what is considered to be excessive behavior around eating and drinking, certainly in comparison to any cultural unease about what it might mean for individuals to eat too little. Recognizing that gluttony stands conceptually in opposition to moderation—and not deficiency—explains the intensity with which gluttony is condemned as immoral, for there is only one conceptual location that bears the burden of criticism, instead of two: eating too little is of minimal concern in the ancient world. We can thus see the intensity of gluttony's censure in the consistent associations of gluttony with other undesirable values, like irrationality, disease, death, animality, and femininity. When moderation is associated with rationality, health, humanity, and masculinity, the cultural disdain for gluttony becomes palpable. Foucault's interpretation of the meaning of the sexual and dietary regimen among the ancient Greeks thus helps to elucidate the conceptual roots of the West's enduring focus on the moral problem of overindulgence.

Where Gluttony and the Fat Body (Sometimes) Meet

This introduction has emphasized that ancient ideas about gluttony and the fat body in the West both confirm and challenge contemporary ideas about gluttony and fatness. The glutton as exemplar of excessive and damaging social behavior is distinct from the fat body, which can be seen both as abundantly alive and excessively consuming until death. These distinctions are necessary for understanding the nuances of historical difference, as well as providing comparative touchstones with the assumed conflation of gluttony and fatness in the contemporary world.

At the same time, however, gluttony and fatness do make a symbolic connection in the ancient world when both are connected to the idea of excess. When connected to surfeit and overabundance, fatness and the fat body, like gluttony, are symbolically connected to irrationality, death, disease, animality, and femininity. It is this symbolic parallel that confuses and aligns the two ideas, even when they are most often understood as distinct entities, and it is this symbolic parallel that can explain the historical conflation of these two ideas as history marches on.

CHAPTER OVERVIEW

This book explores many aspects of the fat and gluttonous body in the ancient world but cannot include everything. Eating too much, for instance, is sometimes linked with drinking too much: for some writers, gluttony includes drunkenness. In the contemporary world, however, the relationship between gluttony and the fat body is primarily about food; hence that became the focus of this book. In addition, it was necessary to circumscribe the book's focus to excessive eating and gluttonous behavior, within the much larger, more general context of food and eating. Gluttony and the fat body have rarely received focused scholarly attention; hence the purpose of this book.

To highlight the history of gluttony and the fat body, Chapter 1 analyzes biblical ideas of sacrificial fat, human fatness, and gluttony, which set the stage for patterns of thought that both confirm and challenge contemporary ideas about the glutton and the fat body. In both the Hebrew Bible and the New Testament, accusations of gluttony and gluttonous behavior reveal an antisocial attitude that has little to do with fatness. In the Hebrew Bible, in particular, sacrificial fat is associated with God's abundance and stands as a reminder of the human duty to use wisely the gifts that God has given.

Chapter 2 explores the role of the glutton and the fat body in the philosophical work of Plato and Aristotle. Plato's philosophical explanation of the creation of the universe emphasizes the detrimental effects of gluttony and promotes the necessity of moderation in all things as the key to living a good life. Aristotle's understanding of gluttony in the *Nichomachean Ethics* furthers Plato's thinking by developing the idea of the golden mean, a schema in which the middle term between two extremes becomes the goal of the good life. What both of these authors articulate are theories of excess that render it more dangerous, more threatening to social harmony, than its opposites, moderation and abstinence.

Chapter 3 broadens our understanding of the role of fatness and gluttony in ancient culture by examining what the Greek doctor, Hippocrates, has to say about fat bodies and gluttons. Much of Western medicine after Hippocrates uses these texts to formulate ideas about health and dietary regimens. In keeping with Greek ideals of moderation, Hippocrates, too, focuses intently on bodily practices that create balance among all of the bodily elements. But Hippocrates also recognizes that there are many different body types and sizes that require different regimens to keep them healthy. Moderation means finding the appropriate set of bodily habits for the kind of body one has, not creating a midsized body. This chapter also explores the ancient pseudoscience of physiognomy, which uses the size and shape of a person's body features to interpret character. If being fat were considered to be a moral failure in the ancient world, it is in physiognomic texts that we would most certainly find it, for the fat body would reveal one's inner proclivities and dispositions. Instead, physiognomic texts present a complex and ambivalent set of ideas about what the fat body reveals.

Chapter 4 investigates popular images of gluttons and fat bodies in the ancient Greek and Roman world, through the image of Herakles, more popularly known as Hercules, who often plays the glutton in fourth-century BCE Greek comedy; "Trimalchio's Feast," in Petronius' *Satyricon,* a first century CE Roman satire; and the second-century compendium of Greek and Roman dining practices, Athenaeus's *Deipnosophistae,* or *The Learned Banqueters.* These texts confirm the philosophical and medical distinctions made between gluttonous behavior and fat bodies, while also rounding out these ideas by showing how gluttons and fat bodies are situated in the popular imagination.

In Chapter 5, we begin to see the cultural effects of Jewish biblical and Greek ideas about gluttony and fatness in the context of early Christian teachings, while we also find a heightened interest in gluttony. Early Christian writers carry the Greek philosophical emphasis on moderation through to their work, while they also begin to underscore the sinfulness and shame of overindulgence. Philo of Alexandria is an important figure here, because he synthesized Jewish biblical ideas and Greek philosophy, even though his work was preserved primarily by Christians. Food and drink are of significant concern to Philo because the belly has, in both the Bible and Plato, rich symbolic and actual meaning that creates a point of connection between the two worldviews. His emphasis on the evils of covetous desire—its impurity, irrationality, and animality—as it is represented by the belly's cravings, renders biblical morality and philosophical discernment part and parcel of a universally applicable system for human moral behavior. Clement of Alexandria and John Chrysostom are also important figures in this chapter, for they both articulate some of the earliest Christian ideas about bodily practice.

Chapter 6 continues our exploration of gluttony and fatness in the early Middle Ages, with the development of gluttony as one of the seven deadly sins. Here, we trace the development of the sin of gluttony, from its earliest formulation with the monk Evagrius of Ponticus, to one of its most developed monastic expressions in the *Institutes* of John Cassian. Both men emphasize the seven deadly sins, or vices, as a way of organizing the behavioral guidelines of their respective monastic communities. Later, Pope Gregory the Great formulates a popular list of the seven deadly sins for all Christians, not just monks, and, in so doing "translates" the theological implications of gluttony for the lay Christian. The Epilogue looks ahead to the 14th century, when penitential texts provided clergy and lay people alike with lists of sins and their appropriate penances. The late medieval penitential text, *Jacob's Well,* places Gregory's ideas in an everyday context that defines sinful behavior in the life of the Christian. The text viscerally describes "the ooze of gluttony" and its potential for ensnaring the unsuspecting Christian in its sinful trap.

To trace the history of the glutton and the fat body and to elucidate the variety of ways in which the overindulgence and appropriate use of food have been defined and moralized gives us fresh insight into the ways in which ancient people and cultures understood the meaning of bodily makeup and practices, and provides greater appreciation for the role that food practices play in establishing and maintaining the social order. To reflect on how the ancient world perceived gluttony and fatness also allows us to recognize that contemporary Western discourse about fat and gluttonous bodies is not obvious or inevitable, but rather a reflection of a historical moment in time.

BIBLICAL REFERENCES AND DATING

What is most commonly known as the Christian Old Testament was initially, and remains, the sacred text of the Jews. As Judaism and Christianity became distinct religions, Christianity added its New Testament to the Old Testament to create its sacred text. Throughout this book I refer to the Old Testament as the Hebrew Bible to make a historical distinction between the Hebrew Bible and the New Testament, to distinguish the ways that each text treats questions of gluttony and fatness, and to recognize the distinctive religious and cultural context of the Hebrew Bible that sets it apart from later Christian interpretations of its meaning. Unless otherwise specified, all biblical passages are taken from *The New Oxford Annotated Bible with Apocrypha,* ed. Michael Coogan, 3rd edition, New Revised Standard Version, Oxford: Oxford University Press, 2001.

This book follows contemporary scholarly practice by using the dating system of BCE, "Before the Common Era" and CE, "the Common Era," which correspond to BC (Before Christ) and AD (Anno Domini)—"In the Year of Our Lord" but avoid specific religious reference.

1

"All Fat Is the Lord's"

> All fat is the Lord's. It shall be a perpetual statute throughout your generations, in all your settlements: you must not eat any fat or any blood.
>
> —Leviticus 3:16–17

As one of the primary sources for cultural ideals and moral thought in Western culture, the Bible begins to lay the foundation for ideas about fat, fatness, and gluttony that we will see throughout the historical time period of this book. Indeed, the Bible has much to say about food and eating in general and is thus an excellent text for understanding the role of the glutton and the fat body within the social and moral boundaries that food creates. Levitical food laws (Leviticus 11, especially) help to identify the ancient Israelites as a people in covenant with a monotheistic deity, while Paul's discussions of those same laws during the earliest days of Christianity in Corinth reveal the complexities of negotiating communal meals in a time of radical religious change (I Corinthians 8–10). In the book of Genesis, the first human sin occurs through disobedient eating (Genesis 3); that sin is redeemed, according to Christian theology, through the eating and drinking of the body of Jesus Christ in the Eucharistic meal (i.e., Matthew 26:26–29). In the Hebrew Bible, God's power over nature is demonstrated when He rains food from heaven and makes water flow from a rock for the hungry and thirsty desert wanderers released from captivity in Egypt (Exodus 16–17), while in the Christian New Testament, Jesus's divinity is revealed through his miraculous feeding of five thousand hungry followers with a few fish and seven loaves of bread (Matthew 15:32–29). What and how people eat, and with whom they eat, defines and delimits their roles within their communities and their relationship with God.

Within the greater context of biblical food symbolism, this chapter focuses specifically on fat, fatness, and gluttony in biblical texts. The Bible is an excellent example of the ancient separation of fatness and gluttony: while the Hebrew Bible does discuss fatness—both human fat and the sacrificial fat of animals—as well as gluttony, the New Testament, while showing much interest in gluttony, has nothing to say about human or sacrificial fat. We begin, then, by exploring sacrificial fat and human fat in the Hebrew Bible, which exemplifies the interpretive schema set out in the introduction: the text recognizes an opposition between abundance/life and scarcity/death. Here, abundance is associated with God's immortality, favor, and generosity, and scarcity with human mortality, human disregard of God, and disobedience in the face of God's wishes. In addition, the Hebrew Bible disparages human excess by showing that there are always negative consequences when humans misuse the abundance given to them by God. One of the ways that the text marks humans' abuse of God's abundance is connecting excessive eating and human fatness with human indifference toward God's role in providing abundant resources to them. Moreover, when humans misuse God's abundance, they confuse the symbolic order: the orderly opposition of abundance/life and scarcity/death is disrupted as excess abundance becomes associated with death, irrationality, animality, uncontrollability, and impurity, for when humans refuse to acknowledge their limits with regard to God's abundance, they attempt to be like God and ignore their mortality. To show how the Hebrew Bible understands human excess as overstepping an important definitional boundary between humans and God, we explore the prohibition against eating sacrificial fat in Leviticus, the story of the fat Moabite king Eglon and his Israelite assassin, Ehud, as well as other passages where human excess exemplifies human disregard of God's power. Indeed, an examination of the Hebrew Bible's perspective on fat and fatness offers a symbolic explanation for the pervasive cultural fear of and disdain for the fat body in the West.

While the fat human body is often perceived to be a reflection of human arrogance in the face of God's abundance, accounts of gluttony in both the Hebrew Bible and the New Testament point to its destabilization of relationships between humans. Like biblical accounts of fatness, gluttony in the Bible is also associated with death, excess, and uncontrollability, but in the case of gluttony, these associations are made in the context of the human community. What is interesting here is that biblical incidents of gluttony are quite distinct from those that address the question of fatness: the two ideas are never specifically mentioned together. Nor is there a perceived causal connection between fatness and gluttony; it is unclear whether all fat people are gluttons or whether gluttony inevitably leads to fatness. What appears to be the case is that, whether fat or not, the glutton ruptures social boundaries that threaten community stability. Thus, accusations of gluttony—whether the accused is actually participating in gluttonous behavior or not—become a marker for social disruption. In a world where proper behavior around food is paramount, the misuse of food has particularly damaging social consequences.

Explorations of the meaning of sacrificial fat, human fatness, and gluttony in the Bible give insight into the ways that the ancient Israelites or Jews—and early Christians—ordered their world, revealing an important aspect of the boundary between humans and God, as well as circumscribing proper human behavior. The improper use of food, whether it be linked to human fatness or gluttonous excess, carries a symbolic weight that goes beyond our contemporary discourse about the medical hazards of the fat body. In the worldview of the Hebrew Bible, abundance, and all that goes with it, can only be God's.

"ALL FAT IS THE LORD'S"

An important aspect of the Hebrew Bible's understanding of the meaning of the fat human body can be found in the prohibition against eating the fat of sacrificed animals, which is found in the book of Leviticus. This biblical book includes regulations that articulate important aspects of the covenant between God and the Jews. The covenant, or promise, is first made with Noah in Genesis 9:17 after the flood, and again with Abraham in Genesis 12–15. It establishes a special relationship between God and his people, in which God makes certain promises to his people and requires the people to behave in certain ways. The aspects of the covenant that Leviticus specifies include the correct way to make animal and grain sacrifices, as well as moral and ethical guidelines for daily living, like what one can and cannot eat, how one should conduct business or farm, and how best to treat others. This set of guidelines for living, as Mary Douglas points out in her book, *Purity and Danger: An Analysis of Concepts of Pollution and Taboo,* is based on a complex and intricate system of purity and impurity that reveals boundaries between God and humans, and humans and animals. The prohibition against eating sacrificial fat, and the meaning of the fat human body, need to be understood in the context of a broader set of religious regulations that establishes the parameters of divine and human character and behavior.

This section examines the meaning of the prohibition against eating sacrificial fat, a prohibition that is always paired with the prohibition against the eating of sacrificial blood. And although the meaning of the prohibition on eating blood has been well-established, few scholars—with the exception of Mary Douglas—have attempted an interpretation of the ban on eating fat. Douglas's complex analysis of the prohibition in her book, *Leviticus as Literature,* helps to show that the prohibition on eating fat marks God's recognition of the human tendency toward excess, and the necessity of human restraint in the face of God's abundance. Scholars' difficulties in deciphering this prohibition reflect a contemporary unwillingness to acknowledge the positive valuation of sacrificial fat present in the text, a stance that ironically prevents them from seeing the text's subtle moral censure of the fat human body.

The book of Leviticus is one of the Priestly writings of the Hebrew Bible and, as such, focuses primarily on the regulations of Israelite worship. Probably compiled from various existing sources during the sixth century BCE, Leviticus offers a fairly comprehensive account of the proper ritual relationship between the Israelites and their God. The first seven chapters of Leviticus concern the proper performance of ritual sacrifice, which was an important feature of Israelite worship: 1:1–6:7 lists the basic rules for animal and grain sacrifice, while 6:8–7:38 recapitulates those explanations with specific guidelines for priests. Chapter 1 explains the burnt offering, which was the most common kind of animal sacrifice because it could perform a number of different functions, including atonement (Leviticus 1:4), purification, and thanksgiving.[1] This kind of sacrifice may have occurred daily and required the complete burning of an unblemished male animal, except for its skin, which would be kept by the priest (Leviticus 7:8).[2]

Chapter 2 describes the cereal or grain offering, which was done on the occasion of presenting the first fruits of the harvest to God (Leviticus 2:14) and could have also been used as a substitute for an animal in the burnt offering.[3] Grain offerings require that a small portion of the choicest grain be burned, while the rest is given to the priest. Chapter 3 details the peace or well-being or fellowship offering, which could be used as a confessional offering, a free-will offering, or to fulfill a vow.[4]

What is distinctive about the peace offering, in contrast to the burnt offering, is that the entire animal is not burned; rather, only parts of the animal—the kidneys, fat, and part of the liver—are burned. The rest of the animal is eaten during a sacrificial meal, and meat is given to the priest. One connection between the sacrificial rituals described in Chapters 1–3 is that all of them state that the "priest shall turn the whole into smoke on the altar as a burnt offering, an offering by fire of pleasing odor to the Lord" (Leviticus 1:9, 13, 17; 2:12; 3:5, 11, 16). Chapters 4–5 concern the purification offering and the guilt offering, which are done to cleanse the temple when inadvertent sins, deliberate sins, and sins of omission are committed. All of these sacrifices functioned to restore and maintain the covenant between Israel and God through human acts of purification and dedication.

In all of these sacrificial rituals, there are specific rules for handling the blood, the fat and entrails, and the meat of the animal. The proper handling of the animal's blood—usually pouring it on the side of the altar, sometimes collecting it for other uses—is crucial, and in the peace or fellowship offering (Leviticus 3:1–17), the purification offering (Leviticus 4:8–10), and the guilt offering (Leviticus 7: 1–10) particular attention is paid to the burning of internal organs, like the kidneys and liver, and the animal's fat. Indeed, Leviticus 3:16–17 states that, "All fat is the Lord's. It shall be a perpetual statute throughout your generations, in all your settlements: you must not eat any fat or any blood." Thus, fat, along with blood, plays a key role in the sacrifice as the only parts of the animal specifically prohibited for human consumption.

In Leviticus 7:14, there is a biblical explanation for the prohibition on eating blood. According to the text, humans are forbidden to eat blood because "the life of every creature—its blood is its life"; therefore, God says, "I have said to the people of Israel: You shall not eat the blood of any creature." This is an odd phrase because ingesting blood would usually require drinking, not eating, and the text is clear that the prohibition is against the eating of blood. Scholars have therefore argued that the prohibition refers specifically to the "eating of flesh with the blood still in it."[5] Jean Soler notes that this prohibition marks a change in biblical ideas of what humans should eat: in the Garden of Eden, God gives the humans and animals plants to eat; after the cataclysmic flood, during which all living creatures except for Noah's righteous family are eradicated, God recognizes the human tendency toward violence and makes a concession to that tendency by allowing humans to kill animals for food, as long as this killing is properly ritualized. In Genesis 9:4–6, God says to Noah, "Only, you shall not eat flesh with its life, that is, its blood. For your own lifeblood I will surely require a reckoning: from every animal I will require it and from human beings, each one for the blood of another, I will require a reckoning for human life." As Soler explains, "instead of the initial opposition between the eating of meat and the eating of plants, a distinction is henceforth made between flesh and blood. Once the blood (which is God's) is set apart, meat becomes desacralized—and permissible."[6] The blood prohibition underscores the distinctions between God (as provider of food), humans (as eaters of animals), and animals (as food for humans).

Moreover, in the Genesis post-flood narrative, humans are not only entrusted with particular ways of killing animals, they are forbidden from killing one another. According to Jacob Milgrom, the biblical texts declare "that human society is viable only if it desists from the shedding of human blood and the ingestion of animal blood" and assert that humans can "curb their violent nature through ritual means" by recognizing that all life is sacred.[7] Thus, the ritual treatment of animal blood symbolizes the respectful use of specified animals for human consumption and the considerate treatment of humans by one another in daily life. The blood prohibition clearly has significant theological and societal importance.

The fat prohibition, on the other hand, has no explicit biblical justification. Although the prohibitions on eating blood and eating fat are textually connected, there is no obvious explanation for their connection. Leviticus does specify that the kind of fat that plays a role in the sacrifice is not the kind of fat that one finds embedded in the flesh of meat.[8] As one commentary on the Torah suggests, "one cannot eat meat without getting some of the fat that is mixed in with the muscle. Tradition sensibly understood *chelev* in the technical sense of 'prohibited fat.' It is hard fat—according to Rabbi Akiba, that which is layered, covered by a membrane, and capable of being peeled off."[9] Thus, the forbidden fat—*chelev*—is suet fat, "the fat that covers the entrails, and all the fat that is around the entrails; the two kidneys with the fat that is on them at the loins, and the appendage of the liver, which you shall remove with the kidneys" (Leviticus 3:10). If a sheep is being sacrificed, the fat includes "the whole broad tail, which shall be removed close to the backbone" (Leviticus 3:9–10). This could be a significant amount of fat, as the sheep prevalent in this geographical location have a fatty area around the tail that can weigh up to 33 pounds.[10] Prohibited fat, then, is the fat that plays a role in protecting the internal organs of the animal and functions "as an energy reserve in maintaining the life of the animal."[11] In the case of sheep, the fat tail is prohibited, as well.

Without a biblical statement parallel to the explanation of the blood prohibition for the fat prohibition, a number of interpretations of the fat ban have been suggested, and it is in these interpretations that we can see scholars' difficulties in seeing sacrificial fat as a positive symbol of abundance associated with God. One reading suggests that suet fat represents human emotions, selfishness and remorse. Since the kidneys and entrails are used metaphorically in the Hebrew Bible to refer to "the seat of the emotions," Gordon Wenham speculates that the suet fat, along with these other organs, could represent "the dedication of the worshipper's best and deepest emotions to God."[12] Wenham's reading of the suet fat as a desirable offering of the best part of human feelings to God finds a contrast in Nobuyoshi Kiuchi, who argues that since the burned fat gives off a pleasing aroma to God, it is the destruction of the fat, and not the fat itself, that God finds appealing. Citing Psalms 119:70, where the arrogant are described as having hearts that are "fat and gross," and Job 15:27, where the defiant cover their faces "with their fat," Kiuchi argues that "fat symbolizes something that the Lord detests."[13] Because of this, "the burning of the fat symbolizes the destruction of detestable things within a human's inner being."[14] Kiuchi also points out that the association of the suet fat with the kidneys, which are often connected to a "person's inner being," suggests that fat symbolizes human egocentricity.[15] In this reading, suet fat represents the human desire to relinquish a focus on worldly things in order to renew fellowship with God.[16] For Wenham and Kiuchi, the suet fat represents human emotions given to God for distinctly different purposes, one as a giving up of the best part of the human to God, and one as a removal of a negative aspect of humanity. Such readings fail to provide a coherent understanding of the ban on sacrificial fat.

Questions about whether suet fat should be read positively or negatively continue in other interpretations of its meaning. Since the other foods offered in sacrifice must be the choice portion (Leviticus 2:2), some scholars have often framed discussion about the fat ban in the context of whether suet fat could be considered to be the "choice" portion of the animal. Milgrom argues, for instance, that suet is the "choicest of the animal's portions," placing the Hebrew word used for suet, *chelev,* in another biblical context, Genesis 45:18, where "the fat of the land" is associated with the best, most productive land, and he is not alone in this interpretation.[17] Such a reading requires that the suet fat be considered the most desirable to eat portion of the animal, even more desirable than, say, a juicy porterhouse steak. Most scholars reject this notion, arguing either that the reading of *chelev* as "best" "must be rejected out of hand because all of the suet . . . is inedible,"[18] or by suggesting that what is the best offering for God is "not regarded as choice food for humans."[19] Derek Tidball argues that we need to "disabuse ourselves from thinking about this matter from a dietary viewpoint" precisely because the "portions of the animals that were offered to God as choice cuts are the very portions most Westerners today despise."[20] Rather, Tidball argues, we need to think about suet fat not with regard to its nutritional value, but in regard to its cultic symbolism of prosperity and abundance.[21] All of these interpretations of the fat prohibition in the biblical texts suggest that we should understand the fat of the sacrifice in both nutritional and symbolic ways. It seems likely that suet fat was a part of the ancient Middle Eastern diet; the fat tail of the sheep, in particular, is still considered a delicacy.[22] J. R. Porter calls the fat tail of the sheep "an item of particularly tasty food."[23] *The New Interpreter's Bible* notes that suet fat was used as "a substitute for butter and oil" and that it was "especially palatable in boiled rice."[24] Mary Douglas points out that, even today, people who live in polar regions "practically live on blubber."[25] Traditional English cooks consider suet an "esteemed ingredient" in the creation of Christmas pudding, dumplings, and pies.[26] So, although in the United States the most common use for suet is for bird food, this fatty part of an animal is more valued in other cultures and cuisines and is not considered inedible, by any means. To forbid the ingestion of suet fat in the context of Israelite ritual would confirm the idea that suet is desirable human food. Since the best—best of the crop, best animal—is reserved for God and forbidden to humans in other sacrificial contexts, the prohibition against eating suet fat should also be considered to be the best, reserved for God. And, if the suet fat of the animal is reserved for God, it represents abundance and life, much like the blood of an animal represents life. As further analysis of biblical texts shows, just as the prohibition against eating blood stands as a warning to humans to be mindful of the sacredness of life, the prohibition against eating fat stands as a warning to humans about the dangers of excess.

Fat in a Cosmic Context

To understand how the fat of the sacrifice represents God's admonition against the misuse of God's abundance as exemplified in human fatness, we need to understand the ways that biblical sacrifice reflects the Hebrew worldview. In her book, *Leviticus as Literature,* Mary Douglas uses a structuralist analysis to elucidate the cosmic significance of sacrifice, its connection to life and death, and its expression of the covenant relationship between God and the Israelites. Recognizing, like Milgrom and others, that sacrifice in Leviticus reflects a concern for respecting the sanctity of all life, even when animals are used as food for humans, Douglas shows how sacrifice, along with the taboos it enacts, reflects the Hebrew understanding of cosmos and covenant. According to Douglas, "sacrifice invokes the whole cosmos, life and death. . . . With sacrifice, Leviticus expresses its doctrine of blood, of atonement, of covenant between God and his people."[27] We can see these ideas about sacrifice in the symbolic correspondence between the body of the sacrificed animal, the land, and the human body; sacrifice gives definition to animal, human, and divine existence. Through sacrifice, the ancient Israelites make a connection to God that expresses the divine order of things.

In addition, sacrifice always enacts and reflects cultural taboos, or prohibitions. Taboos, Douglas argues, point to the location of cosmic, cultural, social, and bodily boundaries, many of which are blurry, permeable, indistinct, and therefore, conceptually dangerous. Taboos create "a vocabulary of spatial limits and physical and verbal signals to hedge around vulnerable relations."[28] We find taboos and prohibitions when an important conceptual boundary is in danger of being breached. Eating blood is prohibited, for instance, because it reveals the danger in humans killing animals for food when they should not kill one another. The prohibition against eating blood signifies the distinction between killing animals and killing other humans.

Taboos thus reveal and represent boundaries. Another example of how taboos work can be seen in the relationship between humans and God. For example, if humans are made in God's image, what are the boundaries between God and humans? What does it mean to be made "in the image of" God? Where do animals fit in the scheme of things? Sacrifice addresses these kinds of cosmic questions, clarifying boundaries through particular, prescribed acts, and pointing out the places where the distinctions are precarious. As Douglas states, "A strong prohibition on eating warns that the order of sacrifice is being used to demonstrate the boundaries of God's pattern of the world."[29]

By understanding the role of prohibitions, then, we can understand the prohibition against eating suet fat in the context of the cosmic and religious geography of the Hebrews. Douglas points out that the arrangement of the tabernacle or temple as specified in Exodus 25–40 reflects the geographic zones of Mount Sinai: the tip of the mountain, the sacred location from which God descends to speak to Moses, corresponds to the location of the most sacred part of the tabernacle, the site of the ark of the covenant, which contains God's word (see Figure 1.1). In the sacrifice, the tip of the mountain and the site of the ark are paralleled by the entrails, intestines, and genital organs, which are always put on the top of the sacrificial fire and make a link between the tabernacle and the fertile, creative power of God.[30] Below the entrails, intestines, and genital organs sits the suet fat on the sacrificial

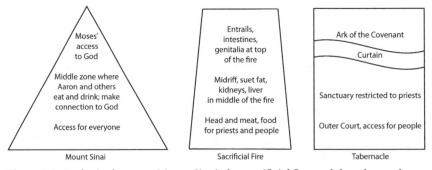

Figure 1.1 Analogies between Mount Sinai, the sacrificial fire, and the tabernacle

fire, taking up a middle position between the head and the genitals, just as it does in the actual body of the animal. The middle part of the sacrificial animal corresponds to the middle of Mount Sinai, the place restricted to Aaron and his sons in Exodus 24:1–9 while Moses receives the law, as well as to the part of the tabernacle restricted to the priests. The suet fat thus represents a dangerous middle zone, where human contact can be made with God. The suet fat is forbidden because "it corresponds in the body to the boundary of a forbidden sacred space on the mountain."[31]

Douglas's reading offers an explanation of the prohibition on eating suet fat that reveals its place in the cosmic and social order. She draws a parallel between the prohibition on eating blood and the prohibition on eating fat by underscoring the notion that both prohibitions reveal important boundaries that explain the relationship between God, humans, and animals. The blood prohibition reveals the boundary between humans and animals and clarifies the idea that humans must acknowledge a restriction given to them by God that they must respect the life of the animals that they kill for food. The fat prohibition marks a boundary between humans and God and clarifies the restrictions that are necessary when humans come in contact with God. Exodus 24:1–2 is clear about what is required for the selected representatives to meet God: "Come up to the Lord, you and Aaron, Nadab, and Abihu, and seventy of the elders of Israel, and worship at a distance. Moses alone shall come near the Lord; but the others shall not come near, and the people shall not come up with him" (Exodus 24:1–2). Douglas's ideas support the oppositions working in the text, for God is contrasted to the human, distance is contrasted with closeness, while the mediating point is the place where humans and God meet—carefully. It is a reminder of God's transcendence as well as God's immanence, for Aaron and the others see God and eat a meal; it is a place where there is life and community in the presence of God.

The notion that the ban on eating suet fat marks a distinction between humans and God is further buttressed by the idea that the space where humans and God meet is also a place where Aaron and the others eat a sacred meal. The location of human connection with God is thus the symbolic belly of the mountain, and human contact with God is made while humans participate in an activity that both distinguishes them from and aligns them with God: eating. God does not need to eat to live, as humans do, and yet God supplies humans with the food that fosters life. God does not eat, as humans do, but God "ingests" the fat of the sacrifice. When associated with the prohibited fat of the sacrificed animal, the sacred meal that takes place in the belly of Mount Sinai both reflects a distinction between God and humans and reminds humans that the food they eat comes from God, the source of all abundance.

Thus, the prohibition against the eating of suet fat marks multiple boundaries between humans and God: it suggests both the restrictions necessary when humans meet God, and the recognition that it is God who gives humans the sustenance to live. Suet fat, like blood, is associated with life: it covers and protects vital organs without which humans and animals cannot live. Suet fat is associated with the belly, with eating, digestion, and health.

Like blood, suet fat symbolizes the specificity of human life: eating suet fat would be like eating blood. In Leviticus 7:22–27, we see that the punishment for eating fat or eating blood is the same: both infractions require being "cut off from your kin." The text's parallel treatment of blood and fat suggests that the fat prohibition plays a similar cultural role to the blood prohibition: if the blood prohibition recognizes the human tendency toward violence, the fat prohibition recognizes the human tendency to take for granted the abundant gifts given to them by God, which is reflected in humans' penchant for excessive eating.

Support for the idea that the prohibition against the eating of fat is a warning against human excess plays out in a number of places in the biblical text where the subject of the fat human body is raised. Human fat is used as a marker for the dangers of human excess, the result of which is an inevitable turn away from God. Deuteronomy 31, for example, focuses on preparations for Israel's future as it faces Moses's impending death. In one last conversation between God and Moses, God predicts that the Israelites will break the covenant and forsake him. Significantly, the primary reason for their disobedience is their inability to make a connection between their abundance and God's favor. God says, "For when I have brought them into the land flowing with milk and honey, which I promised on oath to their ancestors, and they have eaten their fill and grown fat, they will turn to other gods and serve them, despising me and breaking my covenant" (Deuteronomy 31:20). Although it may certainly be the case that "fat" in this passage points in a general sense to the Israelites' wealth and resources, it is telling that fortune and fatness are connected. For this verse articulates both the idea that all fat, all abundance, belongs to God, and, that when humans become fat, they reject God and render their society untenable, even though the source of their fatness is given to them by God. Eating too much, taking advantage of God's offering of abundance, leads to human forgetfulness: once sated, once filled with milk and honey, God's children will ignore their dependence on God and "their prosperity and comfort will lead them to forget the true source of their well-being, which they will attribute to false gods."[32]

Deuteronomy 32:15 repeats this earlier claim. Here, Jeshurun, a poetic name for Israel, "grew fat, and kicked. You grew fat, bloated, and gorged! He abandoned God who made him and scoffed at the Rock of his salvation." Fatness not only likens humans to animals who kick their masters, it makes them disobedient and unfaithful. A similar account can be found in Nehemiah 9:25–26, where God's prediction to Moses of the disobedience of future generations is realized. Here, the people ate, "and were filled and became fat, and delighted themselves in your [God's] great goodness." Reveling in God's abundance, however, the people "were disobedient and rebelled against you and cast your law behind their backs." Such passages reflect back to the first sin in the Garden of Eden, which was committed through an act of eating. In a symbolic sense, Adam and Eve "overate" because they were unable to display the necessary self-restraint in the face of God's abundance; they ate beyond what was required with the one food they were forbidden to eat.

These passages note the human challenge of being appreciative of all that is given to humans by God while not misusing that abundance. In this sense, just as the blood prohibition marks a dangerous place where humans can kill animals for meat but not kill one another, the fat prohibition recognizes the dangerous place where humans gladly receive God's abundant gifts but risk abusing them and forgetting that God has given them those gifts in the first place. Just as curbing acts of killing is necessary for the creation of a viable human culture, it seems that so, too, is curbing human excess: for humans to live in accordance with the covenant and with one another, greed, gluttony, and excess need to be controlled. Philo of Alexandria, a first-century Jew who blended Greek philosophy with Jewish thought, and whose ideas on gluttony and excess will be explored more thoroughly in Chapter 5, picks up on this idea in his commentary on Mosaic law. He reads the prohibition against the eating of fat as a call for human self-restraint: "The fat is prohibited because it is the richest part and here again he [Moses] teaches us to practice self-restraint and foster the aspiration for the life of austerity which relinquishes what is easiest and lies ready to hand, but willingly endures anxiety and toils in order to acquire virtue."[33] For Philo, the taboo on suet fat enacts the necessity of human restraint when faced with the fact of God's abundance.

In the biblical prohibition against the eating of suet fat we see one of the myriad ways that Israelite theology attempts to explain the meaning of living in covenant with God and understand the differences and similarities between human and divine life. Humans are created in the image of God, yet God does not have a body. As Howard Eilberg-Schwartz points out, this contradiction creates difficulties for the representation of God in human thought. "While God does a variety of humanlike things, including speaking, walking and laughing, God does not perform 'baser' human functions, such as eating, digesting, procreating, urinating or defecating."[34] These "baser" functions connect humans more closely with animals, not God. Yet, over and over again, we read that the smoke of the burning fat on the sacrificial fire creates a "pleasing odor" for God. Some scholars see in this idea of the "pleasing odor" a parallel to animal sacrifice in the ancient Greek world, where the thighbone of an animal is wrapped in fat and burned so that the smoke of the burned fat can be ingested by the gods, who do not eat meat.[35] In the Israelite context, the fat transforms and disappears into smoke in the hot fire so that there is no confusion about God eating or needing to eat the fat: God can "ingest" the fat through its pleasing odor. As the smoke from the burning fat reaches toward the sky, it creates a visual expression of the parallel connections between humans and God, the earth and the sky, death and life, and mortality and immortality. The prohibition against eating suet fat is thus one of the ways that Israel remembers, reflects, and repeats the real connection of the people with God on Mount Sinai. Like the blood prohibition, the ban on fat recognizes the covenant and makes a distinction between human and divine life by articulating a human promise to control their use of God's material goods.

The prohibition against the ritual eating of suet fat thus raises the issue of human excess in the context of the covenant. The ritual prohibition against the eating of blood, for example, plays out in daily life not only in the specific rules for slaughtering animals, but in rules about how to deal with human blood.[36] Certainly, the ritual prohibition against eating suet fat carries over into daily eating habits, which are also governed by a clear list of dietary laws found in Leviticus 11; no one would eat suet fat at a daily meal. And, although it is clear from the passages from Deuteronomy and Nehemiah discussed earlier that when humans become fat they may turn away from God, there are no specific rules for how to avoid a fat body. This textual silence about fat and fatness, in a context where there are very specific rules about multiple aspects of bodily existence—what to eat, how to dress, how to deal with diseases and bodily fluids, to name a few—is puzzling. If all fat is the Lord's, is there anything else to be said about human fatness?

From Cosmic Fat to Human Fat

In addition to the idea that becoming fat leads humans to turn away from the source of their abundance, human fatness in the Hebrew Bible is also symbolically connected to dirt, impurity, animality, uncontrollability, and death. Judges 3 tells the story of the defeat of the Moabite king Eglon, by the Israelite Ehud. Enslaved to the Moabites for 18 years, the Israelites cry out for a deliverer. Ehud crafts for himself a sword that he can hide under his garments and goes to Eglon. Once there, he thrusts the sword into Eglon's very fat belly: "the hilt also went in after the blade, and the fat closed over the blade, for he did not draw the sword out of his belly; and the dirt came out" (Judges 3:22).

There are a number of elements in this story that highlight the symbolic meaning of the fat body. First, the Moabite king, "Eglon," whose name means "young calf," is "a very fat man" (Judges 3:17).[37] King Eglon is thus likened to a fat, young calf, which aligns him with an animal that would be a prime candidate for sacrifice; Ehud thrusts his sword into Eglon's belly, where the suet fat is located on the sacrificial animal. Being fat redefines Eglon's human body as a base, animal body, distancing his human body from its more refined and godlike features, which serves simultaneously to undermine the distinctions between humans and animals, and emphasize the distinction between the Moabites and the Israelites. The same Moabites who refused to offer food and drink to the Israelites during the Exodus (Deuteronomy 23:3–5) reveal their continued selfishness through the example of their fat and excessive king. Commentators also characterize Eglon as ridiculous, greedy, pleasure-loving, and gullible, unflattering qualities all associated with his fatness.[38] Such connections show the unappealing results of ignoring the prescribed need for bodily control.

In addition to the negative character traits associated with fatness, Eglon's fat body creates a barrier to capturing his assailant, which, though advantageous to the Israelites, undermines the possibility of seeking justice for his death. The effects of Eglon's fatness allows Ehud's escape: the "dirt" or excrement that comes out of Eglon's fat body after his death tricks Eglon's guards into thinking that he is relieving himself, thereby giving Ehud time to flee the scene of his crime. Eglon's fatness is a hindrance that becomes associated with the excrement that comes out of his body at the time of his death.

This connection between fatness and excrement suggests a connection between fatness, pollution, and an inability to control the body. Here Douglas's work on purity codes in *Purity and Danger* is helpful in better understanding the meaning of the biblical story. Douglas argues that, in any given culture, "where there is dirt, there is system."[39] Cultural definitions of dirt and pollution function like the taboos we saw earlier in the prohibition against eating sacrificial fat, for how a culture defines dirt and pollution marks a boundary with regard to how a culture defines order and purity. In addition, these purity codes are most often associated with the body, and particularly with bodily fluids and substances—blood, semen, feces—that suggest that the body's boundaries are unstable or unpredictable; a leaking body represents disorder. Moreover, the individual body and its boundaries can represent the cultural body and its boundaries. As Douglas suggests,

The body is a model which can stand for any bounded system. Its boundaries can represent any boundaries which are threatened or precarious. The body is a complex structure. The functions of its different parts and their relation afford a source of symbols for other complex structures. We cannot possibly interpret rituals concerning excreta, breast milk, saliva and the rest unless we are prepared to see in the body a symbol of society and to see the powers and dangers credited to social structure reproduced in small on the human body.[40]

Although Douglas specifically refers to rituals that concern the body in this quote, her understanding of the role of purity codes can also be seen in the story of Eglon's death. In the Israelite world view, Eglon's fat, animal body personifies ideals and behaviors inimical to Israelite values, and his death suggests the triumph of an Israelite belief system in which human fatness, as a marker of greed, decadence, and willful disregard of God, is disdained.

In addition, the details of the story further illuminate the meaning and the function of the covenant for the Israelites. Refining Douglas's ideas of purity and pollution, Howard Eilberg-Schwartz notes that fluids that pollute are associated with death while fluids that do not pollute are associated with life.[41] He observes that the priests in Leviticus "never say that excrement is a source of impurity"; only in Deuteronomy 23:10–15 is excrement mentioned as a pollutant, and only in the very specific context of a military encampment.[42] Eilberg-Schwartz speculates that the distinction between those bodily fluids that pollute and those that do not has to do with whether or not the fluid is controlled. He notes that the ejaculation of semen during a sexual act is associated with "direct action and conscious thought," while menstrual blood is released passively: "The difference between the ejaculation of semen and the release of nonseminal fluids or menstrual blood is the difference between a controlled, conscious act and a passive involuntary occurrence."[43] Thus, there is a symbolic constellation of associations between purity, life, and control, and pollution, death, and uncontrollability.

The connection between fatness and excrement in the story of Eglon and Ehud also follows this pattern because Eglon's excrement is uncontrollable. The note on this passage in the Oxford Annotated Bible even reads "Eglon's anal sphincter explodes with the excrement coming out."[44] Moreover, "the practical association between impurity, death and lack of control embodied the abstract and familiar idea in Israelite religion that a person must exercise self-control in order to fulfill his or her covenantal obligations and thus be closer to God."[45] Eglon's fat body thus represents everything that undermines the proper performance of the covenant, with its fatness, its uncontrollability, its dirt. In this way, we can see that the story of Eglon and Ehud functions to reveal the proper order of things by emphasizing the meaning of disorder. Human fatness undermines order by highlighting the base, animalistic qualities of humanity, which, in turn, emphasizes the damaging consequences of human self-indulgence. The story of Eglon and Ehud thus confirms the meaning of the prohibition against eating fat: a viable human culture is possible only when the human tendency toward excess can be controlled. In slaying Eglon, Ehud confirms the value of the orderly worldview that proper adherence to the covenant creates.

BIBLICAL GLUTTONY

In our society today, we make clear connections between gluttony and fatness; the two ideas are inevitably considered together. In the biblical world, however, gluttony is not predictably connected to being fat. Indeed, while biblical ideas about fat and fatness reveal important aspects of the covenantal relationship between humans and God, gluttonous behavior is presented as a destructive behavior that damages relationships between humans. Thus, although both fatness and gluttony may indicate a misuse of God's abundance, their effects are distinct. Human fatness undermines the proper fulfillment of the covenant, while gluttony undermines the proper function of society.

Gluttony in the Hebrew Bible

The primary discussion of gluttony in the Hebrew Bible is found in Deuteronomy 21:18–21, which provides guidance for parents with disobedient children. According to the text, parents in need of communal assistance "shall say to the elders of his town, 'This son of ours is stubborn and rebellious. He will not obey us. He is a glutton and a drunkard.' Then all the men of the town shall stone him to death. So you shall purge the evil from your midst; and all Israel will hear, and be afraid." Here, gluttony, along with drunkenness, requires the intervention of the town elders because these behaviors are clearly antisocial and cannot be tolerated; they threaten the stability of society. Further support for damaging effects of gluttony can be found elsewhere in the Hebrew Bible. Proverbs 23:20–21 suggests that gluttony creates economic imbalance in society, "for the glutton and the drunkard will come to poverty." Proverbs 28:7 also makes the connection between gluttony and the lack of parental respect, for "those who keep the law are wise children, but companions of gluttons shame their parents." Here, even associating with a glutton can lead to disobedience.

The threat is clearly significant, for the recommended punishment for such behavior in Deuteronomy is death. The sentence of death for the rebellious son is, as Elizabeth Bellefontaine notes, found nowhere else in biblical law, and whether the actual punishment was ever carried out continues to be debated.[46] Nonetheless, the fact that a son's rebellion, stubbornness, gluttony, and drunkenness are considered to be actions punishable by death is noteworthy, particularly when, as Jeffrey Tigay points out, eating and drinking too much are not criminal offenses anywhere in the Bible.[47] To connect rebelliousness and stubbornness with gluttony and drunkenness, however, not only suggests the seriousness of the son's insubordination, it links filial disobedience with specific physical activities considered to be excessive, and that lead the doer of such deeds to be a "non-productive, non-contributing parasite in the community."[48] In addition, the connection of gluttony with death further undergirds the symbolic connections made between excessive behavior, uncontrollability, impurity, and irrationality that we saw with the fat body. Uncontrolled, gluttonous behavior represents an impure malignancy in the cultural body that must be excised for the community to be healthy, much in the same way that the fat body reveals humans' disregard for God's abundance that can undermine the fulfillment of the covenant.

Nonetheless, although being fat and being a glutton both suggest a misuse of God's bounty with particularly excessive behavior, these two ideas are nowhere explicitly connected in the biblical text. None of the texts that deal overtly with human fat use the language of gluttony; even in Deuteronomy when the Israelites "eat their fill" and become fat, there is no specific reference to gluttonous behavior. One can also apparently be a glutton without being fat, for there is no indication that the son's behavior with food and drink has resulted in his particularly fat body. Yet, if we read this passage in the context of Deuteronomy 31:20 and 32:15, the son's gluttony becomes analogous to Israel's growing fat; just as Israel's misuse of God's abundance will lead her to forget God's supremacy, so, too, does the son's gluttony lead to his willful defiance of his parents' authority. Thus, while fatness is invoked to highlight a community's rebellion against God, gluttony is perceived to be an individual excess that leads to unacceptable disruption of the community.

Gluttony in the New Testament

While the Hebrew Bible tells the story of the development of the covenant relationship between God and the Jews, the Christian scriptures focus on the life and death of Jesus, and the subsequent formation of the early Christian community. The Gospels of Matthew and Luke relate an incident in which Jesus is perceived to be a glutton and a drunkard, a scene that places Jesus in the company of the rebellious son in Deuteronomy. In Paul's letters, which are the earliest accounts of the fledgling Christian religion, food is a contentious issue: since the new community was peopled by both law-abiding Jews who believed that Jesus was the Messiah, and non-Jews who were convinced that Jesus was the Son of God, the status of the Jewish food rules is a serious question. Must non-Jews who believe that Jesus is the Messiah follow Jewish law? Should Jews give up their adherence to the law? How can a community made up of two groups who have very different ideas of what can and should be eaten come together? Paul repeatedly argues that those who abide by the law may continue to do so, and that those who do not are not excluded from the Kingdom of God. In the book of Philippians, though, echoes of Deuteronomy appear in Paul's condemnation of those outside the Christian community who live by the belly and turn away from God. Thus the New Testament presents a perspective on the glutton similar to that found in the Hebrew Bible: gluttonous acts disrupt the community. Human fatness, however, is nowhere an issue; where food and morality are connected is not reflected on the body. Rather, food becomes a moral issue to the extent that one's actions with regard to food either maintain or disrupt communal harmony.

Jesus, the Consuming Revolutionary

The gospels of Matthew (11:16–19) and Luke (7:31–35) share a scene in which Jesus and John the Baptist are compared, and their characters are assessed, based on what and with whom they eat. Here I focus on the Lukan narrative, because a comparison of these two texts reveals that Luke specifically uses the theme of food as a way to create an image of Jesus. For Luke, Jesus is the one who reveals "the faithful God who feeds his hungry creation, rectifies the ills that plague it, and rejoices to sup with sinners."[49] Food plays such an important role in the gospel of Luke that it may not be an exaggeration to claim, with Robert Karris, that, "in Luke's gospel, Jesus got himself crucified by the way he ate."[50] In this gospel, Jesus's eating practices become one feature of the differences between John the Baptist and Jesus. The beginning of the book focuses on the births of both John and Jesus, and both are presented as part of God's plan for humanity's salvation, though Jesus is clearly revealed to be the Messiah (3:15–16). As the communities around Jesus and John try to understand who they are and what they intend to do, it is clear that they pose challenges to accepted social norms.

The Pharisees—those responsible for interpreting and keeping Jewish law under a hostile Roman government—are scandalized that John and Jesus associate with tax collectors—Jews who are seen as colluding with the Roman government by collecting taxes for it—and sinners—the generic designation for gentiles and Jews who ignore Pharisaic law.[51] One of the significant differences between the two is their approach to eating. In Luke 5:33, Jesus's teaching is questioned because he does not demand that his disciples fast: "Then they said to him, 'John's disciples, like the disciples of the Pharisees, frequently fast and pray, but your disciples eat and drink.'" Jesus's response—"no one puts old wine into new wineskins" (5:37)—indicates that he brings a new perspective to existing religious practices. Jesus does not eschew fasting, for he himself fasts for forty days in the wilderness (4:2); he simply suggests that it is time to rethink the usefulness of current practices. With regard to food, Jesus demonstrates his viewpoint throughout the text by eating with a variety of different people, often under unusual circumstances, and without regard for purity.[52] It is in this broader context that Luke 7:31–35 must be read. In Luke 7:34, Jesus speaks about the community's perceptions of John the Baptist and himself, highlighting how their eating practices reflect their social deviance. "For John the Baptist has come eating no bread and drinking no wine, and you say, 'He has a demon'; the Son of Man has come eating and drinking, and you say, 'Look, a glutton and a drunkard, a friend of tax collectors and sinners!'" In a context where Jesus and John are perceived by the Pharisees to be undermining Jewish law and order, such accusations underscore the alleged threat both teachers pose to the community. Here, even John's practice of fasting, which is not, in usual circumstances, a deviant practice, becomes fodder for character assassination when it is perceived to be excessive.

Indeed, the issue at stake here is the supposed excesses of John and Jesus, which place them outside communal norms. John fasts excessively, so he must be mad, and Jesus eats excessively, so he must be a glutton and a drunkard. In addition, Jesus's gluttonous behavior is associated with the undesirable segments of the population, the tax collectors and the sinners. For Jesus to eat and drink with such people renders him a social pariah.

Biblical scholars interpret this accusation in various ways. Most often, they see the textual link between "gluttony and drunkenness" and "tax collectors and sinners" as an indication that Jesus is violating Jewish food rules and purity codes. This is the argument that Robert Gundry makes in his exegesis of the parallel passage in Matthew. "In other words, ceremonial contamination from the publicans and sinners with whom he eats and drinks exacerbates his gluttony and drunkenness. It is easy to think that Jesus' daring to transgress the boundaries of ceremonial purity led his critics to exaggerate his festive behavior."[53] For Gundry, Jesus may very well cross the line into gluttony and drunkenness because he eats often, in a festive manner, and with people who are ritually unclean. Leon Morris reads the accusation of gluttony and drunkenness in the context of John's asceticism. He argues that, "when he says that he came *eating and drinking,* we should not imagine that he was claiming to be a gourmet. He is not saying that food and drink were at the center of his life; he is saying that, far from being an ascetic, he ate and drank normally, as other people did. In dietary habits he was a normal member of society."[54] Yet, by eating with gentiles, Jesus "inevitably contracted defilement."[55] For these scholars, the charge of gluttony and drunkenness is clearly associated with ritual impurity.

Though it certainly was the case that Jesus probably violated Jewish purity codes when he ate with gentiles, the accusation of gluttony and drunkenness appears to be not only about ritual purity, but also about death, excess, and lack of social control. When eating and drinking as a "normal member of society" becomes fodder for allegations of excess, it suggests the power of the social condemnation of gluttony and creates an important conceptual link between Jesus and the rebellious son in Deuteronomy. Although Fitzmyer dismisses a linguistic connection between the two passages, I agree with Howard Clark Kee that the context of the Deuteronomic passage is directly relevant to the meaning of the Lukan episode.[56] In Deuteronomy, the son who is a glutton and a drunkard is stubborn and rebellious and refuses to obey authority. In the context of Jesus's ministry, he is like the disobedient son who refuses to follow the rules of his religious elders. As Kee points out, Jesus's "aggressive practice of welcoming aliens and the excluded into the community which he is shaping can only be regarded as rebellion and sedition by strict adherents to ritual, cultic and ethnic limits for participation in those who see themselves as the people of God."[57]

The charge of gluttony and drunkenness against Jesus is a serious charge that reflects the social and religious challenge he brings: to alter the culinary practices of a community strikes at the heart of its cultural identity and worldview. Kee further suggests that Jesus's own use of the phrase, "a glutton and a drunkard," shows that he understands how much of a threat his critics perceive him to be, even to the extent that he may be killed. "What is implicit in Jesus' use of this term, 'glutton and drunkard'—which he borrowed from or attributed to the severe critics of his open and inclusive definition of the community of God's people—is that he is prepared for execution."[58] Kee points out that "Jesus' radical redefining of the people of God and of the grounds for participation in this community he perceived to be providing the basis for a plot to destroy him."[59] The allegation of gluttony reflects the perceived danger of improper food practices by evoking the connection between excess, impurity, lack of social control, and death. To be a glutton is to threaten social boundaries and stability in the worst possible way.

Belly-Worship in Paul

The accusation of gluttony against Jesus is the only place in the New Testament where gluttony itself is mentioned. Nonetheless, the social role of food presented in the gospels also plays out in Paul's letters. And, although Paul never mentions gluttony or fatness specifically, his interest in food practices, along with his explicit references to the belly, are relevant to our discussion. In the ancient world, "the belly is a code-word for gluttony," though both terms—belly and gluttony—may refer to a variety of body parts, activities, or attitudes.[60] The belly, for instance, may refer not only to the stomach per se, but also to the genitals. Gluttony may refer to excessive practices that involve food, drink, or sex, or it may be used in a more general sense to denote greed. Paul's references to the belly, as I will suggest, could encompass a variety of different practices, but what connects them all is their destructive effect on community harmony. For Paul, those who focus on the belly represent a serious challenge to his Christian communities.

Written in the 50s-60s CE, the epistles of Paul reveal the challenges of creating and maintaining the earliest Christian communities. Food practices continually present theological dilemmas for Paul, who, as a Jewish convert to Christianity, understood Jewish food law and the challenge food would bring to communities of Christians made up of both law-abiding Jews and gentiles. The question of whether it is appropriate for Christians to eat meat sacrificed to idols, for example, threatens to tear the community at Corinth apart. As he attempts to satisfy both the gentile and Jewish Christians by noting the validity of both sides of the argument, Paul appeals to a higher authority for his perspective: "So, whether you eat or drink, or whatever you do, do everything for the glory of God. Give no offense to Jews or to Greeks or to the church of God, just as I try to please everyone in everything I do, not seeking my own advantage, but that of many, so that they may be saved" (I Corinthians 10:31–33). For Paul, the contentious issue of food practices is one that must be neutralized in order for a community to come together as the body of Christ.

In addition to the challenge of food in creating communal harmony, the symbol of the belly also represents for Paul a threat to communal harmony and belief in God. Here the question is not so much about what should or should not be eaten; rather, a perceived focus on the belly represents for Paul a turning away from God. At the end of the letter to the Romans, for instance, Paul writes,

I urge you, brothers and sisters, to keep an eye on those who cause dissensions and offenses, in opposition to the teaching that you have learned; avoid them. For such people do not serve our Lord Christ, but their own belly [or appetites], and by smooth talk and flattery they deceive the hearts of the simple-minded. For while your obedience is known to all, so that I rejoice over you, I want you to be wise in what is good and guileless in what is evil. The God of peace will shortly crush Satan under your feet. (Romans 16:17–20)

In the same way that accusations of gluttony in the Hebrew Bible and the gospels serve to mark a real or perceived threat to society, for Paul, those who serve the belly will foment dissent in the community.

In the letter to the Philippians, Paul makes a similar claim about those who worship the belly.

Brothers and sisters, join in imitating me, and observe those who live according to the example you have in us. For many live as enemies of the cross of Christ; I have often told you of them, and now I tell you even with tears. Their end is destruction; their god is the belly; and their glory is in their shame; their minds are set on earthly things. But our citizenship is in heaven, and it is from there that we are expecting a Savior, the Lord Jesus Christ. (Philippians 3:17–20)

Here again, Paul uses the belly as a symbol of opposition to healthy Christian community.

Although each of these communities has specific issues that Paul addresses, the symbol of the belly functions similarly in both contexts.[61] In each of these situations, Paul creates oppositions that place the belly-worshipper over and against the Christian. Although Karl Sandnes points this out specifically in his interpretation of Paul's *Letter to the Romans,* reading Philippians alongside Romans highlights the image of obedient, God-serving Christians who will become citizens of heaven.[62] These good Christians stand in contrast to dissenters who serve their bellies or their appetites instead of God, revel in earthly things, and are aligned with Satan.

Scholars have proposed a variety of explanations as to who these dissenters are; the possibilities are similar for both communities. These belly-worshippers could be Christians who continue to observe Jewish food laws.[63] Reading these texts in this light suggests that their meaning is found mainly "on the basis of Pauline polemics against Judaizers."[64] Such an interpretation would necessitate that Paul had strong disagreements with those who continued to practice their Judaism in the context of the new religion. Since Paul specifically attempts to bring communities together regardless of food practices, this reading is not entirely satisfactory. The most straightforward reading of these passages suggests that the belly-worshippers were just that: those who are gluttons, unwilling to practice self-control with regard to bodily appetites. Because Paul was convinced that Christ would return in his lifetime, and he believed that self-control was a crucial part of one's spiritual life, he would necessarily be adverse to any kind of lifestyle that could be perceived as self-indulgent.[65] The designation of belly-worshipper could also be a general reference to the flesh or to selfishness.[66] In this context, the belly would be a metonym for all behaviors and attitudes that turned one away from a spiritual life. The belly becomes a symbol for the flesh, as opposed to the spirit, and includes sexual indulgence, as well as gluttony. Thus, for Paul, those who worship the belly may be guilty of any number of possible attitudes and behaviors; what is certain with regard to any given explanation is that worshipping the belly presents a threat to the kind of community that he seeks to establish. Indeed, what is fascinating about the belly in Paul is precisely that it is a flexible symbol that can carry so many possible meanings. What we thus see in Paul's letters is an expression of a cultural and religious context in which indulgent bodily practices oppose a meaningful spiritual life. The belly becomes the catch-all for all bodily excess.

The belly's association with Satan, destruction, disobedience, and earthly things in Paul's letters also supports and confirms the Hebrew Bible's connections between gluttony, death, impurity, and lack of control. Paul's engagement with the question of the status of Jewish food law in early Christian communities reveals a continuing concern with purity issues, even as these laws begin to change for Christians (see Acts 10–11; I Corinthians 8). And, Sandnes is right to point out that the association of belly-worship with Satan in Romans evokes God's punishment for the snake/Satan in Genesis 3:14: "Because you have done this, cursed are you among all animals . . . upon your belly you shall go, and dust you shall eat all the days of your life." Here, a specific connection between the belly and death is fashioned. Moreover, those who worship the belly present a serious threat to Paul's communities, for those who wallow in the fleshly body will not become heavenly citizens; their lack of corporeal control will lead not only to physical death, but more importantly, to the exclusion from eternal life in heaven.

Indeed, those who are disrupting the communities in Rome and Philippi are the conceptual counterparts to those in Deuteronomy 31:20 who "have eaten their fill and grown fat" and by focusing on their bellies, have forgotten their commitment to God. Although Paul never connects belly-worship to the fat human body, it is clear that, for him, indulgence of the belly either leads to the willful neglect of God, or stands as a marker of an already depraved spirit.

CONCLUSION

Biblical ideas about sacrificial fat, human fat, and gluttony help to create a foundation for understanding important aspects of the meaning of the fat body and gluttony in the ancient world, and even today. In the Hebrew Bible, the prohibition on the eating of suet fat, for instance, reveals a fundamental connection between God, fat, and abundance that places restrictions on human behavior. To live up to the covenant, humans must learn to curb their excessive tendencies. Indeed, as the story of Eglon and Ehud suggests, human fatness is not only associated with negative character traits, such as self-indulgence and foolishness, it reveals a connection with death, impurity, and lack of control that underscores the importance of the discipline required for humans to live up to covenantal expectations. Indeed, specific references to fat human bodies in the Hebrew Bible reveal a human love for indulgence that places in jeopardy a positive connection between God and humans, even when human fatness is the result of God's gift of abundance in the first place. Human usurpation of God's "fat" in the fat human body implies a turning away from God, a lessening of human awareness that it is God who is responsible for their wealth and prosperity.

Moreover, even if most humans today no longer live in the kind of covenantal relationship specified between humans and God in the Hebrew Bible, the contemporary disdain for the fat body can be at least partially understood as a continuation of these ancient ideas in more secular contexts. Symbolic associations of fatness with death, animality, and uncontrollability persist, in contemporary medical discourse that highlights the associations of obesity with death regardless of data that might contradict such connections, or the association of fat people with animals and dirt—fat pig!—or the often expressed assumption that fat folk should simply learn to control themselves and lose weight. Though contemporary public discourse does not usually make direct connections to the role of God in such formulations, the idea that fat people transgress important symbolic boundaries continues unabated to this day and can help us see the historical tenacity of cultural disdain for the fat body.

While the Hebrew Bible reveals a negative perspective on the fat body, both the Hebrew Bible and the New Testament criticize the glutton, but not for the reasons that we might assume. Although we tend, in the contemporary world, to equate gluttony with the fat body, the Hebrew Bible makes no such clear connection. Instead, we find a biblical parallel between the fat human's rejection of God and the glutton's rejection of society. The son who is a glutton and a drunkard disrupts familial and social relations to the extent that he is to be cut off from the community, perhaps even killed. Excess in food and drink, the Hebrew Bible reveals, causes social disruption that is to be strenuously avoided. For Paul—and the New Testament, in general—gluttony and belly-worship represent a threat to the order, purity, and cohesion of the early Christian community. Accusations of gluttony against Jesus reveal the profound impact of table fellowship on the formation and sustenance of community; practices perceived to deviate from the norm contribute to the perception that Jesus is a danger to his community. Those whom Paul designates as belly-worshippers present an equally difficult challenge to fledgling Christian communities who are already struggling to create food practices acceptable to all.

As in the Hebrew Bible, the New Testament makes no clear connection between one's attitude or behavior with regard to food and the appearance of one's body. And, although one's behavior with regard to food was important—certainly, the worship of the belly was considered inappropriate—the New Testament offers little guidance with regard to what exactly constitutes belly-worship. No specific rules exist for the amount of food that a given person could consume before that person was considered to be a belly-worshipper. Nor is there guidance with regard to the kinds of foods that would lead to overindulgence. Indeed, though biblical references to gluttony, fatness, and the belly both reflect and shape Western cultural views that associate the fat or gluttonous body with immorality, any direct connection between gluttony and fatness in the Bible remains elusive.

2

Philosophizing Excess in Plato and Aristotle

> The creators of our race . . . knew that our gluttony would lead us
> to consume much more than the moderate amount we needed.[1]
>
> —Plato

> Now in the natural appetites few people go wrong, and that in
> only one direction, namely excess.[2]
>
> —Aristotle

If we are to understand the contemporary disdain for the fat body, it is impossible to ignore the Greeks. Two of the West's most famous philosophical forefathers, Plato (427–347 BCE) and Aristotle (384–322 BCE), addressed the nature of bodily appetites, excess, gluttony, moderation, and temperance in their philosophical works. While the writers of the Hebrew Bible explore ideas about fat, fatness, and gluttony in the context of the human relationship with a monotheistic God and interhuman relationships in a God-centered world, Plato and Aristotle write from a perspective that places humans at the center of philosophical inquiry. While the biblical texts reveal a concern that indulgence will result in human indifference toward God, Plato and Aristotle contend that human excesses threaten the possibility of fulfilling human potential. In their philosophical instructions we find themes already seen in the Hebrew Bible, like the idea that overindulgence distracts one from living the proper life, or that gluttony is a source of societal disruption. Like the writers of the Hebrew Bible, Plato and Aristotle also see little connection between gluttony and fatness. Where Plato and Aristotle differ from the biblical writers is that they treat gluttony as a philosophical problem that requires an exploration of the nature of indulgence and its role in human life. Indeed, Plato and Aristotle articulate ideas about human indulgence that we continue to see today.

This chapter explores how Plato and Aristotle understand gluttony and fatness in relation to the ideal of moderation and the good life. Both thinkers maintain that moderation in all physical behavior is necessary for living a good life; from this perspective, either too little or too much food, drink, exercise, or sex hinders the possibility of realizing human potential. Examining the role of eating in human life, however, is more crucial than exercise or sex—which is required of some, but not all, humans for the propagation of the species—because, simply, everyone must eat to live. And, when it comes to food, while the ostensible goal may be to eat neither too little nor too much, moderation is understood primarily in relation to excess: both authors have difficulty presenting a philosophical argument against eating too little. Instead, Plato and Aristotle recognize in human beings a pervasive and consistent tendency to eat excessively in defiance of any and all rational attempts to convince them to eat otherwise. The philosophical challenge is to explain why, despite its threat to moderate living and the good life, eating excessively remains irrationally seductive and difficult to resist. This chapter argues that explaining human obstinacy with regard to excessive eating plays a crucial role in the formulation of both thinkers' ideas of what it means to be human and to participate meaningfully in human society. Moreover, for both of these authors, there is no connection between overindulgent behaviors and the appearance of the body: neither author focuses on the fat body as the excessive body. Neither Plato nor Aristotle acknowledges a causal connection between overindulgence and fatness; any body—fat or thin—can be seduced by the pleasures of eating.

In addition, both authors rely on an oppositional schema where excess and deficiency function as the extremes against which the goal of moderation is measured, and they continue to forge the symbolic connection between overindulgence and animality that we saw in the biblical texts; indeed, Plato forges further links between excessive eating, irrationality, and femininity, emphasizing the role of overindulgence as a threat to proper masculinity. Plato also underscores the relationship between gluttony and the origins of disease that suggests a pervasive interest in rendering the gluttonous body the sick body. And although Aristotle is interested in the male body and its health, as is Plato, his understanding of gluttony is focused much more on the nuances of the pleasures of food for the man who is self-indulgent or self-controlled, morally weak or morally strong.

We begin with Plato's account of the creation of the world in the *Timaeus*. In this dialogue, Plato analyzes the ways in which the human body is designed to facilitate the best possible moral life. Key to this design is the creators' attempt to thwart humans' innate penchant for gluttonous excess by creating the intestines. Yet, despite this physical barrier to gluttony, internal struggles between the body and soul can result in excessive eating, which continues to present a primordial threat to the moderate, good life and thus stands as something to be feared and avoided. Plato's association of gluttony with irrationality, animality, femininity, immorality, and inhumanity suggests the dangers of excessive eating for the conceptualization of the moderate life.

We then turn to Aristotle, whose understanding of gluttony is found in the *Nicomachean Ethics*. Like Plato, Aristotle associates human appetite with animality, recommends that appetite be controlled by reason, promotes the life of moderation or temperance with regard to food and drink, and is uninterested in whether the body is fat. Where Aristotle differs from Plato is in his explanation for why humans indulge excessively. What for Plato was a natural, physical inclination towards gluttony becomes, for Aristotle, an occasion for exploring the role of pleasure in human life. For Aristotle, the proper human attitude toward food and drink is less about eating and drinking too much and more about the pleasures we receive from eating and drinking at all. Aristotle thus expands the definition of gluttony to include the misuse of pleasure and the myriad ways that we seek it. The challenge of food and drink in human life is that we are, often, gluttons for pleasure.

PLATO ON GLUTTONY

Twentieth-century philosopher Alfred North Whitehead once characterized the European philosophical tradition as "a series of footnotes to Plato."[3] To study Plato is to enter into a world of philosophical reflection on metaphysics, epistemology, ethics, politics, and human nature. In comparison to these weighty topics, an exploration of Plato's understanding of gluttony might seem rather frivolous. Yet, the idea of gluttony plays a fundamental role in Plato's conception of the pursuit of knowledge and the good life. Brief references to gluttony can be found in the *Phaedrus,* one of Plato's dialogues on love, and the *Republic,* which concerns itself with the question of justice and is nowadays considered to be Plato's greatest dialogue, but it is in the *Timaeus,* Plato's dialogue about creation, that we can best see his understanding of the philosophical meaning of gluttony.

The *Timaeus* was the most popular and influential dialogue—it was the only Platonic dialogue available in Latin translation—until the late Middle Ages, and up to that time, it was considered to be "the definitive expression" of Plato's philosophy.[4] Today, however, this dialogue is not widely read: current scientific knowledge about the origin of the universe directly contradicts Plato's mythic version of world creation, and our understanding of bodily functions moves beyond the logic of the body as Plato sees it. Because of Plato's scientific missteps in the *Timaeus,* it is often simply easier to focus on other texts in the Platonic corpus that underscore his philosophical authority. Yet, as Carlos Steel suggests, the cosmological, scientific, medical, and physiological aspects of creation in the *Timaeus* serve Plato's "overarching ethical-political purpose . . . about how to live the best life."[5] Indeed, the dialogue's focus on establishing the primordial relationship between "the body of the universe" and the bodies of humans serves Plato's overall philosophical project: to explore what it means for men to create for themselves the conditions under which they could live a good life.[6] Thus, whether Plato is scientifically correct about the workings of the body is less important than the fact that the physiological functions of the body have philosophical significance. So, for instance, as Francis Cornford remarks, the shape and form of the human intestines, which play an important role in Plato's exploration of the meaning of gluttony, serve "the higher interest of the soul," while Plato barely mentions their "necessary" function.[7] Plato's philosophical understanding of bodily functions and human behaviors—like gluttony—can thus add nuance to our understanding of Plato's model for the good life.

It is important to note that Plato's presentation of the relationship between rationality and the appetites in the *Timaeus* is not the only model of this relationship to be found in Plato's thinking. In the *Timaeus,* the unruly appetites need to be controlled by the rational soul. In Plato's *Republic,* 207–209, the appetites also contain the capacity for intelligence and can be trained to work harmoniously with the soul.[8] Since scholars continue to disagree over which of Plato's dialogues were written when, we cannot determine which of these models came earlier or later in his thinking. It seems clear, however, that the relationship between rationality and appetite was one that kept Plato thinking, and his thorough explanation in the *Timaeus* of the human need to control the appetites through reason plays an important role in the understanding of gluttony in the West.[9]

The Creation of the Gluttonous Body: Irrationality, Disease, Impurity, and Femininity

In the *Timaeus,* Plato offers a conception of the creation and purpose of the world that hinges on the idea of Intellect, as personified in a "divine craftsman."[10] This creator's task is to form a good and beautiful world out of the materials available to it. These materials have inherent properties that delimit what can be made out of them and how they will behave; they "represent the causal role of Necessity" and constrain what the creator can do with them.[11] The creator is, however, in most cases able to use these limitations to his advantage, thereby showing that Intellect is able to persuade Necessity to do what is best. Thus, the world is formed out of the interaction between Intellect and Necessity, and intricate explanations of these two separate ideas form the first two sections of the dialogue.

The final section of the dialogue—which is the primary focus in this chapter—shows how Intellect and Necessity are intertwined in the human body. Here, Plato makes a connection between the intellectual/psychological and the necessary/physiological and shows how the interactions between them work. Plato explains the rationale for the male body's physiology—the locations, functions, rationales for various parts of the body—in tandem with the psychological functions of the human soul—reason, emotion, and passion. (The female body is addressed later in this chapter.) He also explains how human activities enhance or detract from the well-being of the mind or soul and body. Male bodies, Plato explains, were created with the *potential* for wisdom and virtue, and therefore, happiness; achieving that potential, however, is not easy because of the ways in which the soul and the body fail to interact in harmony.[12] Plato's explanation of the body's creation underscores the notion that the process of achieving happiness is about developing the skills and knowledge that will allow the soul and body to work together amicably.

Male human beings, who are formed by the progeny of the divine craftsman, are created with two souls, an immortal soul and a mortal soul: the immortal soul is encased in a "round mortal body"—the head—and the rest of the body, which is created as a vehicle for the head, contains the mortal soul.[13] The soul is thus both divine and corporeal, where the immortal soul is more divine than corporeal (even though it is located in the head) and the mortal soul is more corporeal than divine (because it is located in the rest of the body). Because both of these souls are simultaneously divine and corporeal, it is difficult to find the proper language to describe the immortal and mortal souls. Plato argues that the souls' existence and functions are both separate from, and intimately connected to, the body, which makes it difficult to determine when he is making a distinction between the body and the soul, or the immortal and the mortal soul.[14] What is clear is that the immortal soul houses intelligence and reason, and the mortal soul "contains within it those dreadful but necessary disturbances," the emotions and passions, like pleasure, pain, boldness, fear, lust, and irrationality.[15] Men need these emotions—and the sense perceptions that create emotions—because humans must live in an external world and require the ability to interact safely with it.[16] But they are also bothersome because they have the potential to "stain" or "pollute" the immortal soul.[17] Feelings and senses are essential to human life, yet carry with them the potential to contaminate reason. Moreover, the physical body has the capacity both to support and undermine the mind's work. Here, Plato links the mortal soul/body with pollution and immorality, which is set over and against the immortal soul's connection to purity and morality. Indeed, the divine craftsman says that if men "could master these emotions, their lives would be just, whereas if they were mastered by them, they would be unjust."[18] Justice depends on reason's capacity to control, and not surrender to, emotions and senses.

Mary Douglas's work is again helpful in understanding the implications of Plato's linkage of immortal soul with purity and mortal soul/body with pollution. As we saw in our analysis of the Hebrew Bible, a culture's definition of dirt and pollution reveals its sense of order: that which disrupts order or creates ambiguity is defined as polluting. Pollution threatens order, and all cultures find ways to explain or alleviate the dangers of pollution. Often, Douglas argues, these explanations are found in rituals that function to "create unity in experience," by putting on public display "symbolic patterns" in which "disparate elements are related and disparate experience is given meaning."[19] One function of ritual, then, is to help people live with the inevitable ambiguities of life. Plato's analysis of the physiological and psychological functions of the human body, and the potentially stressful relationship between the mortal body/soul (pollution) and the immortal soul (purity) functions as a conceptual parallel to Douglas's understanding of pollution rituals by attempting to bring together and give meaning to two disparate elements of human experience: why we often desire that which we may rationally know is not beneficial to us. Why don't logic and reason always win out over feeling and emotion? Why do we continue to engage in behaviors that we know are bad for us?

Plato's explanation for this can be seen in his emphasis on the interaction between Intellect/immortal soul and Necessity/mortal soul: we prize rationality but need emotions, passions, and senses; hence, we must figure out how to keep those emotions, passions, and senses in check so that rationality can prevail. Because the allure of the passions might overwhelm rationality, Plato goes on to connect the seductive aspects of the mortal soul/body to pollution, irrationality, femininity, and animality, thereby creating a conceptual alignment in which rationality becomes connected to culturally valued ideas of purity, masculinity, and humanness. In this way, Plato can provide a philosophical rationale for the intensity of desire *and* make a case that men should work to control their desires for the good of the community. Plato would concur with Douglas's assertion that "the whole universe is harnessed to men's attempts to force one another into good citizenship."[20] Rational, good, and pure will, philosophically, if not actually, trump irrational, bad, and impure every time.

The interconnectedness of mortal soul/body and immortal soul/mind thus allows Plato to explain the psychophysical tension that exists between desire and rationality. Indeed, the tension between body and soul is more complex than initially imagined, for the ascription of purity to the immortal soul and impurity to the mortal soul works to create layers of meaning that associate purity with masculinity and rationality, and impurity with femininity and irrationality. For not only is the immortal soul located in the head, and the mortal soul located in the body, the mortal soul, Plato explains, is actually made up of two parts. And one part of the mortal soul is superior to the other. Knowing that the mortal soul, with its emotions and passions, would interfere with the rational workings of the immortal soul, the divine craftsman's progeny not only separated the head from the rest of the body with the neck, they also "built the hollow of the trunk in sections, dividing them the way the women's quarters are divided from men's."[21] Here Plato makes reference to the common practice in Greek homes of dividing space according to gender. Just as men and women did not generally enter one another's space in a Greek home, the two parts of the mortal soul also do not mingle with one another. The superior part of the mortal soul is found above the midriff: this is the part of the mortal soul that deals with emotion and sense perception, "exhibits manliness and spirit," and is ambitious; it is located with the heart and lungs.[22] This manly part listens to and understands reason and can restrain the second part of the mortal soul, the womanly part below the midriff, the stomach, in which the appetites and irrationality are found.[23]

The part of the soul that has appetites for food and drink and whatever else it feels a need for, given the body's nature, they settled in the area between the midriff and the boundary toward the navel. In the whole of this region they constructed something like a trough for the body's nourishment. Here they tied this part of the soul down like a beast, a wild one, but one they could not avoid sustaining along with the others if a mortal race were ever to be. They assigned its position there, to keep it ever feeding at its trough, living as far away as possible from the part that takes counsel, and making as little clamor and noise as possible, thereby letting the supreme part take its counsel in peace about what is beneficial for one and all.[24]

The stomach, then, is associated conceptually with the women's quarters and is the seat of the appetites. What is housed there is the beastly part of the soul, which needs to be tied down (no wonder our stomachs growl!). Plato's ascription of what he takes to be masculine and feminine character traits, with their related moral associations, to different parts of the mortal soul, distinguishes and values "manly" ambition over "womanly" and animal appetites, further distancing purity, rationality, and masculinity from pollution, irrationality, femininity, and animality.

Moreover, the stomach is formed in such a way as to keep the greedy appetite quiet and docile, so that it does not disturb the immortal soul. It is placed as far away as possible from the head, for even if it were to understand reason, it would have little regard for it.[25] Indeed, the appetites cannot even understand reason, so the liver was created to mirror "images and phantoms" sent from the mind to "frighten" the appetites into submission to reason.[26] Thus, although Plato recognizes that the appetitive soul is necessary for human life, the danger of the appetites is that they threaten the very humanity of men because they are irrational like animals, and they have the perilous potential of obstructing the ability to reason. By linking the inferior, appetitive part of the mortal soul with willful irrationality, impurity, animality, and femininity, Plato makes a compelling case that attention to the rational, pure, human, and masculine immortal soul is even more desirable than succumbing to those seductive and alluring appetites.

As if these negative aspects of the stomach's appetites were not persuasive enough, Plato continues his explanation of the psychological functions of body parts by underscoring the function of the intestines. As the character Timaeus explains, "The creators of our race knew that we were going to be undisciplined in matters of food and drink. They knew that our gluttony would lead us to consume much more than the moderate amount we needed."[27] Plato defines gluttony as a lack of discipline with regard to food and drink, an innate and inevitable aspect of our appetites. Indeed, gluttony is simultaneously an inescapable part of, and a severe menace to, human existence, so dangerous that "to prevent the swift destruction of our mortal race by diseases and to forestall its immediate, premature demise, [the creators] had the foresight to create the lower abdomen, as it's called, as a receptacle for storing the excess food and drink."[28] To prevent gluttony from overpowering rationality, the creators "wound the intestines round in coils to prevent the nourishment from passing through so quickly that the body would of necessity require fresh nourishment just as quickly, thereby rendering it insatiable."[29] While the stomach is tied down like a wild beast feeding at its trough, the intestines ensure that humans have the capacity for satiety and thus perform an important moral function: they assist in helping humans gain control over our natural proclivity for excessive eating and drinking.

In his explanation of gluttony, we see how Plato reads physiological bodily functions from a psychological and moral perspective. As Daniel Russell points out, Plato's body parts do not act the way that they do because of where they are located in the body; rather, the parts are located in the body because of their psychological functions. Plato here is "antecedently committed at the psychological level" to the function of the appetites and ambitions, around which he then builds the physiology of the soul.[30] The psychological temptations of the appetites and ambitions require that the lungs, heart, and stomach be separated, physiologically, from the head. Of course, Plato is writing the story of creation after the fact, fashioning an explanation for why things are the way they are. In so doing, however, he is able to underscore why humans must live with tensions between desire and rationality, which exist together, though perhaps uneasily, in the body. The fact that bodies contain both the stomach (which is prone to gluttony) and the intestines (which allow for satiety) shows that the creators fashioned men with the potential for rational control of the body—which Plato values considerably—even when the pleasures of irrational desire may seem more appealing. This explanation of the physiological and psychological function of body parts thus explains the power of the irrational appetites, and how difficult it is to keep them under control. Through his use of the language of purity and pollution, he underscores the importance of maintaining control of the desires that would, if left to their own devices, lead humanity into chaos.

At this point in the dialogue, Plato has connected appetites with irrationality, impurity, animality, and femininity, and then specified gluttony as a most dangerous appetite, for it leads to disease, death, and the potential destruction of the human race. Eating and drinking to excess, succumbing to the stomach's beast, is, however, even worse than this, for "gluttony would make our whole race incapable of philosophy and the arts, and incapable of heeding the most divine part within us."[31] Among all of the appetites, it seems, gluttony stands, in the *Timaeus,* as the greatest threat to philosophy. Gluttony threatens to make men lose their capacity to pay attention to the immortal soul, thereby disregarding all of the checks and balances put in place in the creation of the manly body to control and master the appetites. Since philosophy, for Plato, is the practice that assists men in fulfilling their human potential, gluttony's ability to disrupt, and even prevent, the exercise of reason is of significant concern. The only way that Plato can adequately counteract the lure of gluttony is to emphasize that succumbing to gluttony renders the manly, rational being an impure, feminized, irrational animal prone to diseases that threaten the very existence of the human race.

As if gluttony has not already played a significant role in the potential downfall of humanity, Plato continues its association with danger and destruction by showing its instrumental role in the genesis of physical and mental diseases. Greek ideas about how the body works (which will be explained more fully in Chapter 3) make a clear connection between the constitutive elements of the universe and the constitutive elements of human beings. Like the universe, humans are made out of earth, fire, air, and water, which are associated with the qualities of cold, hot, dry, and wet, respectively. Theories of the humors—of which there are many—also link the body's liquids—blood, phlegm, yellow bile, and black bile—with the aforementioned qualities and even with the seasons of the year, so that, for instance, blood, which is hot and wet, is associated with the season of spring.[32] In humoral theories in general, all of the constituent elements and qualities of the body have their proper place but are not fixed in the body. Various movements by these elements and qualities either promote health or cause disease. Plato's humoral theory in the *Timaeus* is not clearly explained, though he assumes the body's make-up of elements and talks generally about the hot, cold, wet, and dry qualities of unspecified body parts. What is clear for Plato is that the elements, humors, and qualities must be found in their appropriate bodily locations, for when, for instance, the elements "unnaturally increase themselves at the expense of the others" or move from an appropriate place to an inappropriate place, "conflicts and diseases" occur.[33] For Plato, physical health is associated with the balance of the humors, elements, and qualities in such a way that "only when that which arrives at or leaves a particular bodily part is the same as that part, consistent, uniform, and in proper proportion with it, will the body be allowed to remain stable, sound, and healthy."[34]

Maintaining the health of the soul also requires balance and harmony, with a focus on controlling excess. "Mindlessness," of which there are two forms, madness and ignorance, is one of the diseases of the soul that is dependent on the body.[35] Madness can be the result of both "excessive pleasure and pains."[36] "When a man enjoys himself too much or, in the opposite case, when he suffers great pain, and he exerts himself to seize the one and avoid the other in opportune ways, he lacks the ability to see or hear anything right. He goes raving mad and is at that moment least capable of rational thought."[37] Plato is thinking primarily of sexual overindulgence here, which he defines not as something that is done willfully, but rather as a disease "caused primarily by the condition of a single stuff which, due to the porousness of the bones, flows within the body and renders it moist."[38]

Even more dangerous than madness is ignorance, which results from a lack of proper proportion between the size of the body and the size of the immortal soul. Plato makes his case in a roundabout way, first asserting that, "all that is good is beautiful, and what is beautiful is not ill-proportioned. Hence we must take it that if a living thing is to be in good condition, it will be well-proportioned."[39] Additionally, Plato makes the case that the proportionality of the body and soul parallel the body and soul's health and disease, and virtue and vice: "In determining health and disease or virtue and vice no proportion or lack of it is more important than that between soul and body."[40] The proper balance between the body and soul is thus crucial to health, which is further associated with beauty, for when "a vigorous and excellent soul is carried about by a too frail and puny frame, or when the two are combined in the opposite way, the living thing as a whole lacks beauty, because it is lacking in the most important of proportions."[41] A small body with a too large immortal soul can become diseased, or the soul can "wear the body out."[42] A too large body with a small immortal soul is an even greater problem:

But when, on the other hand, a large body, too much for its soul, is joined with a puny and feeble mind, then, given that human beings have two sets of natural desires— desires of the body for food and desires of the most divine part of us for wisdom—the motions of the stronger part will predominate, and amplify their own interest. They render the functions of the soul dull, stupid, and forgetful, thereby bringing on the gravest disease of all: ignorance.[43]

If either the body or the immortal soul is out of proportion to the other, the stronger part will control the other. In the case of the large body and the small soul, the desire of the body for food—the need to eat excessively— will overrule the desire for knowledge. Here, eating to excess is particularly harmful, for it overwhelms the immortal soul, rendering it incapable of seeking wisdom. Powerless in the face of the body's great desires, the immortal soul succumbs to the disease of stupidity. For Plato, then, proportionality between body and soul leads to virtue and health; to create and maintain such proportionality is so crucial that Plato leaves his creation story for a moment to focus on ways in which humans can achieve such proportionality. It is in this discussion that the distinction between bodily appearance and bodily behavior becomes clear.

Bodies out of and in Balance: The Fat Philosopher and Physical Regimen . . . Oh, and Women

Plato's insistence on the value of balance and proportion, and his preference for the well-proportioned body, may appear tacitly to condemn the fat body, and his focus on excessive eating as particularly dangerous could lend support to this conclusion. Yet, Plato never censures the fat body. Indeed, Plato does not argue that fatness is either a specific cause or result of the lack of proportionality; it simply seems to be fact that some people are born with body parts that are too long or too big in proportion to the rest of the body. Moreover, Plato's focus on proportionality allows for the possibility that if a large body has the appropriate large soul to go with it, balance occurs. Translator Donald Zeyl concurs that Plato's reference to large (*meta*) bodies may include, but does not necessarily mean, the fat body, and that there could certainly be large and well-proportioned bodies.[44] From this perspective, a fat body is not necessarily out of proportion, it is only out of proportion if the body rules the soul. Thus, for Plato, a fat person can be a philosopher, while the gluttonous man cannot: the *appearance* of the fat man carries with it no inevitable moral judgment, for the soul could easily be proportionate to the body. The man who *behaves* gluttonously, on the other hand, cannot be a philosopher because such behavior precludes the possibility of doing philosophy. Such men could, certainly, be fat. But in Plato's schema, the glutton is not necessarily or inevitably fat; rather, fatness only becomes an indication of "stupidity" if the body is out of proportion to the soul. The fat body, then, is an ambiguous body whose appearance may or may not reveal virtue or vice. What is unambiguous is that gluttonous behavior is thoroughly condemned.

Plato's focus on the need for proportionality between body and soul leads to his recommendation that each individual develop a physical and mental regimen that exercises both body and soul. To avoid disease it is important to train both the body and soul, "so that each may be balanced by the other and so be sound."[45] Indeed, one must provide the body and soul with "the nourishment and motions that are proper to it."[46] Only in this way can our bodies and souls become aligned with "the thoughts and revolutions of the universe."[47] Aligning the body and soul with universal harmony creates "the most excellent life offered to humankind by the gods, both now and forevermore."[48] Thus, when it comes to bodily practices with regard to food, the glutton, who only eats and refuses to provide for the immortal soul its necessary nourishment, will remain out of balance. Plato also seems to suggest that the large or fat person, who exercises both body and soul in the proper ways, can maintain the appropriate balance.

Plato's insistence on balance, harmony, and moderation also exposes his fear of some forms of excessive behavior. Even though Plato promotes the idea that health depends on a regimen that balances physical and mental work, insisting that "the mathematician, then, or the ardent devotee of any other intellectual discipline, should also provide exercise for his body by taking part in gymnastics," he also maintains that the primary threat to bodily health is physical, not mental, excess.[49] For instance, "diseases and degenerations" of the body occur when the bodily elements of earth, air, fire, and water "unnaturally *increase* themselves at the expense of the others."[50] Inappropriate movement of a given element "causes offense by *passing beyond*" the proper boundaries of bodily proportion.[51]

Moreover, since Plato's primary goal is to show "how a man should both lead and be led by himself in order to have the best prospects for leading a rational life," it is clear that "we must give an even higher priority to doing our utmost to make sure that the part that is to do the leading is as superbly and as perfectly as possible fitted for that task."[52] In other words, although maintaining a balance between the different souls is important, it is even more crucial that we nurture the immortal, rational soul. This is "the most sovereign part of our soul" and it is "god's gift to us, given to be our guiding spirit."[53] In the end, then, Plato reveals his final agenda: to show that humanity must strive toward the divine, we must privilege the immortal soul over the physical body. Russell comes to a similar conclusion, though he suggests that Plato sees the body solely as an obstacle to reason.[54]

Yet, it seems to me that Plato's fear of bodily excesses and the dangers that they pose to order and harmony leads him to overemphasize the immortal soul in order to achieve the balance between body and soul that he wishes to promote. Thus, Plato writes, "if a man has become absorbed in his appetites or his ambitions and takes great pains to further them, all his thoughts are bound to become merely mortal."[55] However, "if a man has seriously devoted himself to the love of learning and to true wisdom, if he has exercised these aspects of himself above all, then there is absolutely no way that his thoughts can fail to be immortal and divine, should truth come within his grasp."[56] Here, Plato describes an excessive devotion to learning and wisdom, to exercising one's mental capacities "above all," yet this kind of excess poses no problems for the harmonious body and soul. Rather, the human search for immortality demands excessive care for the mind. "And to the extent that human nature can partake of immortality, he can in no way fail to achieve this: constantly caring for his divine part as he does, keeping well-ordered the guiding spirit that lives within him, he must indeed be supremely happy."[57] Only by focusing intently on the immortal soul can we align the "revolutions in our heads that were thrown off course at our birth" to the "harmonies and revolutions of the universe" and, finally, achieve the goal of creating "that most excellent life offered to humankind by the gods, both now and forevermore."[58]

Finally, Plato explains briefly how other living things were created, namely women and animals. Plato's focus on the male body in the *Timaeus* is quite apparent at this point, because the explanation of how women are created occurs almost as an afterthought in the text. Plato's understanding of the role of gluttony in human life occurs primarily in his description of the male body's creation. The gluttonous male body, with its propensity for excessive eating, threatens social order and stability because it resists rationality and causes disease; these features of gluttony make it one of the factors in the secondary creation of women. In the first generation of men were those who resisted rationality, and were cowardly or unjust; they "were reborn in the second generation as women."[59] Here Plato reveals a creation scheme in which women are born because of those men, as we have previously seen, who were unable to gain control over their desires and came to exhibit negative behaviors. Unlike Plato's more egalitarian views on men and women found in the *Republic,* in this text Plato firmly aligns masculinity with rationality and femininity with the appetites.[60] Making a connection between the diseases of the first generation, the creation of women, and "the desire for sexual union," Plato further concretizes the associations between disease, femininity, lack of control, and animality, for the very existence of woman is the result of inadequacy in the male.[61] Animals, too, are formed from males whose mortal souls could not be controlled by the immortal soul, whose bodies would not succumb to reason. Again, we see Plato's attempt to explain why the world is the way it is, and in this case, he suggests that women, though secondary creations, are nonetheless crucial to the continuation of the human race. The very existence and idea of woman is aligned with those "dreadful but necessary disturbances"—emotions and passions—that need to be controlled, but are also essential for human existence.[62]

For Plato, a focus on balance, harmony, and moderation reveals a fear of the pleasures of physical excesses that threaten to lure humans away from fulfilling their potential to be in harmony with the universe. While Plato argues that we overindulge because it is in our nature as human beings to do so, it is also our natural proclivity for excessive eating that lends philosophical weight to the necessity of learning to control our bodies. The immortal, rational soul, which is associated with manliness, has the best opportunity to master the appetites, which are associated conceptually with femininity, animality, and disease. By linking the possibilities of moral living with manliness, Plato encourages the association of gluttony, excess, appetite, and femininity, suggesting that excessive attention to physical pleasure is the surest way to immorality, inhumanity, and infirmity. Thus, while the needs of the physical body must be acknowledged, it is crucial that they also be controlled in order to create the conditions whereby the soul can strive to gain knowledge, and practice rationality. To be sure, Plato sees physical excess as the greatest danger to a life of moderation and balance, though the measure of that excess is not necessarily or only written on the physical body. Plato is certain, however, that to consume gluttonously—whether one is fat or not—throws off the delicate balance between body and soul, Necessity and Intellect, and threatens all that one needs to live the good life.

ARISTOTLE ON GLUTTONY

The question of how to live a good human life is also of concern to Aristotle, Plato's student, who lived and wrote in the fourth century BCE. Aristotle's understanding of the significance of the human relationship to food can be found in the *Nichomachean Ethics* throughout his discussion of virtue and vice. Virtue, in particular, is crucial for Aristotle, because it is only by living a virtuous life that a person can be happy. Happiness is the good to which all human life aims, and "the good of man is an activity of the soul in conformity with excellence or virtue."[63] To be virtuous means developing a "constant habit" that allows one to "almost automatically make the morally right choices on every occasion."[64] Moreover, the right moral choices occur, according to Aristotle, when one is able to act or feel in moderation. This regard for moderation is known as the doctrine of the mean, which, according to Martin Ostwald, is "Aristotle's most original contribution to moral theory."[65] The doctrine of the mean privileges moderation as a virtue in relation to two vices, an action or feeling that is excessive and an action or feeling that is deficient. Significantly, when it comes to self-control and self-indulgence with regard to food, little can be said for the vice of deficiency: for Aristotle, as for Plato, moderation in eating is about controlling excess. Thus, despite his focus on virtue as the mean, Aristotle confirms Plato's fear that eating to excess is a greater threat to human happiness than eating too little.

In addition, Aristotle's interest in eating to excess has less to do with the quantity of food one ingests and more to do with the quantity and quality of pleasure that indulgence brings. Developing habits of virtue means that one is able to choose the appropriate mean in any given situation, based on a "rational principle" that is able to discern what the mean is.[66] Those who are unable to develop certain habits of virtue, like the self-indulgent, pursue excess by choice, reveling in pleasure unchecked by reason. Others, namely those who are morally weak, pursue pleasure even though they know better. Thus, Aristotle makes a distinction between those who simply eat too much—the self-indulgent "belly-gorgers"—for whom he has little concern, and the morally weak, who gain excessive pleasure from their appetites, whether they eat too much or not. Here, Aristotle adds an important dimension to the understanding of gluttony by defining it according to the intent of the person who is eating excessively. In so doing, Aristotle delves into the psychology of pleasurable eating.

Virtue in Moderation, Vice in Excess

For Aristotle, as for Plato, the human has a soul that consists of two parts, the rational and irrational. Unlike Plato, Aristotle is uninterested in the souls' locations in the body; nonetheless, he assigns two functions to the irrational soul: the first is the part of the human that is common to all living creatures, "the part which is responsible for nurture and growth."[67] This part of the irrational soul "has no share in reason at all" and functions simply to keep living creatures alive.[68] The second part of the irrational soul corresponds to Plato's belly beast: it is the "seat of the appetites and of desire in general."[69] This part of the irrational soul can be (but doesn't necessarily want to be) persuaded by reason.[70] Virtue corresponds to the two kinds of soul: there is intellectual virtue, which corresponds to the rational soul, and moral virtue, which corresponds to the irrational soul. One aspect of human happiness, then, is to become morally virtuous by using rationality to persuade the appetitive part of the irrational soul to "comply with reason."[71]

But what is virtue? According to Aristotle, intellectual virtue is taught, and it requires experience and time to flourish.[72] Moral virtues, like courage, generosity, and gentleness, in contrast, are formed by habit: we must practice moral virtues over and over again in order for them to "stick." For example, we become self-controlled by exercising self-control.[73] In addition, exercising virtue depends on learning to recognize the role of pleasure and pain in our actions: "For moral excellence is concerned with pleasure and pain; it is pleasure that makes us do base actions and pain that prevents us from doing noble actions."[74] Thus, we must learn to enjoy working against too much pleasure: "A man who abstains from bodily pleasures and enjoys doing so is self-controlled; if he finds abstinence troublesome, he is self-indulgent; a man who endures danger without joy, or at least without pain, is courageous; if he endures it with pain, he is a coward."[75] Thus, the practice of virtue is about educating ourselves with regard to acting in "the best way in matters involving pleasure and pain."[76]

Aristotle also contends that "the nature of moral qualities is such that they are destroyed by defect and by excess."[77] To show that this is the case, Aristotle uses a bodily analogy to make his moral point:

We see the same thing happen in the case of strength and of health, to illustrate, as we must, the invisible by means of visible examples: excess as well as deficiency of physical exercise destroys our strength, and similarly, too much and too little food and drink destroys our health; the proportionate amount, however, produces, increases, and preserves it.[78]

Aristotle goes on to suggest that virtue responds in a similar manner to the body in relation to excess and deficiency, for "a man who revels in every pleasure and abstains from none becomes self-indulgent, while he who avoids every pleasure like a boor becomes what might be called insensitive."[79] The excess of self-indulgence and the deficiency of insensitivity stand in contrast to the mean of self-control. We thus have two vices—deficiency and excess—for almost every virtue or mean.

What exactly the mean is, however, is a complicated matter. While the mean of a thing is "a point equidistant from both extremes," the mean relative to individuals is "neither too large nor too small, and this is neither one nor the same for anybody."[80] Again, Aristotle uses a food example to illustrate his point: "if ten pounds of food is too much for a man to eat and two pounds little, it does not follow that the trainer will prescribe six pounds, for this may in turn be much or little for him to eat; it may be little for Milo [a famous wrestler] and much for someone who has just begun to take up athletics."[81] Although Aristotle is using food, a tangible substance, to suggest the challenges of properly determining the more ethereal idea of the moral mean—determining how to experience the right kind of pleasure or pain in its correct quantity, to act well at the right time, toward the right objects and people, for the right reason—he also highlights here the difficulty of developing specific moral prescriptions about food. If one person's excess in food is another's deficiency, gluttony becomes particularly difficult to define.

To complicate matters further, Aristotle also notes that some virtues do not have excesses or deficiencies, making it difficult to determine the mean. For instance, adultery cannot be made right by committing it with the right woman at the right time; adultery is always wrong. It is also impossible for any self-indulgent act to have a mean, excess, or deficiency. As Aristotle says, if this were the case, then "we would have a mean of excess and a mean of deficiency, and an excess of excess and a deficiency of deficiency," which would be logically unsound.[82] Yet, as Aristotle noted, if it is difficult to determine the mean relative to any individual, what it means to call an act self-indulgent will also, necessarily, be difficult to determine.

Self-Indulgence vs. Self-Control

In Book 3, Aristotle takes up the issue of self-indulgence and self-control with regard to food and other bodily pleasures. Self-control is "a mean in regard to pleasures" and is specifically a mean in regard to the pleasures of the body, not the pleasures of the soul.[83] He distinguishes these because one cannot be excessive in the pleasures of the soul, like learning.[84] Even more exclusively, the particular pleasures of the body concerned with self-control and self-indulgence are those pleasures of touch and taste, which Aristotle specifies as eating, drinking, and sexual intercourse.[85] Moreover, people who are self-indulgent do not discriminate with regard to food, like "wine tasters and chefs do when they prepare delicacies."[86] Rather, the self-indulgent enjoy food because they find pleasure "exclusively through touch in eating and in drinking as well as in sexual intercourse."[87] Aristotle supports his argument by citing the example of "a certain gourmet" who "prayed for a throat longer than a crane's, implying that he derived his pleasure from touch."[88]

Aristotle then takes up the question of human appetite for food and drink. He distinguishes "natural" appetite—the appetite that all living creatures have to live and be nourished—and personal appetites that are particular to a given human being, like a specific liking, say, for brownies or broccoli. It is in making this distinction that Aristotle abandons momentarily his notion of the mean, for with regard to the natural appetites, "few people go wrong, and that in only one direction, namely excess. For to eat and to drink anything until one is more than full is to exceed the natural amount, since natural appetite merely means filling a deficiency."[89] Those who overindulge their senses using food and drink submit unthinkingly to the "senses most widely shared by living beings"; such immoderation "is considered reprehensible for a good reason, for it inheres in us not as human beings but as animals."[90] These "belly-gorgers" eat beyond their natural satiety, and hence, are characterized as animals, for only those who are "all too slavish develop this trait."[91]

At the same time, Aristotle argues that it is virtually impossible to find men "deficient in regard to pleasures."[92] He calls this potential deficiency "insensitivity" but says that "such insensitivity is not human."[93] Nor is it, however, animal, for "even the animals discriminate between different kinds of food and enjoy some and not others. If there is someone to whom nothing is pleasant and who does not differentiate one thing from another, he must be anything but a man. There is no name for such a creature, since he is scarcely to be found."[94] Thus, deficiency with regard to the pleasures of food is almost unthinkable; even though the category of deficient pleasure is necessary for the structure of Aristotle's argument, it is a rather empty category, for when it comes to indulging one's natural appetites, only excess poses a serious problem.

While Aristotle seems to dismiss the excesses of the belly-gorger as irrational and animalistic, he is still interested in determining why there are people who are self-indulgent. As Charles Young puts it, "why don't the appetites simply vanish when the needs that occasion them are satisfied, at least in normal cases?"[95] Young points out that it is because we have personal appetites that the appetite requires the practice of virtue: were we all simply to listen to our hunger and eat until we were satisfied, there would be no reason for moral concern about food. What Aristotle is interested in is why it is that humans often wish to—and do—eat too many brownies or too much broccoli. In other words, Aristotle is interested in *why* people are gluttonous.

Aristotle's explanation focuses on the role of pleasure in human inclinations toward gluttony. Unlike the belly-gorgers, who simply eat to excess, those who are self-indulgent seek pleasure in a variety of ways. They find pleasure in things they should not, they find greater pleasure in things than others do, or they find pleasure in them in the wrong way.[96] Aristotle unfortunately gives no examples of these particular pleasures, though he is clear that "a self-indulgent man has appetite for everything pleasant or for what is most pleasant, and he is driven by his appetite to choose pleasant things at the cost of everything else."[97] He may give a clue when he suggests that the self-controlled man takes "no excessive pleasure in touch and taste," does not desire "beyond his means," and finds moderate pleasure in "the pleasant things that contribute to his health and well-being."[98] From this perspective, self-control with regard to food means that one will eat only enough food to satisfy hunger, eat a variety of foods that are not too expensive, and eat foods that are conducive to health. While it is true that, as Young suggests, Aristotle makes a distinction between foods that are "healthful," like broccoli, and those that are "treats," like brownies, it seems to me that Aristotle's point is about excessive pleasure no matter what kind of food inspires it.[99] For, in making a case that it is the delight in different kinds of pleasure that controls the self-indulgent man, he excludes nothing in the realm of taste as a potential source of pleasure, and even eating too much broccoli is not conducive to health. For example, the person who experiences more pleasure than others do when eating broccoli is self-indulgent in a similar way to the man who spends all of his money to buy the double-fudge pecan brownies he frequently enjoys. The real problem for the self-indulgent man is that he "loves such pleasures more than they are worth."[100] Unlike the self-controlled man, who "follows right reason," the self-indulgent man focuses too intently on the pleasures of the body, hence failing to be properly attentive to reason.[101]

Indeed, Aristotle's disdain for the self-indulgent can be seen in the fact that the pleasures involved in it are shared with other animals, and "appear slavish and bestial."[102] Because "the senses involved in self-indulgence are those most widely shared by living beings," self-indulgence is "considered reprehensible for a good reason, for it inheres in us not as human beings but as animals."[103] Being self-indulgent emphasizes the animalistic, and hence, irrational, aspects of the human being. Moreover, self-indulgence is also associated with "the naughtiness of children."[104] The difficulty here is that we are self-indulgent because we seek pleasure, as children do, without a sense of reason. So, Aristotle says,

if appetite and desire do not obey and do not subject themselves to the ruling element, they will go far astray. For the desire for pleasure is insatiable in a senseless creature and knows no bounds, and the active gratification of appetite will increase the appetite with which we were born, and if the appetites are great and intense, they push aside the power of reasoning.[105]

Thus, the greater the desire for pleasure, the more likely it will be that the desire for pleasure will supersede reason. Without reason, a human cannot be virtuous, and hence, cannot be happy.

Aristotle's disdain for the self-indulgent person is further highlighted in Book 7, when he considers the difference between the self-indulgent and morally weak man. While the morally weak man "is the kind of person who pursues bodily pleasures to excess and contrary to right reason, though he is not persuaded (that he ought to do so)," the self-indulgent man "is persuaded to pursue them because he is the kind of man who does so."[106] Thus, a morally weak man understands the virtue of moderation but "loses himself under the impact of emotion and violates right reason."[107] The self-indulgent man, on the other hand, neither understands nor wants to understand the virtue of moderation and is instead "persuaded that he must abandon himself completely to the pursuit of such pleasures."[108] The self-indulgent man is the worst kind of man, the morally weak man can be persuaded through reason, while the best man is the man who exhibits moral strength, the kind of man "who remains steadfast and does not lose himself, at least not under the impact of emotion."[109] The self-indulgent man thus seeks pleasure for its own sake and ignores the dictates of reason, while the morally weak man "feels more joy than he should (in bodily things)" and is unable, on every occasion, to win the struggle between reason and pleasure.[110] The morally strong man "does find pleasure in such things, but he is not driven by them."[111] Indeed, the goal is not to avoid pleasure, for it is rare to find a person who experiences "less joy than he should at the things of the body"; rather, for Aristotle, the key to the moderate life is to feel pleasure, and to be able to regulate pleasure through the use of reason.[112]

Aristotle's focus on the role of pleasure and reason in the consumption of food shifts the focus away from the body itself; like Plato, Aristotle is uninterested in whether or not the body is fat. Certainly, he is interested in the question of the body's health; as we saw earlier, he uses the idea of health as a way to illustrate the doctrine of the mean; eating too much or too little food destroys health, while the proportionate amount "produces, increases and preserves it."[113] Yet, because the mean must be determined for each individual, and because Aristotle is primarily concerned with the amount and kind of pleasure one gets from food, what the body looks like is of little consequence. In Aristotle's scheme of things, a fat person who receives the appropriate pleasure from food would be more virtuous than a skinny person who receives excessive pleasure from eating. For Aristotle, as for Plato, the mere size of the body does not reveal or reflect the soul's relationship with reason, virtue, or happiness.

Aristotle's formulation of what it means to be happy and to live a good life provides a crucial foundation upon which ideas about gluttony and excess are fashioned throughout Western history. Aristotle's focus on the ways in which the pleasures of the body can distract from rational thinking and lead to unhappiness bolsters Plato's similar claim and creates a coherent cultural message that the pleasure-seeking body must be controlled by the rational mind. Indeed, as we shall see, Aristotle's focus on the mean of moderation becomes standard fare when talking of the proper human relationship to food, as does his emphasis on the threat of excess—as opposed to deficiency—to that mean.

CONCLUSION

An exploration of the meaning and significance of gluttony for Plato and Aristotle reveals both similarities to and differences from biblical concerns. With their interest in a bodily discipline that benefits intellectual pursuits, and their focus on the dangers of excessive eating and pleasurable indulgence, Plato and Aristotle provide an expansive and influential definition of gluttony. For both Plato and Aristotle, gluttony is aligned with the irrational soul, which is, in turn, associated with the appetites and bodily desire. Gluttony threatens the possibility of the good, moderate, happy, rational life by diverting attention from intellectual to bodily pursuits. In addition, both philosophers see gluttony as a behavior that reveals humanity's animalistic, irrational nature. As such, gluttony is to be avoided. To live a good life, humans must develop physical regimens and moral self-control as ways to counter the natural human proclivity for gluttony. Both philosophers understand excessive eating in a contextual framework of conceptual oppositions. While Plato aligns gluttonous excess with disease, impurity, animality, and femininity, moderation becomes characteristic of the healthy, pure, masculine human. For Aristotle, moderation is the goal of human existence; even more than Plato, Aristotle is interested in why humans pursue pleasure even when they know that such pursuit is morally disadvantageous.

Indeed, both philosophers underscore the problem of gluttony and focus on moderation as the key to the good life. Aristotle's doctrine of the mean, where virtue stands as the median between the two vices of excess and deficiency, provides the foundation for his entire ethical system. Nonetheless, for both authors, excess creates a greater challenge to the virtue of moderation than does deficiency. What Plato and Aristotle offer to the history of ideas of gluttony and fatness in the West is a conception of excess that renders it more dangerous, more threatening to social harmony, than its opposite, abstinence. Finally, despite their intense interest in the challenge of gluttony, neither philosopher makes a connection between gluttony and being fat, which emphasizes the idea that bodily behavior and bodily appearance remain distinct. Unlike today, when the immorality of gluttonous behavior is always written on the fat body, an understanding of the philosophical importance of gluttony in the work of Plato and Aristotle offers a significant contrast to the assumptions that underlie contemporary Western ideas about the gluttonous and fat body.

3

Inside and Out: Medicine, Health, and Physiognomy in the Ancient World

It is possible to infer character from features . . . For if there is an affection which belongs properly to an individual kind, e.g. courage to lions, it is necessary that there should be a sign of it: for . . . body and soul are affected together.[1]

—Aristotle

Because our contemporary understanding of the fat body is shaped by medical knowledge, it is important that we understand how the ancient world perceived the fat body from a medical perspective. This chapter begins its examination of the fat body in ancient medicine by looking at the works of Hippocrates, who is considered to be the first doctor in the Western world. In addition, this chapter explores texts from the ancient pseudo-science of physiognomy, a quasi-medical discourse that interprets character from physique; as the opening quote from Aristotle suggests, the physical appearance of a body—animal or human—reveals its inner moral dispositions, reflecting the notion that body and soul work together. As we move in this chapter into the world of Greek and Roman medicine and physiognomy, we find that the biblical and philosophical uncoupling of fatness and gluttony holds; the fat person is not necessarily a glutton, and the glutton is not always fat. In the Greek and Roman worlds, gluttony does continue to be censured, and medical texts underscore the importance of self-restraint when eating and drinking. But while the gluttonous body—whether fat or not—exhibits bad behavior that threatens social order and stability, the fat body—even when it is the result of eating too much food—does not inevitably reveal something about a person's behavior that presents a threat to society. As we saw in the biblical texts, and in Plato and Aristotle, it is the *behavior* of the glutton, and not the *appearance* of the fat body that is subject to the most moral disapproval. This chapter shows that the distinction between behavior and appearance reveals an underlying recognition that being fat is not inevitably or always connected to gluttonous behavior or bad character. A fat body does not necessarily reveal—though it can—important aspects of one's character.

Indeed, Greek and Roman medical writers reveal concepts of the fat body that highlight its multiple moral and social meanings, providing telling contrasts and challenges to, as well as confirmation of, contemporary views. Ancient medical texts ask us to think very differently about bodily composition and function. They challenge us to define the fat body using means other than BMI: how fat is the person designated as "fat" or "fleshy" or "big"? They ask why some bodies are fat and others are not, a question that assumes that there are more reasons than overeating that create fat bodies. They ask what it means to be healthy. In addition, if the body's appearance reveals character, as physiognomy suggests, a fat body should clearly mark behaviors—like greed or lack of self-discipline. Yet, physiognomic texts reveal that the fat body is an ambivalent symbol, one that does not clearly or consistently reflect moral failure. Because of the questions they ask and the perspectives they reveal, ancient medical and physiognomic texts show us the importance of understanding the historical and cultural contexts that shape a society's perspective on the fat body.

THE BODY IN ANCIENT MEDICINE

According to medical historian Helen King, contemporary Western society contends with two different definitions of health.[2] From the biomedical perspective, health is about the absence of disease. Such a scientific definition sees medical knowledge of the body as authoritative; health and illness can be measured and assessed with a variety of tests and evaluative techniques. Viewing health in this way underscores the importance of the medical doctor as the expert who can propose cures for illnesses and assist patients in establishing bodily routines that are believed to create the best possibilities for a healthy life. A more social view of health is found in the World Health Organization's 1946 description of health as "a state of complete physical, mental and social well-being and not merely the absence of disease or infirmity."[3] This definition rejects a purely medical perspective on the body and contends that human health should be viewed more holistically, taking into account not only the condition of the individual's body, but how that body lives in the world. While medical experts treat the bodily aspects of human health, in this definition, overall health is related to other aspects of human life, like economic status, educational opportunities, or adequate housing. Thinking of health more holistically allows us to think about bodily health as one part of a much bigger picture of what it means to be "healthy."

The ancient Greeks also had two competing ways of thinking about the origins of human health that reveal a conceptual parallel to our own. The famous doctor Hippocrates speculates that the beginning of human life was fraught with disease because humans ate the same raw foods as the animals; as doctors worked to create a diet of prepared and cooked foods appropriate for humans, humans became healthy.[4] In this story, doctors become the key players in the creation of human culture with their role in developing a cuisine that included cooked foods, which, not incidentally, reveals the importance of food as a pivotal contributor to human health. This story also suggests parallels with the biblical text, where prohibited foods and foods cooked in particular ways signify distinctions between God and humans, thus revealing an important aspect of the Israelite worldview. Here, the Greek understanding of the distinction between humans and animals is played out in the development of human culture, signified by cooked food.

A different view can be found in the poet Hesiod's *Works and Days,* which posits a primordial world of human health and perfection that was destroyed when Prometheus stole fire from the gods, and in retaliation, the gods created Pandora and sent her to earth with a box entrusted to her care. Disobeying the orders of the gods by opening the box, Pandora released disease into the world along with all sorts of other human afflictions.[5] This story suggests not only that disease is the result of rebellion against the gods and woman's curiosity, but also that health is to be appreciated as a reminder of the time before suffering began, a remembrance of primordial human happiness. Further parallels can be seen here with the story of Adam and Eve in Genesis, as human sin and suffering are portrayed as the result of woman's curiosity and human disobedience. As a comparison of these modern and ancient definitions show, stories about the origins and meaning of health vary significantly from ancient to modern times. Nonetheless, what is shared by both cultures is that health can be defined from a scientific, medical perspective, and a societal one, where health and happiness are inextricably linked.

Medical and social definitions of health in the modern and ancient worlds emphasize the historical and cultural contexts that influence any given culture's understanding of the fat body. In the contemporary world, medical science influences all aspects of our understanding of the fat body—fat = overeating = unhealthy—and it is easy to dismiss evidence that may present a challenge to the dominant mode of thinking. Indeed, it is hard to imagine anything other than that our views are correct, true, scientific, and inevitable. Yet, historical comparisons can reveal the conceptual shifts that belie the seeming facticity of those assumptions. As King points out, ancient Greek stories of the origins of human health show that "health is only a pawn in the bigger game, whether that game is myth explaining how all the perceived evils of the world derive from the same point, or medicine claiming the credit for all that is good."[6] To see that ancient ways of thinking about health and the body are inevitably wrapped up in broader cultural ideologies may allow us some conceptual space to identify the broader cultural ideas in which our own ideas about health and the fat body live.

Acknowledging the role of medical and cultural ideologies in understanding the fat body raises two important issues. First, whether the Greeks are "right" about how the body functions is not the issue; what we might consider to be the scientific accuracy—or lack thereof—of ancient medicine could allow an easy dismissal of anything the Greeks had to say. So, for instance, if the Greeks were to say that being fat is not a deterrent to health, one possible reaction would be simply to say that they were wrong about the unhealthy effects of being fat because they lacked the kind of detailed knowledge of the body that we have today. A response like this ignores the ways in which different kinds of bodies are treated in the whole context of Greek medicine and refuses to acknowledge that the meanings and perceptions of different kinds of bodies are culturally determined.

Another issue that arises when we recognize the way that ideology influences our understanding of the past is the attempt to suggest that, despite all of their differences, the Greeks, like many people today, believed that being fat was detrimental to health. A number of scholars have made this case, suggesting that contemporary ideas about the unhealthy effects of being fat have been consistent over time. Internationally known expert on obesity George Bray has suggested that "the concept that obesity was a risk to health was clearly identified in the works of Hippocrates and frequently over the ensuing centuries,"[7] while Helen Christopoulou-Aletra and Niki Papavramidou claim that "in classical antiquity, particularly in the *Hippocratic Corpus,* obesity was considered the cause of disease, and in the extreme, death."[8] And Sander Gilman claims that "fat has been a pathological category in the West from the earliest state of medical culture."[9] Yet, this chapter argues that a more holistic reading of ancient medical texts renders a broader perspective on the fat body. While it is possible to read Hippocrates in a way that affirms our contemporary views, Hippocratic texts also raise a number of questions, like how the fat body is defined, how being fat is related to disease, how body composition is related to the natural world, and how moderation is understood; all of these questions underscore the idea that Hippocratic texts think quite differently about the body from a medical perspective than we do in the contemporary West. Thus, the challenge of Hippocratic texts is to understand the conceptual differences in the ways that ancient medical texts perceive the meanings of fat and gluttonous bodies, and to think about them in relation to our own. For instance, Hippocratic texts are more circumspect about the fat body and its prospects for health. Thus, although a number of contemporary writers try to make the case that ancient doctors regularly recommend weight loss or express disapproval of the fat body much as many doctors do today, an in-depth look at ancient medical treatises suggests a rather different way of thinking about health.

FAT HIPPOCRATIC BODIES

Knowledge of ancient perspectives on health and medicine begins with a collection of sixty or so texts in the Hippocratic Corpus. Written between 420–370 BCE, and compiled in Alexandria around 280 BCE, these texts, though attributed to Hippocrates, "the Father of Medicine," are likely the work of more than one author, so explanations and perspectives vary, depending on which text is being examined.[10] At its core, though, Hippocratic medicine is concerned with the maintenance of health, which requires knowledge about the body's make-up and the best ways to treat disease. How diseases are treated, of course, depends on the body's constitution, for which the texts provide various explanations, all of which are quite different from those with which we are familiar today.

Hippocratic texts understand the body as an integral part of the universe, made up of elements found in nature, which work together in harmony to create health. The texts diverge in their explanations of the constituent elements of human beings: sometimes the human is considered to be made up of earth, air, fire, and water—the fundamental building blocks of nature—and at other times, the focus is more specifically on black bile, yellow bile, blood, and phlegm, fluids that also reflect the qualities of earth, air, fire, and water. The qualities of hot, cold, wet, and dry also play a role in understanding how the body works. Usually, some combination of the elements and qualities are put into play so that, for instance, the elements of blood, phlegm, yellow bile, and black bile (or sometimes phlegm, bile, blood, and water) work together with the qualities of hot, cold, wet, and dry, where fire is hot and dry, and water wet and cold.[11] A person enjoys "the most perfect health when these elements are duly proportioned to one another in respect of compounding, power and bulk, and when they are perfectly mingled," suggesting that the best body is the moderate body, one that is "nimble and well-proportioned, who has healthy inward parts, and who is neither too fleshy nor too thin."[12] Make no mistake: the Greeks most certainly privilege the moderate body as described here. This is not surprising, given the Greeks' admiration for the warrior and the athlete, as we see in numerous examples of Greek art, and in ancient literary works like Homer's *Iliad*. More on the moderate body later.

For now, it is important to understand that Hippocratic texts recognize that different bodies are constitutionally distinct, and that not every body is exactly alike; rather, each individual has his or her own distinct, innate, perfectly balanced elemental make-up. This is how Hippocratic texts understand how some people may be affected by particular diseases, while others are not: "The constitutions of men are well or ill adapted to the seasons, some to summer, some to winter; others again to districts, to periods of life, to modes of living, to the various constitutions of diseases."[13] In addition, the bodily humors and the qualities shift and change with the seasons. So, for example, "phlegm increases in a man in winter; for phlegm, being the coldest constituent of the body, is closest akin to winter."[14] Finally, the connection between the human body and the natural world through seasonal shifts and changes also underscores the links between the body and the universe, as a whole:

All these elements then are always comprised in the body of a man, but as the year goes round they become now greater and now less, each in turn and according to its nature. For just as every year participates in every element, the hot, the cold, the dry and the moist—none in fact of these elements would last for a moment without all the things that exist in this universe.[15]

The body's constitution and its workings are thus seen to reflect the make-up and operations of the universe itself, suggesting an approach to bodily health that is integrated into and reflects a holistic understanding of the human being as part and parcel of the natural world. Making links between the elements of the body and the elements of nature offers us an opportunity to examine the meaning of moderation, excess, and body size in texts that attempt to strike a balance between what can be claimed to be universally true declarations about all bodies, and the special circumstances and needs of each individual. This weighing of the universal and individual is more explicit in Hippocratic texts than it is today, especially when it comes to ideas about weight and weight loss.

One of the best ways to understand how Hippocrates thinks about the body is to examine the relationship between body and the environment in the text, "Airs, Waters, Places." Here, Hippocrates analyzes the effects of climate and geography both on health and character, focusing particularly on the peoples of Europe and Asia (Asia Minor, which sometimes includes Greeks[16]). Geography and body type are intimately connected, so that those who live in a land without rivers, where the water people drink is "marshy, stagnant, and fenny," will have physiques that "must show protruding bellies and large spleens."[17] Like the physiognomic texts we examine later in this chapter, Hippocrates often associates character traits with particular body types, so people who live in a climate with "sharp contrasts" between the seasons "are likely to be of big physique, with a nature well-adapted for endurance and courage," while others, who "dwell in a high land that is level, windy, and watered, will be tall in physique and similar to one another, but rather unmanly and tame in character."[18] Such connections between body type and character are not without moral valuation; Hippocrates asserts that geographical disadvantages create physically superior people and vice versa.

Where the land is rich, soft, and well-watered . . . and if the situation be favorable as regards the seasons, there the inhabitants are fleshy, ill-articulated, moist, lazy, and generally cowardly in character. . . . But where the land is bare, waterless, rough, oppressed by winter's storms and burnt by the sun, there you will see men who are hard, lean, well-articulated, well-braced and hairy; such natures will be found energetic, vigilant, stubborn and independent in character and in temper, wild rather than tame, of more than average sharpness and intelligence in the arts, and in war of more than average courage.[19]

Soft land = soft body; hard land = hard body, and hard bodies come with intelligence and courage. Yet, at the same time that he makes links between the environment and body type, Hippocrates also understands that the environment is not the only factor that influences character. He argues, for instance, that "violent and frequent" changes in weather create a greater variety in European body types than in Asia, and that "the Europeans are also more courageous" than the Asiatics but then suggests that courage is a character trait formed not only by climate and geography, but also by social institutions and law.[20] In this way, Hippocrates's typology of the peoples of Europe and Asia by body type, geography, and climate can be presented as an objective standard that is subject to revision if cultural influences are found to exist. So, it is possible that the fleshy coward can become "artificially" courageous with "the imposition of law."[21] By accounting for so many factors in his understanding of the body, Hippocrates is thus not only able to create a taxonomy of the character traits of humanity as related to their external appearance, he is also able to account for exceptions to his general rules.

This conceptual dance between the universal truths about bodies and the necessity of dealing with individual deviations from the universal is the primary characteristic of Hippocratic texts and of the Hippocratic understanding of the body and of bodily health. Within a schema that places the body in seasonal cycles and elemental balance, maintaining the body's health consists of preserving the balance between the different bodily humors in the context of varying seasons, climates, exercise, and diet; curing illness focuses on regaining a bodily balance that was lost. Hippocratic medicine recommends an entire regimen for health that consists not only of what a person eats and drinks, but also advocates qualities and quantities of exercise, sexual activity, and sleep. Indeed, "A man must observe the risings and settings of the stars, that he may know how to watch for change and excess in food, drink, wind and the whole universe, from which diseases exist among men."[22] The need to take into account so many factors when making a diagnosis suggests a recognition of the complexities of the body and its functions. When all is said and done, though, Hippocrates states that, while a myriad of factors may lead to good or ill health, food and exercise are the most crucial elements of the body's regimen because they "work together to produce health."[23] He suggests that if "it were possible to discover for the constitution of each individual a due proportion of food to exercise, with no inaccuracy either of excess or of defect, an exact discovery of health for all men would have been made.[24] Such a discovery is impossible, however, for the physician cannot be present at all times in a patient's life to see whether there occurs "even a small deficiency in one or the other."[25] So delicate and exact is the balance that determines health that it is virtually impossible to maintain it on a constant and continuing basis; such is the way that Hippocratic texts can account for periodic illness.

When the body does get out of balance, Hippocratic texts generally recommend that whatever feature is out of balance be countered with its opposite. Hippocratic medicine sees the body as a play of opposites where, for instance, "hunger is a disease, as everything is called a disease which makes a man suffer. What then is the remedy for hunger? That which makes hunger to cease. This is eating, so that by eating hunger must be cured. Again, drink stays thirst; and again repletion is cured by depletion, depletion by repletion, fatigue by rest. To sum up in a single sentence, opposites are cures for opposites."[26]

Within Hippocratic medicine, then, there is a recognition that individual bodies are made up of distinct combinations of humors and qualities that require different methods for bodily balance, which is created by adopting a regimen opposite of the body's natural characteristics. So, the person with the "fleshy (*sarkinos*), soft and red" physique, whose nature is moist, "will find it beneficial to adopt a rather dry regimen," while the person with the "lean and sinewy" physique, whose nature is dry, "should adopt a moister regimen for the greater part of the time."[27] Thus, Hippocratic medicine acknowledges not only that bodies are different—some fleshy and soft, some thin and sinewy—but that these bodies require distinctive regimens to maintain health. Moreover, because of the way that Hippocrates presents ideas about bodily balancing, it seems clear that what is important is balancing what one has, whether one is fat or not. In this context, Hippocrates does not attempt to suggest how these bodies should change to be a different kind of body. Rather, he suggests what kind of regimen would be most advantageous, given the body's humoral make-up. It is important to note that there is no moral judgment here about being fleshy and soft or lean and sinewy. What Hippocrates is interested in is how to create the maximum state of health for the body that exists.

When it comes to the fat body, then, a Hippocratic doctor would need to take into account a wide variety of factors in determining the body's proper regimen. And, what is fascinating about Hippocratic texts—especially in light of the constant contemporary medical recommendation to lose excess weight—is that there is no absolute medical or moral imperative to lose weight if one is fat or fleshy. While Helen Christopolou-Aletra and Niki Papavramidou suggest that Hippocrates thought of weight loss as necessary for health, much in the same way that many suggest today, it seems to me that Hippocrates's understanding of health is more complex than this.[28] It is most certainly the case that humoral balance, moderation, and the proper regimen are keys to defining health in the Hippocratic corpus, and that there are recommendations for those who wish to reduce fleshy excess.[29] But when there are recommendations on how people can lose weight if they so desire, there are also recommendations for those who wish to gain weight. For instance, in "Regimen in Health," Hippocrates states that people who are fat (*pachus*) "and wish to become thin," should "always fast when they undertake exertion," while those who are thin "and wish to become fat (*pachus*)" should "do the opposite of these things."[30] Running exercises that are done wearing a cloak are, for instance, beneficial in making the body moist (sweaty), so they are recommended to those "who have a dry body, to those who have excess of flesh which they wish to reduce, and, because of the coldness of their bodies, to those who are getting on in years."[31] So, certain practices are beneficial to people with a number of different constitutions and depend on the specific way in which the individual's body must attain balance. On the whole, then, Hippocratic texts understand that the humoral make-up of bodies differs, that different body types require different regimens, that people may be constitutionally more or less "fleshy," and that maintaining health requires a regimen appropriate to the season and environment, as well as the age, sex, and occupation of the individual.

Within this overarching need for bodily balance, there are certainly occasions in Hippocratic texts where excess flesh is seen as an impediment to health. Contemporary readers who want Hippocrates to share the belief that reducing fleshy excess always leads to greater health focus only on these texts, without getting a sense of the big picture presented here. What contemporary readers fail to note with their one-sided approach to these texts is that Hippocrates always focuses on balance: if the reduction of flesh is necessary in one case, there may certainly be other cases where the expansion of the flesh is also necessary.

One version of Hippocrates's interest in weight loss can be seen in the four texts called *Regimen*. These texts present an atypical way of understanding the body in the Hippocratic corpus as made up only of fire (hot and dry; causes motion) and water (cold and wet; nourishes), with the two main contributors to health being food and exercise. These texts focus primarily on how excesses and deficiencies of food and exercise contribute to disease, so that the extremes, especially excess, is the focus. From the perspective of these texts, the state of the body is in constant flux, moving back and forth from depletion to repletion, from illness to health, like the movement of a saw through a log, one side pulling and the other pushing.[32] Yet, even within this context, the author admits that it is "impossible to treat of the regimen of men with such a nicety as to make the exercises exactly proportionate to the amount of food."[33] He explains that there are so many factors to consider in the creation of a regimen—the differing constitutions of men, the requirements of people of different ages, the distinct qualities of foods—that all he can do is give general rules that may not be accurate for a given individual. Again, we see the tension here between Hippocrates's desire to make universal statements about regimen even when he realizes that each person requires a very individual set of treatments to attain balance.

Within this specific approach to the body, the author considers the oppositional constitutions of a number of different kinds of bodies. A person made up of "the moistest fire and the driest water," for example, is the best combination, the one that is most perceptive or gives one the best command of one's senses, and the appropriate food and exercise will keep this person healthy and balanced.[34] But, if one of these elements "grows or diminishes," the result is something "most unintelligent" or imperceptible.[35] A person whose water masters fire is "senseless" or "grossly stupid" and weeps for no reason; this kind of person must perform a regimen that is focused on drying and "reduction of flesh."[36] Similarly, the person whose fire somewhat overpowers water "rapidly passes judgment on the things presented to it," moves too quickly from one object to another, and requires a regimen "inclining more to water," less frequent sexual intercourse, and well-diluted drink.[37] Moreover,

to reduce the flesh of such persons conduces to their [ability to be in possession of their senses]; for abundance of flesh cannot fail to result in inflammation of the blood, and when this happens to a soul of this sort it turns to madness, as the water has been mastered and the fire attracted.[38]

If fire further masters water, the person is "half-mad," whether the inflammation results from "intoxication, or from overabundance of flesh, or from eating too much meat."[39] To make connections between too much flesh and stupidity, madness, and lack of intelligence suggests the similarities between the Greeks' moral judgments of the fat body and those we saw in the Hebrew Bible. At the same time, however, these medical texts are also consistently clear that restoring balance is the key. Thus, when there are occasions where "exercise is in excess of food," the patient needs to "get drunk once or twice, but not to excess, to have sexual intercourse after a moderate indulgence in wine, and to slack off their exercises, except walking."[40] One must do whatever is necessary to restore bodily balance, whether that requires self-restraint or self-indulgence.

Another context in which it appears that being fat is unhealthy can be found in Hippocrates's statements about women's fertility. In "Aphorisms," the author declares that, "when unnaturally fat (*pachus*) women cannot conceive, it is because the fat presses the mouth of the womb, and conception is impossible until they grow thinner."[41] In "Prorrhetic 2," the author suggests that women who are "by nature" more likely to become pregnant have these characteristics: "small women conceive better than large ones, thin better than [fat] (*pachus*),[42] pale better than ruddy, dark better than livid."[43] At the same time, however,

Women who are of good colour, who are fleshy (*sarka*) and plump (*pi'eira*) with their vessels hidden, who are free of pains, but whose menses either do not appear at all or are scanty and irregular: this is one of the most difficult of types in which to force pregnancy to occur. If, on the other hand, with the menses appearing unhesitatingly, the body is in such a state and the woman does not conceive, the uterus is to blame that offspring cannot grow—for it must be either retracted or gaping, since the other evils that arise in it are accompanied by pains, paleness and melting of the tissue.[44]

In other words, it may be the size and shape of the body that is at issue in assessing fertility, or it is the uterus itself, which, even when contained in the most perfect body, may malfunction. Thus, initial assumptions about the likely infertility of the fat body are tempered by explanations that simultaneously categorize fertile bodies and explain exceptions to the rule.

We can see this move again in Hippocrates's assessment of women's potential for childbearing as it is related to the environment in which women live. In "Airs, Waters, Places," the author assesses women's fertility in a number of different cultures. Scythians, for instance, spend much of their time riding horses in a cold, damp climate. Because of this, they are a "ruddy" race, whose girls—because they sit in wagons all the time—are "wonderfully flabby and torpid in physique."[45] Such a lifestyle, however, "prevents fertility": the men have little desire for sex because their constitutions are so "moist" and "the constant jolting on their horses unfits them for intercourse."[46] The women are fat and moist, and "the mouth of the womb is closed by fat and does not admit the seed."[47] Such claims suggest a clear Hippocratic disdain for the fat body.

Yet, Hippocrates discusses the fertility of every race he examines in "Airs, Waters, Places," and few of the races have environmental conditions conducive to fertility. People from cities "that lie exposed to the hot winds" ensure that women are "unhealthy," and "barren from disease."[48] Those who live in cities "facing the cold winds" have women who become "barren through the waters being hard, indigestible and cold."[49] Women in damp, rainy climates "conceive hardly and are delivered with difficulty."[50] Indeed, the only women who "very readily conceive and have easy deliveries" live in cities that "lie towards the risings of the sun."[51] Thus, it seems apparent that environmental conditions, which determine body type, are more to blame for infertility than body type itself. Moreover, it seems clear here that body size is not seen to be the result of overeating, as we assume today, but rather reflects the climate, environment, and social practices of the culture in which that body lives.

The difficulty of analyzing the role of body size in relation to fertility is paralleled in another case where being fat is seemingly associated with mortality. Hippocrates's "Aphorism" 44 is one of the most quoted Hippocratic statements by those wishing to suggest that ancient medicine also saw the fat body as unhealthy. In the Loeb translation, the aphorism reads: "Those who are constitutionally very fat (*pachus*) are more apt to die quickly than those who are thin."[52] Footnotes attached to this aphorism suggest that the phrase "die quickly" refers to the idea that the constitutionally very fat "have less power successfully to resist a severe disease." In Edwin Burton Levine's *Hippocrates,* the same aphorism is translated, "People who are excessively overweight (by nature) are far more apt to die suddenly than those of average weight."[53] While it is clear that being constitutionally *pachus* is disadvantageous, it is unclear exactly what that disadvantage is; the meaning of the aphorism is ambiguous. What seems clear in this aphorism is that there are some people who are "by nature" or "constitutionally" *pachus,* a word that is translated as "fat." This suggests that the fat body is not always the result of overeating, but rather may be an inherent feature of a person's humoral and constitutional make-up. The word *pachus,* which is translated as "fat" or "fleshy," also implies stout, heavy (as opposed to wispy), strong, or solid, which conjures up an image of a large, but not necessarily fat or obese person. Moreover, since there is no indication in Hippocratic texts of how determinations of body weight were made, we have no idea what passed for the fat body: is it the contemporary category of overweight? Obese? Morbidly obese? There is no way of telling this in the Hippocratic texts. Certainly, one aphorism with an ambiguous meaning does not allow us to make conclusive claims about the overall understanding of the fat body from a Hippocratic medical perspective, as a number of contemporary readers propose.

Indeed, as the Hippocratic texts show, being fat may simply be the result of one's natural humoral constitution, or, if it is a factor in illness, it may need to be reduced. Ancient Greek medicine suggests that there are numerous factors that go into determining the individual's regimen, including proper amounts and kinds of food, exercise, sex, and sleep. There is no wholesale condemnation of the fat body, nor are there consistent recommendations for weight loss.

THE HIPPOCRATIC GLUTTON

In the Hippocratic texts, the individual body's distinct humoral make-up and regimen for health is understood in the context of universal ideas about what it means to be healthy. The primary way that health is understood is that it is a balance of constituent elements that can become unbalanced through excesses of one kind or another. To achieve health means to counter the imbalance with its opposite—too little food requires eating more; too much food requires eating less—and to maintain health requires moderation. So, it should come as no surprise that excessive eating, or surfeit, as the texts suggest, is not recommended. At the same time, however, it is important to note that overeating is not always or inevitably connected to being fat. For example, in "Regimen 3," Hippocrates discusses the symptoms of surfeit, which may or may not be recognizable as such. Body aches, fever, headaches, constipation, even pneumonia are seen as the result of surfeit, though the patient may think that they are in a state of fatigue rather than surfeit.[54] A recognized lack of ability to discern the source of one's fatigue suggests that surfeit is not necessarily associated with being fat, though one of the many cures is the reduction of flesh. Other cures include vomiting, steam baths, walking, abstinence from sexual intercourse, and "wrestling with the body oiled."[55] Indeed, given the wide range of symptoms and cures for surfeit, it would seem to be a rather common condition experienced by many people, whether they are fat or not.

And although it is certainly the case that excessive eating can lead to disease, as is often emphasized by contemporary readers, such an emphasis fails to note that eating too little is equally damaging. So, it may certainly be true that, "if the foods and drinks that are most nourishing to the body and most sufficient for nourishment and health are employed at an inopportune moment or in an excessive amount, diseases result and, from the diseases, deaths. . . ."[56] But Hippocrates also claims that "if a man takes insufficient food, the mistake is a great as that of excess, and harms the man just as much. For abstinence has upon the human constitution a most powerful effect, to enervate, to weaken and to kill."[57] As is characteristic for Hippocratic texts, both excesses and deficiencies cause problems.

A holistic analysis of Hippocrates's comments on body types and proper regimen suggests that the ancient Greek medical approach to the body requires assent to the idea that there is more than one healthy body type, and that what makes a body healthy is the balance between the elements of the individual's body, whether that body is fat or thin, short or tall. From the Hippocratic perspective, a person's ethnic heritage, along with the culture and environment in which they live, determines the body's humoral make-up and, hence, the body's proper regimen. While gluttony or surfeit can result in impediments to health because excesses (or deficiencies) inevitably cause the body to become imbalanced, there is no inevitable causal connection between surfeit and fatness. Indeed, because of Hippocratic assumptions about the relationship between the body and the natural world, Greek medicine has a broader and more holistic understanding of the healthy body than we appear to have today.

These ideas about the body confirm the distinction between the fat body and the glutton that we saw in the Hebrew Bible. As we turn to physiognomy, an ancient pseudo-science that connects the inner features of the soul with the body's appearance, we will see that these divisions continue to hold.

PHYSIOGNOMY: FAT AND CHARACTER

The ancient pseudo-science of physiognomy emphasizes the connection between the appearance of the body and one's character or disposition. From this perspective, the physical body symbolizes and reveals one's inner nature or soul; the body becomes a visible canvas upon which a person's mental proclivities, temperament, behavioral tendencies, and moral values are exposed. In the ancient world, we see the principles of physiognomy at work both in a few formal treatises, like Pseudo-Aristotle's fourth-century BCE or Polemon's second-century CE synonymously titled *Physiognomics,* as well as informally, in the detailed physical descriptions found in many ancient biographies, like Suetonius's *On the Lives of the Caesars.*[58] Although nowadays we might tend to dismiss such connections as frivolous, less systematic and more informal versions of physiognomy—what Elizabeth Evans calls "physiognomic consciousness"—lives on today in the idea that body language can give clues to psychological states, or that actors are hired for certain roles because they "look the part."[59] Moreover, physiognomic consciousness is at play in the contemporary assumption that a fat body reveals an inner glutton, that fatness exposes a fatal character flaw, a moral iniquity. Indeed, given the clear connection between body and soul that physiognomy assumes, we might expect that in those ancient treatises the appearance of the fat body would reflect and reveal the inner glutton. And, in some texts it does: the copious size of the belly, in particular, is occasionally read as the sign of the glutton. At the same time, however, the large or fleshy belly is also read as an indication of strength or gentleness. Far from being a certain sign of negative character, the fat belly plays an ambivalent role in ancient physiognomy, a rare example of a bodily feature that escapes being labeled as a physical manifestation of personal identity. Despite the clear conceptual connections made between the physical body and the inner self in the ancient world—links made much more systematically than we would ever claim to do—the meaning of the fat body remains ambiguous, and multivalent.

Pseudo-Aristotle: Physiognomics

When the philosopher Aristotle died in 322 BCE, he left behind a thriving academy of students and scholars. Documents from this school survive as part of the Aristotelian Corpus of works, as texts influenced by, but probably not written by, Aristotle himself; the treatise on *Physiognomics* is one of these texts.[60] The existence of this text, along with brief references to physiognomy in Aristotle's *Analytica Priora,* quoted at the beginning of this chapter, and other texts on animals and natural science, suggests his interest in identifying essential characteristics of an animal or person by physical appearance. Indeed, Pseudo-Aristotle's *Physiognomics* remains for us the first systematic articulation of the attempt to understand how the external, physical body reveals inner character or identity; there is no attempt in this treatise to explain why there is such a relationship between the body and soul.[61] What we discover in its examination is that being fat does not consistently reveal character as do other, more stable physical characteristics, like height or eye color or the tone of one's voice. This text reveals that to interpret character from the physical body requires a kind of consistency that the fat body does not seem to provide.

The text of the *Physiognomics* consists of two fragments. In the first part of the treatise, the author introduces the science of physiognomy and describes different physiognomic methods as an introduction to his version of appropriate physiognomy. Physiognomy works because minds "are not isolated and unaffected by the changes of the body."[62] The author finds his evidence for this connection "in cases of drunkenness and illness: for states of mind appear to change a great deal through the affections of the body. And correlatively, the body is clearly affected along with the affections of the soul in cases of love and fear and grief and pleasure.[63] We can see that soul and body react and change with one another because, for example, when a person is inwardly sad, he frowns, or if a person is released from physical pain, he may feel happier. This type of exchange is common, changeable, and not always entirely accurate. For as the author points out, "the same facial expression may belong to different characters: the brave and the shameless, for example, look alike, though their characters are far apart."[64] Thus, while facial expressions and moods may highlight the interaction between body and soul, they do not accurately reveal an essential aspect of the person or animal's identity. Other physiognomists have attempted to judge human character based on animal body types, or have divided humans into different races based on bodily characteristics, or have attempted to identify the physical characteristics that belong to men with different personalities.[65] The author disputes each of these methods because in each of these cases, judgments are made based on connections between body and soul that are, as in the example given, superficial and not innate.

In contrast to these other physiognomists, the author of the first fragment is interested in ascertaining which kinds of fixed physical and mental characteristics simultaneously reveal and reflect one another and are appropriate marks of identity. He asserts that it is possible to make such connections because "no animal has ever been born that has the appearance of one animal but the mind of another."[66] Nonetheless, elucidating these connections is difficult, given that there are so many characteristics that are common to so many different animals. So, for instance, "when investigating the external marks of courage, we ought to collect all brave animals, and then to inquire what sort of affections are natural to all of them but absent in all other animals."[67] Physiognomists are thus confronted with the painstaking task of finding common permanent characteristics in disposition that are revealed in permanent physical characteristics.

Because of the challenge of finding permanent characteristics, the physiognomist must limit the signs with which the science of physiognomy deals, focusing on the "more convincing among its conclusions."[68] Those signs are "movements, gestures of the body, colour, characteristic facial expression, the growth of the hair, the smoothness of the skin, the voice, condition of the flesh, the parts of the body, and the build of the body as a whole."[69] To give an example,

Signs of a courageous man: stiff hair, the carriage of the body upright, bones, flanks and extremities of the body strong and big, the belly broad and flat, the shoulder blades broad and set apart neither too closely nor too loosely knit, a sturdy neck.[70]

This is the description of the classical Greek warrior/athlete, with broad shoulders and lots of muscle. The coward, who should logically be physiognomically the opposite of the brave man, has "a small growth of soft hair, the figure stooping and lacking in quickness . . . the extremities of the body weak and small . . . loins small and weak . . . and a shifty, downcast look."[71] These two descriptions highlight how mental characteristics are read through physical appearance; strength of limb, bright eyes, and features that are neither too large nor too small, but "just right," are valued as the mark of courage. Note also that in the description of the brave man, the belly is flat and broad. Yet, in the description of the coward, there is no mention of the belly, an idea to which we will return in a moment.

In the second part of the treatise, the author focuses on animals in order "to distinguish among animals which ones stand out as being brave or cowardly or just or unjust."[72] The first distinction to be made is that of the two sexes; characteristics appropriate to masculinity and femininity are listed. So, for instance, females are "tamer and gentler in disposition than the male."[73] Females are also "more mischievous than the male, and (though feebler) more reckless."[74] Some of the physical characteristics that identify femininity are smaller heads, weaker chests, and fleshier thighs, with softer, moister flesh. Males, of course, are "the opposite of all this: his is the braver and more upright nature."[75] The author goes on to point out that the lion is the best example of the male type, with its large, square face, its moderately sized eyes, large chest, and narrow hips. His physical characteristics reveal an inner disposition that is "generous and liberal, proud and ambitious, yet mild and just and affectionate to his comrades."[76]

If such descriptions of character stemming from physical appearance seem to smack to us of stereotyping and prejudice, it is because physiognomy functions as a moral classification schema couched in the language of science. As Maud Gleason notes in her study of Polemon, "the principles of physiognomic science were but the implicit prejudices that had molded his own education, made explicit as a system of universal rules."[77] Being able to read the body's surface as an indication of inner morality was, according to Gleason, a necessary skill "for a technology of suspicion that was indigenous" to the "competitive face-to-face world of educated upper class males."[78] Using physiognomic categories to discern the state of one's opponent's soul was believed to give one a distinct advantage in matters that involved politics, business, and personal reputation.

Since physiognomic treatises reveal much about the ways that Greeks thought about the relationship between bodily features and morality, including how bodies reveal gender, such texts should reveal whether being fat was linked to moral failings. Indeed, Gleason maintains that physiognomy "acknowledged no exceptions to its rules," so, what these texts say about the fat body or fat belly should matter.[79] Yet, these texts undermine such assumptions. Take for example the description of the "mild" man: "robust-looking, well covered with plenty of moist flesh; well sized and well proportioned."[80] Moreover, "a loose build (or 'fat parts') around the belly indicates strength of character, as in the male sex, whilst the opposite is by congruity indicative of a soft character."[81] Being of large size, as long as one is well-proportioned, seems to be fine: "big men with dry flesh, and of the hue that results from heat, are also persistent, and are keen of sense; for the warmth of flesh and complexion counteracts the excessive size so that a proportion conducive to effectiveness is attained."[82] Although there is a clear privileging of the "man whose nature falls in the mean between these two points" for getting things done, because bodily impulses reach the brain easily—not too quickly or too slowly—the biggest problem is the lack of proportion; "an ill-proportioned body indicates a rogue."[83] Thus, a large or fat body that is well-proportioned receives no moral censure.

Attitudes about the significance of the belly are morally distinct in the two parts of pseudo-Aristotle's treatise. In the first part, the author states, "Hearty eaters are indicated when the distance from navel to chest is greater than that from chest to neck."[84] Later in the treatise, the author reiterates, with moral judgment:

When the distance from the navel to the lower end of the breastbone exceeds that from the latter to the neck, it is a mark of gluttony and of insensibility, of gluttony because there is so large a receptacle of food, and of insensibility because the seat of the senses is correspondingly confined and compressed by the receptacle of food, so that the senses have become stupefied by repletion of the stomach, rather than, as is usual, by [starvation].[85]

Here, the author seems to suggest that the large size of the gluttonous stomach suppresses the senses, rendering the person unable to accurately perceive the world around him.

In Polemon's treatise on physiognomy, which contains a similar passage, the large belly suggests that "the instrument of the intellect and understanding" has been limited by the capaciousness of the stomach.[86] Similar passages in other physiognomic treatises suggest further distinctions with regard to the belly. The fourteenth chapter of Polemon's treatise on physiognomy reads as follows:

Thinness and fineness of the stomach is an indication of a healthy intellect, magnanimity, and enthusiasm. Excessive emaciation and thinness of the stomach is an indication of boldness, wickedness of intellect, and gluttony. Largeness of the stomach and great fleshiness, especially if it has softness and droop, indicates much movement, drunkenness, and love of sexual intercourse. If it is very fleshy and strong, that indicates wickedness of deeds, malice, deceit, cunning and lack of intellect.[87]

Note that Polemon's gluttonous stomach is the excessively thin stomach, not the fat stomach, which would be more familiar to us as the beer belly. Another physiognomic text, *Anonymus Latinus,* Book of Physiognomy, written in the fourth century CE and based on Polemon, suggests that

when the stomach is large and congested with flesh which is soft and hanging, it indicates a man without sense who is drunken and intemperate and dedicated to luxury and sex. If the flesh is excessive but solid, it reveals a malevolent man who devises evils. If the stomach has an excessive recess, as if it were empty, it indicates a timid, malicious and greedy man. A stomach which is considerably softer and pressed in shows manliness of mind and magnificence.[88]

In his own translation of this passage, Karl Sandnes suggests that the hollow stomach indicates insatiability, or gluttony, so that the skinny person is gluttonous because he can eat and eat and still remain thin.[89] Such an idea is also found in the 19th-century United States. In his book *Never Satisfied,* Hillel Schwartz notes that, although Americans were eating more high-calorie, high-fat food than people in any other country in the world during this time, they nonetheless remained thin. The explanation for this was that they were "thin *because* they were gluttonous," that is, they could not digest their food properly.[90] Thus, we see further that the fat belly need not be inevitably or historically linked to the idea of gluttony.

Certainly, there are forms of fatness that imply gluttony; that is not in dispute. Yet, whether and how one gets a fat belly seem to be of such a great variety that it is impossible to make clear connections between fatness and moral failing. Indeed, Pseudo-Aristotle's *Physiognomy* ends with an admission that there are certain parts of the body that best reveal mental characteristics, and the belly is not one of them:

It will be found . . . that some signs are better adapted than others to indicate the mental character behind them. The clearest indications are given by signs in certain particularly suitable parts of the body. The most suitable part of all is the region of the eyes and forehead, head and face; next to it comes the region of the chest and shoulders, and next again, that of the legs and feet; whilst the belly and neighboring parts are of least service. In a word, the clearest signs are derived from those parts in which intelligence is most manifest.[91]

Certainly, we find here a bit of a backhanded slap against the belly, which does not serve intelligence; that characterization, in and of itself, might suggest that a person's moral character cannot be judged by the state of the belly because the belly simply has no access to morality or thought. From this perspective, the belly is so far removed from the seat of judgment that it is unreliable as a witness to mental states. At the same time, however, it is precisely because the belly is dissociated from intelligence or morality that it remains an ambivalent sign, not always or inevitably an indication of bad morals, gluttony, or excess.

In the end, physiognomic texts reveal important ideas about fatness and morality in the ancient world. Although the physical body is believed to reveal important aspects of the inner person—his soul, his intelligence, his mental states—being fat in the ancient world is not a certain sign of an inner moral flaw that reveals a proclivity for excessive behavior. Indeed, if both the fat and excessively thin belly can be a sign of gluttony, then the stomach undermines the purported certainty of physiognomic truth and stands as one body part that refuses to make the connection between inner and outer man.

CONCLUSION

Ancient Greek medicine and physiognomy present ideas about the fat and gluttonous body that both confirm and challenge our contemporary views. On the one hand, it is clear that being fat is not a desirable state of being: a fat body defies the cultural preference for the moderate body. At the same time, however, medical texts recognize that being fat can be the result of one's bodily constitution, and can, therefore, be healthy, with the proper regimen. Physiognomic texts also see the fat body and belly as signs with multiple meanings, sometimes revealing inner dispositions, sometimes not. These ancient texts also remind us to question how the fat body is defined in relation to other bodies. In the end, ancient medicine and physiognomy encourage us to see the complexities of the fat body within a particular time and place, and that this is the only way to understand its many variations and meanings.

4

Popular Gluttons and Fat Bodies: The Trickster Herakles, Petronius's *Satyricon,* and Athenaeus's *The Learned Banqueters*

As in other texts we have examined so far, food and eating play an important role in shaping the moral worldview of one of the most popular literary texts from the ancient world, Homer's *Odyssey.* How characters think about and use food indicates their moral shortcomings. Penelope's suitors, for instance, are forever slaughtering all of Odysseus's livestock, eating their "unpaid way through one man's wealth."[1] Food tempts and distracts. When Odysseus's men eat "the honey-sweet, enticing lotus fruit" they forget that they want to go home and instead wish to stay with the Lotus-Eaters forever.[2] Even our hero, Odysseus, has food issues: released from Calypso's island, he finds himself shipwrecked again, and as he tells his tale of woe, he becomes preoccupied with food. "But let me, even in my sorrow, eat. There is no thing more shameless than the belly; however tried we are, whatever pain assails our heart, the hateful stomach claims its right to be remembered."[3] Food and eating are touchstones in the narrative, showing the characters' human limitations and accomplishments, highlighting the strangeness and familiarity of the creatures they meet on their journey.

Almost a thousand years after Homer's *Odyssey* was written, Athenaeus labels Odysseus a "greedy gourmand" in his work, the *Deipnosophistae* or *The Learned Banqueters.*[4] Athenaeus suggests that Odysseus "exhibits extreme greed and gluttony" when he says, "for nothing is more shameless than the miserable belly, which orders us to pay attention to it and gives us no choice, even when we are worn out, and demands to be filled."[5] Odysseus's periodic tendency to indulge his gluttonous appetite renders him a morally complex character whose heroic perfection is tempered by human flaws. And, although Odysseus may be perceived to be a glutton, he is never described as fat. He has "youthful strength," is patient and bright, and is a man of many wiles, but he is not fat.[6] Again, we see here a distinction between gluttony and fatness, where the behavior of gluttony does not necessarily result in a fat body.

The significance of food and eating in Homer's *Odyssey* becomes even more evident when we examine additional Greek and Roman literary texts that convey ideas about gluttony and the fat body, for references to Homer abound. This chapter explores the comic, popular side of ancient images of the glutton and the fat body using the figure of Herakles, the *Satyricon* by Petronius, and Athenaeus's *The Learned Banqueters,* all of which make connections, often humorous, to Homer's *Odyssey,* reflecting the cultural influence of that text, while also giving insight into the ways in which ideas about gluttony and the fat body are located in the popular imagination of the time. Odysseus meets the ghost of Herakles during his journey to the underworld; Aristophanes's comedy, *The Frogs,* mocks Herakles's serious journey to the underworld and emphasizes his gluttony. Petronius's *Satyricon* makes frequent references to the *Odyssey,* turning Odysseus's adventure into a crazy series of random events for its protagonists, including a gluttonous feast given by the wealthy and vulgar Trimalchio. Finally, Athenaeus uses the *Odyssey* as a foundational cultural text that defines dining practices in the ancient world, including gluttony. Whether in comedy, satire, or the literature of the symposium, the meaning of the role of the glutton and the fat body in ancient popular texts rests on perceptions of excessive behaviors and the ways that immoderation reveals and criticizes cultural ideals, practices, and social structures. Just as religious and philosophical texts of the ancient world frequently separate the idea of the glutton and the fat body, so, too, do popular images. As in other texts examined so far, here the act of gluttony is perceived to be an act of social disruption associated with death, animality, femininity, and irrationality, but it is also used as a way to critique social mores and class constructs.

At the same time, however, we can also find in some of these texts ideas that conflate the fat body with the glutton, a strand of thought that continues to this day. As John Wilkins points out, "fat is frequently a political issue in [ancient Greek] comedy, large body-size being invoked within the rhetoric of political invective against greed."[7] This idea continues in later texts, as well, where gluttony and greed go hand in hand. This connection will be particularly evident in the *Satyricon* and *The Learned Banqueters,* where the fat body represents a kind of luxury and self-indulgence that comes under moral scrutiny. In these texts, then, we see again the complexity of ancient ideas about the glutton and the fat body, a complexity that both challenges and supports our contemporary conflation of the two.

HERAKLES THE TRICKSTER

In the *Odyssey,* Book 11, Odysseus travels to the underworld to hear the prophecy of Tiresias. While there, he meets legendary figures like Sisyphus, Tantalus, Orion, and Herakles. Homer's description of these heroes briefly tells their tales: Sisyphus rolls his boulder up the hill again and again; Tantalus stands in a pool of water and thirsts, but he is unable to reach the water that disappears each time he attempts to drink; and Orion hunts on the hillside. In the underworld, Herakles is a ghost, for "the man himself delights in the grand feasts of the deathless gods on high."[8] He walks through the land of the dead gripping his bow, "forever poised to shoot," horrifying even the dead who scatter as he walks among them.[9] Even his ghost inspires fear in those who see him.

Homer's portrayal of Herakles, better known to us by his Roman name, Hercules, the human hero turned god of Greek and Roman myth, supports a common understanding of the mythic figure, the man of superhuman strength who inspires fear as he carries out his 12 labors with power, will, and courage. Many Greek statues of Herakles show him to be a confident, muscular hero (see Figure 4.1).

Herakles, whose name means "Glory of Hera," was the product of Zeus's dalliance with Alcmene. Alcmene's pregnancy so angered Hera, Zeus's wife, that she attempted to stop the birth of the baby. When Alcmene gave birth to her son anyway and named him after Hera, Hera vowed to make Herakles's life as difficult as possible. Herakles's divine parentage resulted in his superhuman strength, which is both a gift and a curse to him throughout his life. It is used for good when he protects humans from monstrous creatures, and it is used for ill when, driven to madness by Hera, he kills his wife, Megara, and, according to some versions of the story, their children, too.[10]

Figure 4.1 Statue of the youthful Hercules. Marble. Roman 68–98 CE

His strength renders him both a superhuman defender of humanity and a man whose physical strength leads to intense suffering; he is "the most moving symbol of the human condition."[11] In ancient Greek myth, however, Herakles is more than the heroic strong man and poignant symbol of human frailty; he also takes on a comic persona as an exemplar of human excess: he is presented as a gluttonous, lecherous fool. Take his "insatiable appetite and excessive drinking" and put them together with his image as "mighty hero and the punisher of the wicked" and he becomes a comic figure of excess.[12] Homer knows these two sides of the hero, as well, for his Herakles lives on Olympus with the gods, feasting, while his fearsome ghost hunts in the underworld. Indeed, Herakles is a mythological trickster figure who plays in the boundaries between the human and divine, culture and nature, protection and violence, tragedy and comedy, masculine and feminine, and human and animal. As both heroic savior and comic foil, Herakles both protects and undermines culture, at once defending and confusing the boundaries that distinguish life from death, the natural world from human society. One of the features of Herakles's character that allows him to function in this way is his gluttonous appetite, a sign of life that often leads to death or distraction. With his huge passion for food, Herakles again underscores the connections between gluttony and social disruption, animality, femininity, irrationality, and death.

The earliest evidence of Herakles as a comic figure is found in the work of Epicharmus, whose plays were most likely performed between 490 and 450 BCE.[13] Much of Epicharmus's writing survives only in fragments, often quoted by Athenaeus in *The Learned Banqueters.* Athenaeus cites Epicharmus's play, *Busiris,* as an illustration of Herakles's gluttony: "If you saw him eating, first of all, you'd die. His throat emits a roar, his jaw rattles, his molars resound, his canine teeth squeak, he snorts loudly and he wiggles his ears."[14] This description emphasizes the sheer force of Herakles's jaws, a frightening portrayal more appropriate for a vicious animal than a comedic glutton. But then Herakles's ears wiggle, and the image moves from the frightening to the funny, highlighting the ridiculousness of the use of such force while eating. In describing him this way, Epicharmus emphasizes the animalistic, irrational aspects of Herakles's excessive eating while also providing fodder for laughter.

In other Greek comedies, Herakles's stomach becomes the driving force behind all of his actions. In the play, *Hesione,* Herakles's gluttony distracts him from the beautiful heroine. More interested in eating than wooing the lovely Hesione, she says, "When he saw two serving men bring in the tray/ With motley side-dishes abounding gay,/He had no eyes for me."[15] Sometimes for Herakles, gluttony even trumps lust.

Or, it trumps education. In the play *Linus,* by the comic poet Alexis, Herakles is a student of Linus. Asked to pick one book from Linus's wide collection of texts by Homer, Hesiod, and any number of other important authors, Herakles picks Simus's *Art of Cookery.* When Linus realizes that Herakles is uninterested in the educational aspects of the text, he remarks that Herakles is "hunger personified." Herakles responds: "Call me what you will. Please understand I want to eat my fill."[16] Such a singular focus on food and eating turns the powerful Herakles into a childish oaf. This characterization of Herakles suggests that the kind of intensity that allows him to protect humanity with his muscular strength is put to unfortunate use when it is directed toward food. Such a characterization also gives evidence to the notion that we also saw in Plato, that gluttony's effect is to distract one from intellectual and philosophical pursuits that would enhance society. Here, Herakles's gluttony stands as living proof of the need to control the animalistic aspects of our human lives.

The portrayal of Herakles as the gluttonous fool is also common in the comedies of Aristophanes. In his play *The Birds,* Herakles is brought in as a comic foil with a serious purpose: to show how the stomach's demands can wreak havoc with the social and political order. The play opens with Pisthetairos and Euelpides, who are tired of living in Athens, going on an adventure to find the Hoopoe, a bird who used to be a man. The protagonists seek the Hoopoe because they think he can tell them whether there is a place "of soft and lovely leisure" they can live.[17] Upon finding the Hoopoe, Pisthetairos convinces him and his friends to establish such a city, and since they are birds and will create their city in the space between heaven and earth, they can rule over all of humankind. In addition, they can also make things difficult for the gods by boycotting the sacrifices, which could lead to the gods' starvation. When they establish Cloudcuckooland and block humans from sacrificing to the gods, Olympus sends a delegation to negotiate peace with the leaders of the new land. This delegation consists of Poseidon, Herakles, and Triballos, a representative of the barbarian gods.[18]

In Arrowsmith's translation of the play, Herakles takes on the accent of a thug from New Jersey who wants to throttle any guy who "dared blockade the gods."[19] When Pisthetairos enters the scene with his cooking utensils and proceeds to slice pickles, Herakles loses his focus on the task at hand and starts paying attention only to the food. "What kind of meat is dat?" Herakles asks, and Pisthetairos responds that he's preparing birds who have been killed for treason. "And dat luscious gravy gets poured on foist?" asks Herakles, uninterested in anything but the food.[20] Poseidon tries to negotiate an end to the blockade of the sacrifices, and Pisthetairos makes his one demand: that Zeus give up his power to the Birds. This demand is unacceptable to Poseidon, but when Pisthetairos ends his request with an invitation to dinner, Herakles immediately votes to accept Pisthetairos's offer and "translates" Triballos's grunts and groans as agreement. Poseidon, frustrated with the negotiations, screams at Herakles, "You contemptible, idiotic glutton! Would you dethrone your own father?"[21] Herakles the trickster, willing to do anything for food, does not seem to care about his father Zeus, his relationship with him, or the potential demise of the gods. He would rather watch the barbecue, and even when Poseidon refuses to leave him behind because he would "guzzle grill and all," Herakles can only respond, "Aw, Unc, but it woulda tasted so good."[22] Although aligned with the gods, Herakles is ruled by his very human stomach and his excessive desire for food to the exclusion of all other concerns. Playing with the distinctions between gods and humans, Aristophanes shows the power of the stomach to undermine the divine order of things. Indeed, the perspective on gluttony presented in this play aligns—though less seriously, to be sure—with the biblical notion that those who pay attention only to their bellies will inevitably turn away from God.

Aristophanes's play *The Frogs* also invokes the gluttonous Herakles. *The Frogs* was first performed in 405 BCE, when the Athenians had been at war with Sparta for almost 30 years and had recently lost two influential playwrights, Euripides and Sophocles. The play is critical of the continuing war, and nostalgic about Greece's cultural past, as Dionysius attempts to go to the underworld to bring back Euripides—and good writing—to Athens.[23] To get to the underworld, Dionysius consults with his brother Herakles, whose 12th labor had been a trip to the underworld to kidnap the hound of Hades, Cerberus. Aristophanes invokes the serious side of Herakles—his heroic labors—only to focus on his gluttony in this play, for when Dionysius asks Herakles for the route to the underworld, he uses Herakles's love of beans— or pea soup—to emphasize how eager he is to make the trip.[24]

DIONYSIUS: Don't laugh at me, brother dear. Truly I am in a bad way. I've got this craving. It's demoralizing me.
  HERAKLES: What kind of craving, little brother?
         D: I don't know how to explain. I'll paraphrase it by a parable. Did you ever feel a sudden longing for baked beans?
         H: Baked beans? Gosh yes, that's happened to me a million times.
         D: Shall I give you another illustration? Expound this one?
         H: Don't need to expound baked beans to me. I get the point.[25]

What is interesting in this interaction is that, although Herakles's gluttony is supposed to get the laugh, he takes his craving for beans quite seriously: his love of beans allows him to understand exactly how intent Dionysius is on getting to the underworld. In that understanding, Herakles becomes the sane one, questioning his brother's need to bring back the dead by suggesting that there are living poets still available to satisfy Dionysius's need for tragedy: "Look here," Herakles says, "there still are a million and one young guys around. You know, Tragic Poets who can outgabble Euripides by a country mile."[26] In addition, Dionysius's silly disguise as Herakles, which consists of Herakles's traditional lion skin (from the Nemean lion conquered to complete his first labor) worn over a "buttercup nightie," appears to be an attempt to make fun of Herakles's masculinity, but it works instead to emphasize his role as ordinary citizen.[27] In this play, at least, Aristophanes makes a comic reversal where Dionysius, not Herakles, is the object of ridicule, even though Herakles more often plays that role in Greek comedy. Here, Herakles's role as trickster is to reverse roles, to become the conventional, even rational character, who stands as evidence of the disintegration of Athenian life. When the gluttonous Herakles is no longer the laughable one, when he is speaking rationally, life in Athens must be quite bad.

Indeed, as the play goes on, Herakles's previous trip to the underworld, marked by his gluttony, becomes the hook upon which the play's comedic reversals hang. During their trip to the underworld, Dionysius and his slave, Xanthias, run into a number of people who remember Herakles and his big appetite, and think he has returned. While Dionysius originally thought that disguising himself as Herakles is a good idea, he soon realizes that not everyone in the underworld remembers Herakles fondly, and he forces Xanthias to wear the costume. At one point, the two stop at an inn, where the maids remember Herakles and tell the disguised Xanthias/Herakles that Persephone, Queen of the Underworld, has had buns baked, beans cooked, and an entire steer barbecued, just for his eating pleasure.[28] Thrilled at this welcome, Dionysius forces Xanthias to give him back the disguise, only to meet up with the inn's hostesses, who also remember Herakles because during his previous visit, he ate 16 loaves of bread, 20 pounds of roast beef, feta cheese—including its packaging—and then refused to pay for it. Now that he has returned, they plot their revenge on the "horrid gourmet," and both Dionysius and Xanthias pay the price—with a beating—for Herakles's previous actions.[29] Here we see a number of reversals and disguises in an underworld turned upside-down to reflect the world above, for as the play continues, the chorus confirms that the world of Athens has lost its grip on reality by privileging "any foreign fool, redhead slave, or brassy clown or shyster" to direct the city, ignoring the "stately gentlemen . . . men of distinction who have been to school."[30]

As Dionysius and Xanthias continue their journey and meet the tragic poets, Dionysius asks them for advice on how to stop the wars in the world above. At this point, the comedic Herakles fades and the conversation turns more serious. The poet who gives the best advice about how to save the city is Aeschylus, who proclaims that the only way to save Athens from war is to reverse again the way that the leaders are currently thinking: "They shall win—when they think of their land as if it were their enemies' and think of their enemies' land as if it were their own, that ships are all their wealth, and their wealth, despair."[31] Ending the play on a serious note, Aristophanes emphasizes the importance of overturning current thinking to save Athens from the continuing devastation of war, a point that has been made by using Herakles's gluttony as a way to shake up the status quo and to get the audience to think differently about the current situation in Athens.

It is Herakles's gluttony, in the context of his heroism, that not only provides the fodder for comedy, it creates a context for dealing with difficult cultural contradictions, and explaining cultural practices. Herakles's gluttony, for instance, challenges Greek ideals of masculinity and femininity. Stories of his strength and heroism place Herakles in the realm of the hypermasculine, and his insatiable appetite also serves as an indication of his "vigorous male sexuality."[32] At the same time, however, his gluttony also feminizes him, because it associates him with the belly, which is connected to the womb. Gluttony—*gastris*—is a word used to describe Herakles, even though it is a word that in Greek comedy is used primarily to describe women.[33] Derived from the Greek word *gaster*, which can mean the belly, gluttony, and womb, *gastris* underscores the aspects of gluttony that associate it primarily with a lack of control. We saw with Plato the idea that the belly is separated from the intellect like the women's quarters are separated from the men's, rendering the belly a feminized space. Plato also asserted that the second generation of humans, which saw the creation of women and sexual desire, comes from the disease and gluttony of the first generation of men. Such ideas are embodied by Herakles's gluttonous belly, which challenges clear definitions of Greek masculinity and femininity, especially in the realm of comedy, where his gluttony helps to create a picture of effeminacy, as in Aristophanes's *The Frogs*. Here again, Herakles is the trickster, mediating oppositions between masculinity and femininity through his gastric excess.

Herakles's gluttony also serves as a means of understanding the cultural significance of meat eating in ancient Greece, which further underscores his role as trickster. One of the most common features of Herakles's gluttony is his ability to eat an entire cow—and the coals it was roasted over—in one sitting.[34] Jeremy McInerney points out that cattle are central to the city-temple constellation in ancient Greece, and that their symbolic value "helped shape some of the most distinctive practices and habits of the Greeks, reinforcing the importance of sanctuaries and framing notions of the divine, of heroic action, of elite performance. . . ." as well as being "instantiated in daily life in the nexus of sacrifice, feast and distribution that was a recurrent feature of Greek life."[35] Cattle occupy an important place in the Greek imagination and play a central role in societal structures and practices. Herakles is an important figure for understanding the centrality of the cow, because it is he who steals cattle from the gods for human use, thereby contributing to the development of human culture.[36] He also consumes them voraciously, like an animal himself. In this way, Herakles moves between the human and animal, both highlighting and hiding the similarities and differences between humans and the animals they sacrifice. We saw this cultural difficulty in the book of Leviticus, as well, where the treatment of the sacrificed animal reflects a recognition that, in sacrifice, humans take the lives of beings also created by God. Although Greek culture does not rely on a single God for creation and order in the universe, it confronts a similar challenge in rectifying the sacrifice of animals. As McInerney points out, "the blood running off the altar may be holy, but the grease dribbling down your chin is not."[37] Herakles embodies and mediates the paradox of animal sacrifice. His gluttonous behavior simultaneously points out and alleviates human and societal contradictions by making culture and defying it at every turn.

Herakles's role in the boundaries between the human and the animal is further confirmed in artistic representations. Herakles is often portrayed wearing the skin of the Nemean lion, which suggests the animal-like strength and power he uses to defend humanity. But the animal skin can represent his role as fierce, strong man, or as comic fool, as we saw in Aristophanes's *The Frogs*.

Terracotta figures of Herakles play with his heroic and comic elements—the lion skin, club, pot belly, and phallus—to create an image that refers to his enormous appetite and lust (see Figure 4.2).

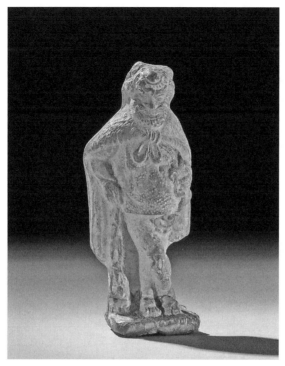

Figure 4.2 Athenian terracotta figurine of Herakles standing with a club and lionskin, his bow and quiver in his left hand. ca. late fifth or early fourth century BCE

Figurines like these, which were produced at the end of the fifth century or early fourth century BCE, appear to support a visual alignment of gluttony with fatness; however, it was common in Greek comedies for all actors—whether gluttons or not—to wear padding on their behinds and bellies, along with large attached phalluses for the men.[38] Other terracotta figurines from the same time period show that all characters have large bellies, a feature which seems to mark them as comic figures, generally (see Figure 4.3). These figurines suggest a visual connection between the fat body and what is funny, an idea that continues to have resonance today with the contemporary stereotype of the jolly fat person, but what the Greek comedies emphasize is the notion that what is funny is found in all different kinds of excess, of which the fat body is merely one possible form.

Indeed, comic representations of Herakles with a fat belly may reflect his gluttony, but the fat belly is also not solely a symbol of gluttony, for other comic figures not considered gluttons are also represented with large bellies, as are female figures who are portrayed neither as gluttonous nor pregnant. Rather, it seems that comedy is generally associated with excesses that can

Figure 4.3 Athenian terracotta figurine of an actor.
ca. late fifth or early fourth century BCE

be represented by making body parts bigger, especially the belly, butt, phallus, and breasts for female characters. Thus, although we do see here a connection between the fat body and the glutton, it is a weak connection, for it seems clear that fatness may not always represent gluttony, and gluttony may not always be indicated by fatness: the fat body may indicate excesses that have nothing to do with gluttony. As is consistent with what we have seen with the fat body and the glutton in the ancient world, the size of Herakles's body is not as important as his gluttonous actions, which reveal the numerous ways that his excessive eating—whether it makes him fat or not—creates and reflects cultural ideals.

PETRONIUS, *THE SATYRICON*

Petronius Arbiter, the likely author of *The Satyricon*, lived in the Roman Empire during the first century CE. A governor of the Roman province of Bithynia, Petronius was a friend of the Emperor Nero until he incurred Nero's disfavor and took his own life.[39] Petronius's suicide was a long, drawn-out affair: the Roman historian Tacitus tells how Petronius slit his wrists and bled slowly to death while he bound and unbound them, conversing with his friends and writing a list of the "emperor's debaucheries," which he then sent tò Nero.[40] He died at the dinner table, an exemplar of the kind of luxurious and leisurely life often associated with Nero's reign.

Petronius's *Satyricon* narrates the decadence of the time with its bawdy romps, genteel stupidity, absurd adventure, and social excess. *The Satyricon* tells of the adventures of Encolpius and Ascyltus, who vie for the attention of the young boy, Giton. The form of the text evokes a number of different literary traditions: it mimics in a comedic way the adventure of the *Odyssey* and, like the Greek satyr play or many of the comedies of Aristophanes, it is full of lasciviousness, silliness, and mockery. It also conforms to the style of the Menippean satire, which combines prose and verse to ridicule the vices, absurdities, and habits of humanity, and it satirizes the literature of the symposium, especially Plato's *Sympoisum*.[41] Indeed, the many different genres represented in the text suggest that one important descriptive feature of the work is its disorder, its rejection of an organized form.[42] Confusion and chaos characterize the text as a whole, reflecting the luxury and debaucheries of Nero's Rome, which occur in the context of greater upward mobility and physical movement in the Roman Empire, in general.[43] Here, we focus on the mayhem of the *Cena Trimalchio,* or Trimalchio's feast, which is one stop on the comic adventure of the *Satyricon.*

Trimalchio's feast is a comic satire on lavish Roman dining, hosted by the nouveau riche Trimalchio, a former slave who, as a freedman, has been able to amass great wealth. Petronius's presentation of the world of the freedman "reflects the disruption of that hierarchical society in which each man knew his place and his prospects."[44] As we have seen repeatedly in the ancient world, gluttony is often used symbolically to indicate social disruption, and we see this again in Trimalchio's dinner, where unrestrained, animalistic excess is evidence of the pleasures and dangers of an unstable, even volatile, social order. Indeed, what is fascinating about Trimalchio's feast is that although the occasion of feasting invokes the appearance of gluttony, it is not the actual eating of the food at the table that exemplifies its gluttonous excess; rather, the feast's gluttony is seen in its excessively chaotic atmosphere, where the food is presented as spectacle with little regard for its taste or appeal, as well as in the feast's associations with excrement and death. The text itself is gluttonous, full of overblown description and detail that overwhelms the reader; in this way, the idea of gluttony expands to encompass all kinds of excess and greed, not just that of food.[45] In the same way that the accusations of gluttony against Jesus in the New Testament have little to do with whether Jesus actually was a glutton but instead indicated anxiety about what was perceived to be his antisocial behavior, so too does the gluttonous excess of Trimalchio's feast reflect a greater social turmoil, anxiety about the chaotic social order, and fear of death—whether those partaking of the feast are actual gluttons or not.

While the text exudes gluttonous excess, little is said about the fat body. There may or may not be fat bodies in the text, but the characters' excessive actions seem to infer their heft. Trimalchio claims to be fat, but whenever fat bodies are mentioned, their fatness is about their wealth, with little attention paid to the actual size of the body. Like gluttony, what is perceived to be the fat body in "Trimalchio's Feast" gives evidence of greed and social disruption.

We are first introduced to Trimalchio and his decadent lifestyle when Encolpius, Ascyltus, their teacher, Agamemnon, and Giton are invited to his house for dinner. Our guests' first encounter with Trimalchio gives a glimpse into the world of the host. On their way to the baths, they see "an old, bald man" wearing only a "long red undershirt" playing ball with a "bunch of curly-headed slave boys."[46] When he drops the ball, he simply takes another from a slave standing by precisely for this purpose, and when he needs to relieve himself, he snaps his fingers and one of his slaves shuffles across the circle "clutching a chamber pot of solid silver" so that Trimalchio can do his business without too much disruption to his entertainment.[47] Here is a rich man who plays ball with slaves, does not wear pants, has a silver chamber pot, and relieves himself in public. With this description, the reader and protagonists move into a world where the public and private have no boundaries, and where there is little regard for social graces.

As the guests enter his house, they walk past frescos on the walls that tell Trimalchio's story from slave boy to freedman to wealthy landowner. Scattered among the art that depicts Trimalchio's life are scenes from the popular entertainment of the gladiator games, as well as pictures of the more refined *Iliad* and *Odyssey*. The frescos are jammed with details, "everything scrupulously labeled," attempting to give the impression of Trimalchio's importance, but merely serving to emphasize excess.[48] Along with the unnecessary detail, this mishmash of scenarios from Trimalchio's life, from high- and low-brow culture, reveal his vulgarity, for at the same time that he aligns himself with the revered figures from Homer's respected tales of war and wandering, his artistic taste reveals his classless, uncouth past. Knowing that Trimalchio is a former slave suggests the lengths to which he will go to show that he has embraced his place in the moneyed class, but all of his attempts at extravagance merely highlight his bad taste. Trimalchio is a rich man with no idea of the refinements traditionally associated with wealth.

As the guests make it past the frescos, they are led into the dining room, where a slave screams, "RIGHT FEET FIRST!"[49] Arbitrary, silly rules are in place that confuse the guests, who try to accommodate. They are shown to their tables, where their hands are washed and they are given pedicures, all by slaves who sing constantly. Encolpius muses that all of this singing makes it seem as though "you were eating in a concert-hall rather than a private dining room."[50] Trimalchio enters the room late and begs the guests' pardon while he finishes a game, adding another dimension to the dining room. Food is served amidst the blaring of an orchestra. Expensive silver dishes are dropped and swept away with the garbage, while slaves "carrying little skin bottles like the circus attendants who sprinkle the arena with perfume" pour wine over the guests' hands.[51] Even the location of the dinner is in question: is it a dining room, a concert hall, a game room, or a circus?

The confusion continues as Trimalchio attempts to present himself as a sophisticated man of refinement. He claims that "at dinner . . . there should be culture as much as food," but for him, culture consists of his amusing yet ludicrous astrological interpretations, "huge Spartan mastiffs" let loose among the diners to mimic a hunting scene, a reading of the estate records, which reveals the purchase of gardens in Pompeii that Trimalchio was unaware that he owned, tumblers performing stunts on ladders and jumping through hoops of fire, a ritual to praise Trimalchio's three household gods— Fat Profit, Good Luck, and Large Income—loud recitations of Homer, an opening of the dining room ceiling to lower a circular hoop on which vials of perfume and garlands made of gold are hung, waiting for the guests to remove them, and numerous other outlandish pursuits.[52] The confusion of so many different kinds of entertainments happening during the dinner reflects Trimalchio's inability to live in an orderly way with so much money, with so many possibilities. He is a dilettante, but perhaps necessarily so, given the plethora of options open to him.

As all of these events occur, food is served. Here is where the guests and readers should be encouraged to be gluttonous, but it is clear that what matters in this feast is the spectacle of the food, not its ingestion. He praises his chef as most valuable, for he can "whip you up a fish out of sowbelly, pigeons out of bacon, doves from ham and chicken from pigs' knuckles."[53] It is the deception of the food that matters, not its flavor; this is food whose main function is to entertain, not to satiate or please the palate. Indeed, Trimalchio seems to pride himself on serving food that fools his guests. For instance, he presents a dish with the zodiac signs on it, each sign covered by its most literal edible (or inedible) representation: the sign of Taurus, the bull, for instance, is represented by a slice of beef, Gemini the twins by testicles and kidneys, Scorpio the scorpion by a crawfish. Trimalchio urges everyone to "eat up," but the guests are rather put off by this "wretched fare."[54] When the slaves remove the zodiac plate and reveal another tray, with "fat capons and sowbellies and a hare tricked out with wings to look like a little Pegasus" surrounded by "little gravy boats, all shaped like the satyr Marsyas, with phalluses for spouts and a spicy hot gravy dripping down over several large fish swimming about in the lagoon of the tray," the guests' reluctance turns to delight, and for this one time during the feast, they turn to the repast with "gusto."[55] A roasted brood sow, with tiny pigs made of pastry attached to her teats, is brought in wearing a freedman's cap, a hat worn by newly freed slaves to indicate their freedom. When carved, thrushes fly out of the sow's belly, and servants catch them to distribute to the guests as gifts. Encolpius is not so interested in the spectacle of the pig; rather, he puzzles over why the pig was wearing a freedman's cap. When he musters up his courage to ask, his neighbor says, "Look: yesterday this sow was served for dinner, but the guests were so stuffed they let it go. Get it? They *let it go*. So today naturally she comes back to the table as a free sow."[56] While yesterday's guests may have eaten their fill, no mention is made of the actual eating of the pork at this feast, and what matters more than the food is the pun about the food. It is the spectacle of the sow that garners the attention of the diners.

The most elaborate food ruse occurs when three more hogs are paraded in front of the diners, and they are asked by the host which one they would like to eat for dinner. A conversation with the cook ensues, with threats from the host regarding the proper roasting of the next course. Shortly thereafter, servants return with a huge roasted hog, and Encolpius wonders how it could have cooked so quickly. As Trimalchio inspects the pig, he thunders, "What! What's this? By god, this hog hasn't even been gutted! Get that cook in here on the double!"[57] Trimalchio calls out the cook, has him stripped, and is about to have him whipped, when the guests intervene and beg for leniency. Trimalchio relents and tells the cook to gut the pig in front of the guests. The cook puts his clothes back on and cuts the pig's belly. Then, "the slits widened out under the pressure from inside, and suddenly out pour, not the pig's bowels and guts, but link upon link of tumbling sausages and blood puddings," whereupon the cook is given a silver crown and a drink.[58] After this, Trimalchio tells more stories about the extent of his wealth, but there is no account of the taste of the food, or that the food is even eaten. Indeed, the clearest expressions of eating use the idea metaphorically: a slave asks the three protagonists, "What's eating you," when he sees that the three are bothered; later, a man ends up "eating crow" when a business deal falls through.[59]

It is clear throughout the feast that the most important aspect of the food is not its ingestion, but rather Trimalchio's ability to use it to create surprise and entertainment for his guests, even when it is in bad taste and includes the humiliation of his previously honored cook. At almost every point that eating could occur, it does not. When an elaborate troop of rhapsodes enters the hall and reads a tale from Homer about Ajax going mad, a slave playing the role of Ajax comes in and elaborately carves a barbecued calf, spearing slices for the guests. But, their "applause for this elaborate *tour de force* . . . [is] abruptly cut short" when the ceiling begins to rumble, the room begins to shake, and the guests must turn their attention to other matters.[60] Although this feast is the result of wealth and leisure, it occurs at such a quick pace that there is no time to eat what is offered. Trimalchio's feast becomes a metaphor for the overwhelming possibilities that open up when the social order turns upside-down, when slaves become rich, when everything is up for grabs.

Despite all of the chaos, we do know that Trimalchio has been eating, because he willingly talks about his bathroom habits. At one point during the feast, he gets up and "[waddles] off to the toilet."[61] While he is gone, a long conversation ensues between some of Trimalchio's guests, in which the fat, wealthy body becomes a subject of conversation. Seleucus relays that he spent the day at the funeral of Chrysanthus. Seleucus talks about the unpredictability of death, and the fragility of the body. "What are men anyway but balloons on legs, a lot of blown-up bladders? . . . And, you know, Chrysanthus might still be with us if he hadn't tried that starvation diet. Five days and not a crumb of bread, not a drop of water, passed his lips. Tch, tch. And now he's gone, joined the great majority."[62] This reference to the "starvation diet" not only suggests the longevity of unhealthy diet practices, it infers—perhaps—that Chrysanthus was a fat man. Later in the conversation, when Phileros describes the "real" Chrysanthus, we find out the extent of his wealth, which is described as his fatness.

He got what was coming to him. He lived well, he died well. What the hell more did he want? And got rich from nothing too. And no wonder, I say. That boy would have grubbed in the gutter for a coin and picked it out with his teeth too. God knows what he had salted away. Just got fatter and fatter, bloated with the stuff. Why, that man oozed money the way a honeycomb oozes honey.[63]

Chrysanthus may have been fat, but what seems relevant in Phileros's description is his monetary, not bodily, heft. Here is an excellent example of the symbolic connection between wealth and bodily fatness that may or may not reflect actual body size. If being fat reflects one's wealth, then it may be the case in many ancient texts that the description of a person as "fat" is more symbolic than real. Yet, when Trimalchio says later that he hopes to become richer, but not fatter, he infers that wealth = fat: there is something about being wealthy that inevitably leads to—or necessitates the imagining of—fatness.[64] Here we see a conceptual constellation that connects wealth, fat, luxury, and leisure, regardless of the actual person's bodily size.

When Trimalchio returns from his long visit to the toilet, he offers an explanation for his departure, and an equally long discourse on the importance of these bodily functions.

"You'll excuse me, friends," he began, "but I've been constipated for days and the doctors are stumped. I got a little relief from a prescription of pomegranate rind and resin in a vinegar base. Still, I hope my tummy will get back its manners soon. Right now my bowels are bumbling around like a bull. But if any of you has any business that needs attending to, go right ahead; no reason to feel embarrassed. There's not a man been born yet with solid insides. And I don't know any anguish on earth like trying to hold it in. Jupiter himself couldn't stop it from coming.—What are you giggling about, Fortunata? [Fortunata is Trimalchio's wife.] You're the one who keeps me awake all night with your trips to the potty. Well, anyone at the table who wants to go has my permission, and the doctors tell us not to hold it in. Everything's ready outside—water and pots and the rest of the stuff. Take my word for it, friends, the vapors go straight to your brain. Poison your whole system. I know of some who've died from being too polite and holding it in."[65]

Trimalchio goes on and on about the importance of defecation, of paying attention to the body's needs, underscoring the notion that the body trumps everything, especially civility and good manners. Despite the perceived importance of cultural mores and polite society, in the end, the body, with its dirty necessities, is the ultimate control.

Indeed, it is precisely the idea of the body's demise that haunts what should be a celebratory feast and raises the specter of death that is so often connected to the symbolic idea of gluttony. A feast is one of the best expressions of life and community and abundance. But Trimalchio is obsessed with his bodily functions and death. One of the first amusements of the feast is the presentation of a silver skeleton, which is made to move into various positions. As servants bend the skeleton into various "suggestive postures" in front of the guests, Trimalchio recites a poem:

Nothing but bones, that's what we are.
Death hustles us humans away.
Today we're here and tomorrow we're not,
so live and drink while you may![66]

This "eat, drink and be merry" idea is found throughout the text of the feast, as Trimalchio cries out again, "'We all have to die, so let's live while we're waiting!'"[67] We find out that Trimalchio is obsessed with time and has hired his tomb to be carved with a lifelike statue of him, so that he will live on long after he's gone.[68] The feast ends with a drunken Trimalchio ordering a brass band into the dining room to play funeral music while he stretches out on pillows and says, "Pretend I'm dead . . . and say something nice about me."[69] The band plays so loudly that they wake up the whole neighborhood, including the fire brigade, who fear that the racket means that Trimalchio's house is on fire. In the ensuing commotion, the three guests abandon Agamemnon and continue on their journey.

At the end of Trimalchio's feast, we are left with gluttonous excess turned into death. Eating and drinking is about life, but this feast would appear to lay waste to that idea, for this is a meal that reflects chaos, unseemly behavior, and the decadence of luxurious living. In "Trimalchio's Feast," gluttony stands for all excesses that lead to death, fatness for unnecessary wealth. Yet, as Trimalchio points out, both slaves and rich men "drink the same mother's milk, though an evil fate grinds [the slaves] down."[70] Gluttony may symbolize the excesses of culture, but in the end, we all die, whether we are gluttons, or fat, or not.

Like other texts in the ancient world, "Trimalchio's Feast" uses an occasion for gluttonous excess as a way to expose the dangers of cultural decadence and the disintegration of social hierarchy. In excesses of the text and the excessive behaviors of the host and the guests at the table, Petronius underscores the symbolic connections of gluttony to animality, irrationality, and death, underscoring the idea that one does not need to eat one bite of food to be cast as a glutton.

ATHENAEUS

One of the most important texts on food and eating in the Greco-Roman world is Athenaeus's *Deipnosophistae,* or *The Learned Banqueters,* a 15-volume work written in the second century CE. Athenaeus was born in Egypt, lived in Rome, and wrote in Greek, reflecting the influence of Greek ideas in all things Roman during the second century.[71] A wide-ranging, un-wieldy, and humorous book, Athenaeus's narrative compiles information from a wide variety of sources on numerous topics, including food, cook-ing, recipes, drinking, medicine, dancing, literature, and philosophy, pre-senting "a detailed survey of the place of eating and drinking in the widest sense in Greek literary culture."[72]

Included in Athenaeus's musings on dining are discussions of gluttony and the fat body. In Athenaeus's text, gluttony is always detrimental to so-ciety, for it is associated with horrific acts of violence, social disintegration, and unsuccessful politics. Stories told about others confirm all of the nega-tive ideas associated with gluttony, while accusations of gluttony between the diners serve as rhetorical strategy to gain argumentative ground during a dinner where philosophical dialogue competes with actual eating. Since it is difficult to eat and talk simultaneously, labeling one's competition glutton-ous serves to emphasize the speaker's lofty desire to engage in philosophical conversation, while the others are accused of being more interested in the immediate pleasures of food.[73] Yet, the diners themselves eat little through-out the text; like the *Satyricon,* much is made of the potential for gluttony at the dinner, but there is little evidence of the actual eating of the repast. Thus, we see again the importance of the symbolic meaning of gluttony as a mis-use of food that threatens social stability, even when the diners themselves can hardly be labeled actual gluttons.

In Athenaeus's text, the glutton is often labeled "pot-belly" (*gastron*), which suggests a connection between being a glutton and being fat. Yet, Athenaeus's discussion of gluttony does not include reference to fatness, specifically; that discourse comes later in the text, in a context quite dis-tinct from that of gluttony. Instead of directly suggesting that gluttony leads to fatness, or that fatness is evidence of gluttony, Athenaeus suggests that, in some contexts, luxurious living leads to fatness. This is the kind of con-nection that we saw in the *Satyricon,* as well, where being fat may indi-cate overindulgence and excess wealth but does not necessarily indicate the kind of moral degradation indicative of the glutton. It is one thing to have the kind of wealth that allows one to indulge in expensive, rich food that may make one fat; it is quite another to exhibit a gluttonous attitude where single-minded focus on the pleasures of food prevails over all other activities.

Accusations of Gluttony as Rhetorical Strategy

In order to give some structure to his dinner conversation, Athenaeus gives some of his numerous speakers more prominence than others.[74] Larensis, a Roman official, is the host of the dinner, while Ulpian of Tyre, a Roman jurist and official, directs the after-dinner conversation. Exchanges between Ul-pian and Theodorus of Thessaly, a cynic called "Cynulcus," or "dog-catcher," are of primary importance here because their frequently quarrelsome con-versations are peppered with mutual accusations of gluttony.

Neither Ulpian nor Cynulcus, though, fits the definition of a glutton, for there is no evidence that they eat excessively or are exceptionally focused on the food itself. Ulpian, for instance, refuses to eat until he has asked whether or not a word was appropriately designated for a particular thing.[75] Ulpian's lengthy discourses on the linguistic aspects of food take primacy over his participation in the meal. At one point during the meal, he suggests that, having "stuffed our bellies enough" it is time to talk.[76] He then begs the Cynics,

since they have been lavishly foddered, to keep quiet, unless they want to gnaw on the jawbones and skulls, which they are welcome to enjoy in their guise of dogs. . . . For they are willing to eat and drink anything . . . That is what you Cynics do, Cynulcus. When you drink—or rather when you drink too much—you prevent pleasant conversation in the same way pipe-girls and dancing-girls do.[77]

Cynulcus, having enough of these insults, turns on Ulpian and cries,

Glutton! Worshipper of your own belly! That's all you know how to do—not how to have a careful discussion, or recall historical events, or offer graceful words on occasion. Instead, you spend all your time asking, "Is it attested or is it not? Is the word used or is it not?"[78]

Although Cynulcus begins by accusing Ulpian of gluttony, his counterattack has little to do with Ulpian's eating habits but rather focuses solely on his obsessive focus on words. Accused of being a belly worshipper, Ulpian's primary response is to inquire as to the origin of the phrase.[79] When no answer is forthcoming, Ulpian digresses with a long speech on the various literary preparations of pork belly.[80]

Myrtilus of Thessaly, a grammarian who sits at the table, similarly accuses Ulpian of being a glutton who has no interest in history. Myrtilus goes even further than Cynculus, charging Ulpian with being a "fat-licker" (*knisoloichos*), or dinner-parasite, a man who eats for free and flatters the host excessively.[81] Though there is no truth to the charge, Ulpian responds in his typical manner by asking where the word "fat-licker" is found. In both of these contexts, gluttony is associated with superficiality and a lack of intellectual seriousness, at the same time that the accusations themselves are baseless. The charge of gluttony has little to do with the actualities of the situation. Indeed, Ulpian is characterized in the text as being fond of criticizing others, lying alone on his couch, watching the speakers, and "not eating much."[82]

Ulpian's accusations of gluttony against Cynculus would appear at first to have more credence, for Cynculus is often hungry. At one point, Ulpian confronts Cynculus, disgusted: "But you, dog, are always starving and do not allow us to share a nice extended discussion."[83] Cynculus is about to leave the feast when fish and other dainties are brought in, and he stays, presumably to eat. Instead, though, he begins to talk about how hungry he is. On another occasion, Cynculus interrupts Ulpian by calling for bread, and when the bread is brought in, a long discussion occurs on the variety of breads found in literary works.[84] At another point, after a long discourse on banquets by Athenaeus himself, Cynculus complains that this long speech has made the diners "as tense as people who are fasting and waiting for the rising star, which has to appear, they say, before those who invented this fine philosophy are allowed to taste any food."[85] Though he is apparently hungry, his craving does not stop him from making a lengthy discourse on the joys of lentils. Even in his hunger, Cynculus privileges conversation over eating in such a way that renders the accusations of gluttony rather baseless. This suggests that charges of gluttony are used rhetorically as a way to add humor to the text and to move the conversation along, rather than to describe the actual behavior of the diners.

Gluttony as a Social Problem

In Book 10, the dinner conversation turns to the subject of gluttony, because, as Athenaeus says, the clever poet must offer his audience a variety of entertainments, much like the "a rich feast that resembles an elegant dinner."[86] From the beginning of the discourse on gluttony, it is clear that such behavior is disdained. Book 9 ended with descriptions of the tragic Herakles, so Athenaeus begins Book 10 by invoking Herakles the glutton. He quotes Ephicharmus's description of the jaw-rattling, nostril-sizzling glutton Herakles in *Busiris,* discussed earlier, as well as the gluttonous Odysseus, who, in addition to being unable to ignore his shameless belly, "offers an unnecessary sententious discussion of his belly."[87] Athenaeus criticizes Odysseus for his impatience and inability to "put up with the situation or . . . [eat] a modest amount.[88] Descriptions of athletes with gluttonous appetites follow, and it is soon clear that Herakles is not the only heroic athlete who is known for his ability to eat great quantities of meat. Theagenes of Thasos also devoured a bull by himself, while the weight lifter Milo of Croton, whom we first encountered in Aristotle, could eat 20 pounds of meat, 20 pounds of bread, and three pitchers of wine (about 8.5 quarts).[89] The athlete Astyanax of Miletus, who was a three-time victor in the Olympic games, once promised his dinner host that he would eat all of the food prepared for the guests, and he proceeded to do so.[90]

These tales of athletic excesses create a context for Athenaeus's critique of what he sees as disproportionate attention to athletics in Greece. Quoting Euripides, Athenaeus suggests that "although Greece has more problems than you can count, there's none worse than the athletes."[91] Athletes "don't learn to live decently" and they are "incapable of being poor or coping with adversity; because the bad habits they develop mean that they have trouble adapting to difficult circumstances."[92] Athletes are not taught "to live decently," for they are enslaved to their jaws and victims of their bellies.[93] Athenaeus heartily agrees with Euripides that good governing is more important than what athletes do; more important are those just and sober men who make good laws and bring wealth to the city. For Athenaeus, then, the athlete's gluttony marks him as unworthy of social praise and points to a necessary reevaluation of cultural priorities that currently place a greater appreciation on the athlete than the wise man. Athenaeus asserts that it is better for society to value those men who control their appetites, work to govern well, and keep society stable, than to give undue respect to the athletes.

The social effects of gluttony are further explored in Athenaeus's accounts of individuals and nations that are satirized for their gluttony. In many cases, gluttonous individuals lead lives full of abusive and inhuman acts, and many of them die from their excessive behaviors. For instance, the tomb of one glutton reads, "After drinking much, and eating much, and making many nasty remarks about others, I lie here, Timocreon of Rhodes."[94] The king of Lydia, Cambles, was so overtaken by his gluttony that "he chopped his own wife up into pieces during the night and ate her; then the next morning, when he found her hand in his mouth, he committed suicide, since rumors about what he had done had already spread."[95] And, when Cantibarus the Persian tired his jaws from eating, he would prop them open and simply have his servants "pour the food in, as if he were an inanimate jar."[96] Connected to death, irrationality, and exploitation, gluttony creates individuals unable to live moral lives within the boundaries of community.

Nations, too, are ridiculed as gluttonous. Boeotia, for instance, is mocked as a nation of "men who are best at eating all day long."[97] When asked what he thought of the Boeotians, a man named Prepelaus said, "Well, what else except that they say what pots would if they could talk, and each of them announces how much he can hold?"[98] Huge portions of food are called "Thessalian" because their dinners consist of "as much as a wagon can carry."[99] People who live in nations where they eat much and talk little live "where everyone has his own outhouse right next to his door."[100] Nations that focus too much on eating are not smart or successful and are associated with excrement and irrationality.

All of these descriptions of the extreme bad behavior of gluttonous individuals and nations leads Athenaeus to his main point: that even ordinary people, when given the opportunity to overindulge in food and drink, will behave badly. Anyone who gathers for a dinner party and eats and drinks too much inevitably treats servants terribly, insults fellow diners, and incites brawling.[101] Athenaeus quotes the comic poet Alexis to emphasize his point:

And you could learn the sort of trouble people's bellies cause them, and the kind of lessons it teaches us, and everything it forces us to do. If you removed this part of our anatomy, no one would deliberately commit a crime or abuse anyone else. But as it is, it's the cause of all our difficulties.[102]

Gluttony is the scourge of civil society, and must be controlled.

Moderation in food and drink leads to the best possible outcome for human interaction, for it leads to comfort, delight and pleasure. One Timotheus, "who was accustomed to expensive dinners of the sort given by generals, was invited by Plato to a drinking party in the Academy"; afterwards "he said that people who had dinner with Plato were happy the next day . . ."

because they had been "entertained in a frugal, but sophisticated style."[103] Eating and drinking in moderation is the mark of a person who is not simply caught up in the pleasures of the moment. And, even the lack of food can give pleasure, as when the bread ran out at a feast given by Arcesilaus and the joking about it "added zest to the occasion."[104] Having a restrained attitude towards consumption will lead to a refined and educated culture.

Luxurious Fat

While gluttony is associated with bad politics, stupidity, rude behavior, death, and abuse, fatness, too, comes under fire from Athenaeus, but for different reasons. Fatness is explicitly discussed in Book 12—clearly distinct from the discussion of gluttony—and is unmistakably associated with luxury (*tryphe*). Luxury includes money, furniture, women, jewels, softness, cosmetics, rich food, copious sex, and a general state of indulgence, practiced by the wealthy and powerful, who are the only people who can afford it. Luxury can deform the body in many ways: "Many other people as well," Athenaeus states, "utterly ruined their bodies as a consequence of their inopportune indulgence in pleasure, some surrendering to obesity, others to a stupor resulting from their enormous self-indulgence."[105] Too much luxury can result in fatness, though it is not the only potential result.

Athenaeus's descriptions of the fat are of those who abandon themselves to luxury and refuse to exercise. Only occasionally is gluttony specifically associated with fatness: "Dionysius, the son of Clearchus . . . grew imperceptibly ever fatter as a consequence of his addiction to luxury and his overeating every day, with the result that he was so obese that he had difficulty breathing and choked."[106] This Dionysius is called a "fat pig" by Menander, who also quotes him as declaring that the "only good way to die" is "to be fat and lie on your back, with an enormous gut, barely able to speak or breathe in and out, eating and saying, 'I feel so good that I'm rotting.' "[107] Yet, Athenaeus is quick to point out that Dionysius was a good leader, ruling as a benevolent tyrant for 33 years. Dionysius was "gentler and more reasonable than any of the tyrants who preceded him."[108] In this case, at least, Dionysius's fatness did not cause or reveal inappropriate behavior. Unlike the gluttonous people he discussed in Book 10, Athenaeus's fat tyrants are not inevitably bad leaders.

And even though Athenaeus invokes the monstrous and the animalistic when speaking of fatness, being thin is also not the solution. He does suggest that it is better to be "poor and thinner . . . than to be much too rich and resemble the sea-monster in Tanagra" (which was a very fat fish), but being thin, according to his examples, does not bring with it particularly moral behavior.[109] Cinesias, who was "so tall and skinny" that he "took a plank of lime-tree wood and wrapped it around himself, to keep him from bending" was accused of being "unhealthy," "conniving," and "the most impious, lawless person alive."[110] It appears that the body's heft is not a wholly transparent sign of a person's moral behavior.

For Athenaeus, then, fatness may be the result of indulgent living, but being fat does not necessarily render a person immoral, a glutton, or a bad leader. As Dorothy Thompson points out, the fat kings that Athenaeus describes, all of whom are from Egypt, ruled their countries for between 25 and 54 years before dying or being overthrown.[111] Thompson also argues that it is not the fatness of these rulers that is a problem for Athenaeus, it is their luxurious living; according to Thompson, Athenaeus "either did not understand or else rejected the luxury and values of Hellenistic Egypt."[112] Thus, although Athenaeus uses fatness as a symbol for a lifestyle that garners his disapproval, fatness does not have the thoroughly negative moral implications that gluttony does. Fatness does not necessarily inhibit good politics, though excessive focus on gluttonous athletes distracts attention away from those who use moderation and govern well. For Athenaeus, it is far worse to be a glutton than to be fat.

CONCLUSION

Popular images of gluttons underscore the symbolic importance of the idea of gluttony as a marker of social disruption, animality, femininity, and death, even when gluttony is presented in a humorous fashion. Popular images of fat people often emphasize their comic aspects, sometimes making connections with gluttonous behavior, more often not. Popular texts emphasize the relationship between being fat and living a luxurious, wealthy life, even though being fat is not, by itself, an indication of moral turpitude. Rather, it is gluttony that has the potential to destroy both individuals and nations, rendering individuals incapable of living well within social boundaries and nations unable to attain political success. It is a good thing, then, that the brave and fearless Odysseus has more going for him than a periodic penchant for behavior that could make him appear to Athenaeus to be a glutton. Indeed, the morally complex character of Odysseus provides for us an alternative model for thinking about our contemporary disdain for the fat body. While we currently tend to allow the moral defects historically associated with gluttony to seep into our appraisal of the fat body, Odysseus reminds us that moral complexities of the gluttonous body need not be confirmed by fatness.

5

Ingest the Word, Not the World: Early
Christian Ideas of Excess and Self-Restraint

But dainty dishes and honeycakes and relishes and all the
elaborate preparations with which the skill of pastrycooks and
other experts at the art bewitches the taste, that most slavish of
all the senses, a stranger to culture and philosophy, a servant not
to things beautiful to see or hear but to the lusts of the wretched
belly, create distempers of soul and body which are often past all
cure.[1]

—Philo

There is no limit to the gluttony these men practice. Truly, in
inventing a multitude of new sweets and ever seeking recipes
of every description, they are shipwrecked on honey-cakes and
desserts.[2]

—Clement of Alexandria

The honey-cakes and desserts that shipwreck gluttonous eaters in the works
of Philo and Clement are reminiscent of Odysseus's men in the *Odyssey*, who
eat the "honey-sweet" lotus and lose all desire to return home.[3] Indeed, popular and philosophical discussions of fat bodies and gluttons in the Greek
and Roman worlds provide fodder for explicitly religious discussions regarding the harmful effects of gluttony by Jewish and Christian writers in the first
centuries of the Common Era. Philo of Alexandria, a Jew who attempts to interpret Jewish theology through the lens of Greek philosophy, and Clement of
Alexandria, who sought to create an explicitly Christian regimen influenced
by Greek ideas, exemplify efforts to highlight similarities between distinct
philosophical and religious ideals. As newcomers to the philosophical and
theological scene in the first century of the Common Era, early Christians
were especially eager to show both the compatibility with and superiority
of their worldview to that of the Greeks by giving old ideas new explanations and analyses. Indeed, Christianity's ultimate success depended on the

ability of its adherents to demonstrate that biblical texts—presented as time-less truth—already contained the wisdom espoused by Greek philosophers, and that its wisdom went further, culminating in a superior mode of moral rigor unmatched by pagan philosophers. Such notions of superiority are fur-ther demonstrated in the writings of John Chrysostom—"golden mouth"—one of the most popular and influential early Christian sermonizers, who exhorted his congregation to appropriate behavior by emphasizing the shamefulness of excessive eating and drinking.

In each of these writers, then, we continue to find the conceptual associa-tions we have seen before: impurity, irrationality, animality, and femininity remain aligned with gluttony, and purity, rationality, humanity, and mascu-linity continue to be linked to self-control. As Christianity enters the intel-lectual and religious picture in the first century, the ideas of self-restraint and moderation with regard to food and eating found in Greek and Roman texts become the strand of thinking that most powerfully links Greek philosophy with Christian theology.

At the same time, early Christian writers begin to expand the definitions of gluttony beyond eating to excess into various other ideas about the misuse of food, where being gluttonous can include eating foods that are delicately prepared or expensive. Indeed, for Christians, the consequences of food mis-behavior intensify: whereas in the Greek context, gluttony could stop one from living the good life here on earth, in Christianity, gluttony becomes a shameful and sinful act that can have the grim consequence of inhibiting the very possibility of an individual's salvation. The Christian focus on a heav-enly afterlife emphasizes the importance of morally appropriate behavior on earth. Thus, as Christianity's influence grows, gluttony's definition expands and its harmful effects are amplified.

In this chapter, then, we witness how three writers—Philo of Alexandria, Clement of Alexandria, and John Chrysostom—shaped an early Christian worldview through their understandings of sacrificial fat, human fatness, and gluttony. All three of these writers offer distinct perspectives on glut-tony that reflect their intellectual backgrounds and interests, and all three articulate different degrees of interest in the fat body. In so doing, these three writers demonstrate the variety of ideas that begin to be associated with the act of gluttony as Christianity grows. Before we turn to Clement of Alexandria and John Chrysostom, whose writings make clear the sinful-ness of gluttony in a Christian context, we examine the works of Philo of Alexandria, a first-century Jew, who, perhaps more than any other writer, created a conceptual bridge between biblical and Greek ideas. An unwitting accomplice in the creation of a Christian worldview through his allegori-cal interpretations of the Hebrew Bible and Greek philosophy, Philo reads similarities regarding the proper use of food and drink in both biblical and Greek texts. In so doing, he offers both a method of textual interpretation and a thematic analysis of those texts that provide a coherent framework for future attempts at bridging the conceptual differences between the two distinct worldviews.

PHILO

In tracing the development of ideas about gluttony and the fat body as Christianity develops, the work of Philo plays a crucial transitional role. Scholars know little about Philo, but as far as we can tell from his writings, he lived from around 15 BCE to 50 CE in Alexandria, a city that, at the time, housed one of the largest Jewish populations outside of Judea, as well as a significant number of Greeks.[4] Philo's writings reveal that he was a Jew deeply influenced by Greek philosophy; as Samuel Sandmel puts it, "Philo's basic religious ideas are Jewish, his intuitions Jewish, and his loyalties Jewish, but his explanations of ideas, intuitions, and devotions are invariably Greek."[5] Yet, Philo's works "were preserved and transmitted by Christians, not by Jews."[6]

One significant reason for Philo's appeal to Christian writers is that he approaches the Hebrew Bible allegorically, that is, he reads the text as saying something other than it appears to say. For Philo, this meant interpreting scripture using ideas from Greek philosophy. While most scholars agree that Philo was a devoted Jew, his method of interpreting texts exemplifies a way to harmonize what might otherwise appear to be two very different ways of thinking about the world, that of the Hebrew Bible and that of Greek philosophy. So, for instance, when Philo interprets the prohibition against eating sacrificial fat in the Hebrew Bible as a call for continence or self-control, he is able to suggest that biblical requirements for behavior parallel those promoted by Plato, for whom the taming of bodily desires is crucial. Indeed, food and drink are of significant concern to Philo because the belly has, in both the Bible and in Plato, rich symbolic and actual meaning that creates a point of connection between the two worldviews. His emphasis on the evils of covetous desire—its impurity, irrationality, and animality—as it is represented by the belly's cravings, renders biblical morality and philosophical discernment part and parcel of what he promotes as a universally applicable system for human moral behavior.

Philo on Desire, Sacrifice, and the Platonic Soul

As James Rhodes points out, Philo's understanding of the sacrifices and the dietary restrictions found in the Hebrew Bible are dependent on his reading of the 10th Commandment, "Thou shalt not covet," as a biblical prohibition against excessive desire.[7] Philo begins his discussion of the 10th Commandment by using the Greek myth of Tantalus to illustrate the idea that desire for what we don't have "breeds fierce and endless yearnings" that can never be satisfied.[8] Tantalus, a Greek king, was invited to feast with the gods, but he stole their nectar and exposed their secrets, thus incurring their wrath. He was sent to Hades, where he stood in a pool of water, trees with ripe fruit hanging over his head. His punishment was never to be able to satisfy his desires for food and drink: when he was thirsty, the "water slipt away"; when hungry "the rich produce of the trees was turned to barrenness."[9] Tantalus's experience of bodily deprivation through continual hunger and thirst suggests to Philo a parallel to the soul's experience of desire:

For just as those unmerciful and relentless mistresses of the body, hunger and thirst, rack it with pains . . . and often bring it to the point of death unless their savagery is assuaged by food and drink, so it is with the soul. Desire makes it empty through oblivion of what is present, and then through memory of what is far away it produces fierce and uncontrollable madness . . . not for what gives gratification to the belly, but for money, reputation, government, beautiful women and all the innumerable objects which are held in human life to be enviable and worthy of a struggle.[10]

The covetous, desiring soul is always tempted by something just out of reach, unsatisfied with what is available. Like the ravenous stomach that seeks more and more food, the desiring soul creeps about, injuring every part of the body, devouring it like a blazing fire.[11] Desire is, for Philo, "so great . . . and transcendent an evil" that it can be seen as "the fountain of all evils."[12]

Philo's use of Greek myth to understand the 10th Commandment not only helps make the connection between the desires of the body and soul, it gives him an entry into reading the Hebrew Bible from the perspective of Greek philosophy. Philo brings Plato into the conversation by suggesting that "those who had feasted abundantly" on the "sound doctrines" of philosophy "made researches into the nature of the soul and observed that its components were threefold, reason, high spirit, and desire."[13] He explains Plato's understanding of desire, focusing particularly on the physical location of desire in the belly. Reason is lodged in the head, the high spirit in the chest, and

to desire they gave the space around the navel and what is called the diaphragm. For it was right that desire so lacking in reasoning power should be lodged as far as might be from reason's royal seat, almost at the outermost boundary, and that being above all others an animal insatiable and incontinent it should be pastured in the region where food-taking and copulation dwell.[14]

According to Philo, however, this arrangement of the soul's components was previously observed by Moses, who created rules to curb desire, especially with regard to food and drink. First, Moses restrains desire by requiring everyone to give portions of the first fruits to the officiating priests and for the sacrifices, for waiting until after the first fruits have been given, "clearly allays passion and thus curbs the restiveness of the appetites."[15] Second, Moses restricts the kinds of food that can be eaten to avoid gluttony.[16] The potentially destructive nature of bodily desire, particularly when the desire for food and drink is excessive, thus becomes the common denominator between Plato and Moses.

Philo's explanation of the rationale behind the sacrifice of the first fruits is made only briefly in Book 4 of the "Special Laws," but it is fully detailed in Book 1, as he analyzes various rules associated with the priesthood. In the section that deals with sacrificial contributions given to priests, Philo explains that priests are given the shoulder, two cheeks, and the maw, or belly, of the oxen or sheep. His justifications for the donation of these particular body parts follow Plato's schema for the arrangement of the soul's components precisely: the shoulder is given because "the spirited element resides in the breast" which is "girded like a soldier armed against attack with the stoutest of fenceworks called the thorax or breastplate," and the jaws are given because they belong to "that master-limb, the head," which in Plato's *Timaeus* houses the immortal soul.[17]

But it is the maw that captures most of Philo's attention. "The maw is an excrescence of the belly, and it is the fate of the belly to be the manger of that irrational animal, desire, which is drenched by wine-bibbing and gluttony, is perpetually flooded with relays of food and drink administered to it, and like a sow rejoices to make its home in the mire."[18] Here desire is the irrational animal, rolling around in the dirty morass of incontinence. Should one wonder why this portion of the animal should be given to the priest, who presumably would not be indulging in his baser appetites, it is because we are to "let continence, that pure and stainless virtue which disregards all concerns of food and drink and claims to stand superior to the pleasures of the stomach, touch the holy altars and bring with it the appendage of the belly as a reminder that it holds in contempt gluttony and greediness and all that inflames the tendencies to lust."[19] The priests are the recipients of the belly precisely because it represents the virtue and purity of continence when placed upon the sacrificial altar.

Philo's explanation of Moses's second dietary restriction on certain kinds of food follows a similar train of thought. In the "Special Laws," Book 4, Philo claims, "All the animals of land, sea or air whose flesh is the finest and fattest, thus titillating and exciting the malignant foe pleasure, he sternly forbade them to eat, knowing that they set a trap for the most slavish of the senses, the taste, and produce gluttony, an evil very dangerous both to soul and body."[20] Not eating delicious meat, like pork, trains people to have self-control, and allows people to live an Aristotelian middle way: "He approved neither of rigorous austerity like the Spartan legislator, nor of dainty living, like him who introduced the Ionians and Sybarites to luxurious and voluptuous practices. Instead he opened up a path midway between the two."[21] For Philo, the dietary restrictions found in the Hebrew Bible confirm and support the creation of the good life as described by Plato and Aristotle.

As Philo continues describing the reasons for Mosaic dietary restrictions, he turns to the prohibition on the eating of suet fat. Chapter 1 argued that the biblical prohibition on eating suet fat made a connection between fat, wealth, and God, and that human fatness represents a willful ignoring of God. Philo's reading of the Mosaic dietary restrictions confirms this reading. Addressing the rationale for the prohibition on eating improperly slaughtered meat, Philo censures those who "extend their unrestrained and excessive luxury beyond all bounds and limits" by preparing meat in forbidden ways, by strangling animals in a way that entombs "in the carcase (sic) the blood which is the essence of the soul."[22] Those who fail to follow the prohibition on eating blood are, for Philo, an example of incontinence and gluttony.

The same goes for the prohibition on the eating of fat. "The fat is prohibited because it is the richest part and here again he teaches us to practice self-restraint and foster the aspiration for the life of austerity which relinquishes what is easiest and lies ready to hand, but willingly endures anxiety and toils in order to acquire virtue."[23] For Philo, the prohibition on the eating of suet fat reveals to humans the necessity of developing self-control. His reading expands prohibitions on eating sacrificial fat beyond the specificity of Judaism, for the idea of self-restraint, promoted by Greek philosophy, becomes for him a mere repetition of a universal ideal already expressed by Jewish dietary restrictions.

In addition to his connection between sacrificial fat and human self-restraint, Philo also makes a more symbolic argument about sacrificial fat and its relation to human fatness. In "The Posterity and Exile of Cain," Philo again addresses the question of human desire. As he traces the genealogy of Cain through his son Lamech and his wife Sella (Zillah), he raises the issue of bodily pleasure by pointing out that their daughter's name, Noeman (Na'amah), means "fatness" (Genesis 4:22). Strong's *Concise Dictionary of the Words in the Hebrew Bible* suggests that Na'amah means "pleasant," suggesting perhaps that Na'amah was pleasingly plump.[24] Regardless of the name's actual meaning, Philo uses his interpretation of Noeman's name to focus on the evils of desire: "for when those, who make bodily comfort and the material things of which I have spoken their object, succeed in getting something which they crave after, the consequence is that they grow fat."[25] Such fatness, for Philo, represents a turning away from God. Here he cites Deuteronomy 32:15, which, as we saw in Chapter 1, makes a connection between human fatness and ignoring God. Indeed, people "suffering from the effects of fatness and enjoyment spreading increasingly, swell out and become distended till they burst," but those who become symbolically fat with wisdom love virtue: "those who are fattened by wisdom which feeds souls that are lovers of virtue, acquire a firm and settled vigour, of which the fat taken from every sacrifice to be offered with the whole burnt offering is a sign."[26] "Richness of mind"—symbolically, sacrificial fat—is, in this reading, "God's gift and appropriated to him" for "all the fat is a due for ever to the Lord" (Leviticus 3:19).[27] Though this is a rather tortured rhetorical attempt at making a parallel between sacrificial fat and wisdom, Philo articulates a parallel between the believer and the philosopher, whose fattened, immortal soul strives for, and represents, wisdom. In addition, the pleasure-seeking body, which is merely mortal, "usurps the place of God" when it eats too much and grows fat.[28] The sacrificial fat thus becomes a metaphor for the triumph of the Platonic immortal soul over the mortal soul, while human fatness symbolizes the human disregard for God.

Continence and covetousness, both focused on the belly, are thus for Philo two significant behaviors at war in the human body and soul. Indeed, the difficulties of intemperance, inordinate desire, and gluttony are primordial in their origins, stemming back to the Garden of Eden. In his allegorical reading of Genesis, "On the Creation," Philo argues that the first sin was that of humans succumbing to pleasure. The enticing serpent is, according to Philo, "a fit symbol of pleasure, because in the first place he is an animal without feet sunk prone upon his belly; secondly because he takes clods of earth as food; thirdly because he carries in his teeth the venom with which it is his nature to destroy those whom he has bitten."[29] A human unable to resist the temptations of pleasure

is exempt from none of these traits, for he is so weighted and dragged downwards that it is with difficulty that he lifts up his head, thrown down and tripped up by intemperance: he feeds not on heavenly nourishment, which wisdom by discourses and doctrines proffers to lovers of contemplation, but on that which comes up out of the earth with the revolving seasons, and which produces drunkenness, daintiness, and greediness.[30]

For Philo, Eve's inability to spurn the temptations of the snake brought Eve and Adam "out of a state of simplicity and innocence into one of wickedness" marked by an inability to refuse earthly temptations.[31]

Philo makes another connection to Plato's *Timaeus* when he discusses the fact that the serpent, or Pleasure, "does not venture to bring her wiles and deceptions to bear on the man, but on the woman, and by her means on him."[32] Here, Philo again reads the Genesis story allegorically, suggesting that the mind corresponds to Adam, and the senses to Eve, "and pleasure encounters and holds parley with the senses first, and through them cheats with her quackeries the sovereign mind itself."[33] As in Plato, if the rational, masculine mind is overcome by the irrational, feminine appetites, "reason is forthwith ensnared and becomes a subject instead of a rule, a slave instead of a master."[34]

Thus, to be lured by earthly pleasures is to ignore rationality and masculinity, and it is this that makes Philo's concern about the pleasures of food significant. Although Philo mentions drunkenness as a serious temptation, it is daintiness—the excessive focus on the pleasures of taste—and greediness—the excessive focus on overeating—that seem to provoke in him the greatest fear. These cause

the cravings of the belly to burst out and fanning them into flame, make the man a glutton, while they also stimulate and stir up the stings of his sexual lusts. For he licks his lips over the labour of caterers and confectioners, and twisting his head about all around strains to catch some of the steam and savour of the delicacies. Whenever he beholds a richly spread table, he flings down his whole person and tumbles upon the dishes set out, eager to devour all at once. His aim is not to sate his hunger, but to leave nothing that has been set before him undevoured. Hence we see that no less than the serpent he carries his poison in his teeth. These are the agents and ministers of excess, cutting and chewing all eatables, handing them over first to the tongue, the judge of savours, for its decision, then to the gullet.[35]

Philo's description of the glutton likens him to a snake, twisting his head to taste the scent of the foods, focusing his eyes and mouth on devouring everything that is laid before him. The glutton focuses on eating not to satisfy hunger, but rather, to satisfy a desire for pleasure, and in so doing, succumbs to irrationality.

Philo's ability to make symbolic connections between the Hebrew Bible and Greek philosophy created an intellectual context within which ideas about pleasure, desire, and bodily restraint become, for him, universals, applicable to either Jews or Greeks. His ability to read Mosaic food rules as a call for bodily self-control suggests the compatibility of Jewish and Greek modes of thought concerning the body and its need for discipline. His clever—though tortured—explanation of how humans should not become physically fat, but rather, strive to become metaphorically "fat" with virtue, just as the Platonic immortal soul strives for wisdom, along with his understanding of the primordial threat of pleasure and desire, underscores his emphasis on the soul's striving, not on the body's comforts. For Philo, it is these attempts to curb bodily desires and to promote self-control that align biblical and philosophical perspectives on living a good and righteous life. And, as we turn to the work of Clement of Alexandria, we see how Philo's attempts to highlight the compatibility of the Hebrew Bible with Greek philosophy offers a way for Christians, too, to find congruence with Greek philosophy.

CLEMENT OF ALEXANDRIA

Titus Flavius Clemens, known to us as Clement of Alexandria, was born around 150, probably in Athens. Whether he was born a pagan or a Christian is the subject of much scholarly speculation, but whatever the religious character of his early life, his texts reveal great familiarity with both Greek texts and Christian scriptures.[36] He made his way to Alexandria around 180, where he began studying with Pantaenus, who was the head teacher at the catechetical school there. Under Pantaenus's leadership, the school became an important center for the training of priests and the development of Christian theology. After Pantaenus's death, Clement became the head of the school. He died in 215.

Clement was "the first Christian to mention Philo by name," and he used Philo's work to bolster his own ideas about what it meant to be a Christian.[37] In his work, Clement is deeply concerned with what it means to live the proper Christian life. Bodily habits, including eating and drinking, play a significant role in the expression of personal morality. In his attempts to distinguish the Christian from those around him or her, proper attitudes toward food and the creation of a Christian dietary regimen parallel to that of the Greeks is crucial.

Clement's importance for understanding the moral history of gluttony and corpulence in the West stems from his writings, especially *The Paidagogos,* or *Christ, the Educator,* which summarize the catechetical teachings of the Alexandrian school and give insight into what Clement taught both Christians and pagans about how to gain salvation, from proper belief to appropriate bodily practices, including eating and drinking. Finding a way to talk about eating and drinking is important for Clement for a number of reasons. In the second century, Christianity was still a new religion, seeking to establish its distinct moral vision. Judaism emphasized that one way of promoting right relationship with God was through adherence to a set of daily bodily practices, including dietary laws that deemed certain foods fit for consumption and other foods prohibited; Greek culture also saw proper use of food as one aspect of living the good life. Christians, too, were in need of directions on how to live a good Christian life, and how to create right relationship with God even when they had no explicit daily, bodily practices or dietary laws, except for occasional fasting. Clement sought to fill this void by teaching Christians how to demonstrate their beliefs by behaving in certain ways. As Peter Brown puts it, "Clement's writings communicated a sense of the God given importance of every moment of daily life, and especially of the life of the household."[38] In addition, Clement was a Greek dealing primarily with Greek converts to Christianity. It was crucial for him to make connections between Greek philosophical ideas and practices and the life of the Christian. To synthesize these ideas would take an articulate and well-educated man, and we find these qualities in Clement, whose writings contain citations from 348 classical authors, including Homer, Plato, and Philo, as well as over 5,000 scriptural references.[39] Using all possible resources, Clement blended Jewish, Christian, and Greek ideas about proper food practices and, in so doing, highlighted what he saw as universal moral obligations, intrinsic to all of these systems of thought.

Thus, when reading Clement, we see his continual attempts to emphasize the connections between Judaism—read primarily through Philo—Christianity, and Greek culture. The very title of his text, the *Paidagogos,* reveals Clement's interest in making connections between Greek culture and Christianity. In Greek culture, the *paidagogos*—"tutor" or "educator"—was a family slave assigned to accompany a boy wherever he went, making sure that the child had the right equipment for school or other activities.[40] The *paidagogos* was also responsible for the boy's behavior and comportment; in this way the *paidagogos* was a tutor of ethics and virtue much in the same way that an academic teacher imparted intellectual knowledge and skills. The goal of the *paidagogos* "is to improve the soul, not just to instruct it; to guide to a life of virtue, not merely to one of knowledge."[41] And in a textual move that owes a great debt to Philo, Clement interprets Jesus Christ as the *paidagogos* for all of humanity through his reading of Philippians 2:7, where Paul explains that Jesus, though in the form of God, "emptied himself, taking the form of a slave, being born in human likeness." Clement's text, then, presents Jesus guiding his followers to a less sinful existence through comprehensive moral instruction, including advice "on the practical needs of life."[42] As Veronika Grimm suggests, Clement's genius is that the moral authority for his Christian etiquette is Christ himself, who teaches Christians about their relationship to bodily practices like eating, drinking, gossiping, and sex, as well as the proper place of luxury items like make-up, perfume, and fine clothes. Clement's Jesus is intimately involved in all aspects of a Christian's life.[43]

From the beginning of Book Two of *Christ, The Educator,* it is clear that Clement's purpose is to teach Christians how to "exercise control" over the body in order to purify body and soul.[44] "For, if a man is completely purified and freed from the things that make him only dust, what could he have more serviceable for walking in the path that leads to the perception of God than his own self?"[45] Clement's use of the idea of a bodily purity that cleanses the soul for its walk with God would have been familiar to his audience and gives him an opportunity to create a conceptual context within which Jewish, Greek, and Christian ideas come together.

One significant aspect of bodily purity is that of proper food habits. Clement begins his discussion of food with a reference to Paul's disdain for those whose god is the belly (Philippians 3:19), stating that while "other men, indeed, live that they may eat, just like unreasoning beasts . . . our Educator has given the command that we eat only to live. Eating is not our main occupation, nor is pleasure our chief ambition."[46] We have already seen the connection between the lack of reason and animality in Plato, Aristotle, and Philo, and here Clement adds Paul to the mix. But Clement goes one step further: recognizing the potential pleasure in food and eating, he rejects any acceptance of culinary gratification and seeks to convince his reader that food should not be a source of pleasure. Clement does not want to argue for an appropriate amount of pleasure derived from food, as is seen in Plato and Aristotle; for him, food is not about pleasure at all. Eating is simply a means to an end and is necessary only to the extent that it keeps our bodies alive to hear the word of God so that we may gain eternal salvation.

Clement uses a number of different arguments in his attempts to convince Christians that pleasure in eating is unacceptable. He suggests for instance, that if food is simply sustenance for the bodies that allow us to hear God's word, then Christians' "food should be plain and ungarnished, in keeping with the truth."[47] Food should be "suitable to children who are plain and unpretentious, adapted to maintaining life, not self-indulgence."[48] Maintaining life requires "health and strength," and "a disposition easily satisfied with any sort of food" will be sufficient for this purpose.[49] Here Clement agrees with Philo that daintily prepared foods can be dangerous to the Christian life. If the proper use of food is to maintain health and strength, then any food will do. Although he never gives specifics about what "any sort of food" is, Clement's main point seems to be that a good Christian will eat what is available and not put any energy into making meals pleasurable. Such an approach replaces prohibitions against eating certain kinds of foods with a prescription to find all food sufficient. Indeed, even if a good Christian finds himself at the banquet of an unbeliever, who places before him rich and exotic foods, the good Christian, "should consider the rich variety of dishes that are served as a matter of indifference, and despise delicacies as things that after awhile will cease to be."[50] Nonetheless, to be a proper guest is important, as is having a proper attitude towards food: "We do not need to abstain from rich foods completely, but we should not be anxious for them. We must partake of what is set before us, as becomes a Christian, out of respect for him who has invited us and not to lessen or destroy the sociability of the gathering."[51] And, according to Clement, a good Christian who gives thanks to God for whatever food is given will "not indulge excessively in pleasure."[52]

Indeed, finding pleasure in food can also create significant problems for an individual's health and wealth. Seeking "excessive variety in food must be avoided," for, according to Clement, eating too many different kinds of food leads "to every kind of bad effect: indisposition of the body, upset stomach, perversion of taste due to some misguided culinary adventure or foolish experiment in pastry cooking."[53] While Plato, too, made a link between gluttony and illness, Clement further underscores the connection by citing the claim of one Antiphanes, a doctor from Delos, who "said that rich variety in food is one of the causes of disease."[54]

In addition, seeking variety in one's diet is, for Clement, inevitably connected to expense. When one is satisfied with simple foods, it seems, one spends neither too much time nor too much money satisfying bodily pleasures. When we "reject simplicity of diet" we "engage in a frantic search for expensive menus that must be imported from across the sea."[55] Seeking variety in food and spending lots of money on food defines for Clement the glutton: "such grasping and excitable people seem to scour the world blunderingly for their costly pleasures, and make themselves heard for their 'sizzling frying-pans,' wasting the whole of their lives in hovering over mortar and pestle, omnivorous fellows who cling as close to matter as fire does."[56] To Clement, such a man "seems nothing more than one great mouth."[57] For those who think that a little indigestion or a few more dollars are a small price to pay for a truly excellent meal, Clement begs to differ; from his perspective, seeking the pleasures of the body can only lead to harm.

Eating too much food is also a problem for Clement, for he values self-control and self-sufficiency. "Self-sufficiency, in dictating that food be limited to the proper amount, ministers to the health of the body, and besides, can distribute some of its substance to its neighbor."[58] Here, Clement again refers to eating for one's health, and he suggests the value in the equitable distribution of food so that one person does not eat up the communal resources. He argues that, if one's diet exceeds "the limits of self-sufficiency, it harms man by dulling his mind and making his body susceptible to disease."[59] Eating too much is, for Clement, also indicative of the pleasures of food:

Indeed, the pleasures of a luxurious table inflict untold damage: gluttony, squeamishness, gourmandizing, insatiability of appetite, voraciousness. Carrion flies and wheedling weasels and gladiators . . . are of the same type, for the first have sacrificed reason, the second friendship, and the last life itself for the pleasures of the belly, creeping upon their bellies, beasts that merely resemble man, made to the likeness of their father, the ravening beast. . . . Are not such men who waste their lives on dishes and frivolous elaborate preparations of highly seasoned foods, whose minds have become base, are they not hidebound to earth, living for the passing moment as though they did not live at all?[60]

Here, Clement, sounding much like Philo, attaches attention to food and the desire to eat elaborately prepared food to a person's inability to move beyond earthly pleasures and, presumably, move towards the pleasures of salvation. Clement thus concurs with the biblical notion that too much attention to food leads to the rejection of God and the abandonment of more heavenly pursuits. In addition, it is important to note that Clement confines the pleasures of food to the pleasures of feasting. Food that inspires a pleasurable response seems to be food that is exotic and delicate; Clement does not seem to recognize the possibility that "sufficient" food, or plain and ungarnished food, could cause one to gain pleasure or overindulge.

Moreover, while overindulgence is of great concern to Clement, the fat body seems to be of little or no concern. Clement mentions body weight only once, when he states that the person satisfied with "any sort of food" will have a disposition that "restricts the weight of the body."[61] It is unclear, however, whether the body whose weight is restricted is a particularly thin body. What is certain is that Clement looks favorably upon the body that exhibits, in his mind, health and strength, "not the unbalanced and unhealthy and miserable state of men such as athletes fed on an enforced diet," whose body weight is presumably unrestricted.[62] While an athlete's diet has, for Clement, negative implications for health, he never suggests that the problem with athletes is that they are too fat. It is more likely that the athlete's diet leads to excessive strength, which creates a lack of humoral balance in the body.[63]

What is of fundamental concern to Clement is that Christians use God's gifts, including food, properly. "We ought not to misuse the gifts of the Father, then, acting the part of spendthrifts like the rich son in the Gospel; let us, rather, make use of them with detachment, keeping them under control. Surely we have been commanded to be the master and lord, not the slave, of food."[64] If we fail to have control over food, we become unreasonable, like animals, for, "unquestionably, it is contrary to reason, utterly useless and beneath human dignity for men to feed themselves like cattle being fattened for the slaughter, for those who come from the earth to keep looking down to the earth and ever bowed over their tables."[65] Indeed, the most important thing that a Christian can do with regard to food is to practice moderation. "Lack of moderation, an evil wherever it is found, is particularly blameworthy in the matter of food. Gourmandising, at least, is nothing more than the immoderate use of delicacies; gluttony is a mania for glutting the appetite, and belly-madness, as the name itself suggests, is lack of self-control with regard to food."[66] Here, Clement references the apostle Paul, whose focus on self-control and moderation Clement extols, though for him, the practice of self-control makes humans "more akin to God."[67] For Clement, the need for moderation in food is crucial to the purpose of human life: "We have been created, not to eat and drink, but to come to the knowledge of God."[68] So instead of indulging in earthly pleasures, we should look to heaven for nourishment and feed on the metaphorical delights of God's truth: "It is an admirable thing indeed for a man to depend upon divine food in contemplation of the truth, and to be filled with the vision of that which really is, which is inexhaustible, tasting pleasure that is enduring and abiding and pure."[69] Just as we saw with Philo, the best and purest form of eating has nothing to do with physical eating at all; it is about ingesting knowledge of God to gain salvation.

Clement's book of Christian etiquette, *Christ, The Educator*, blends Jewish, Greek, and Christian ideas to create the proper regimen for the salvation-seeking Christian. The Christian practitioner should avoid pleasure of all kinds in food and eating, seeking simple foods to create a body capable of being attentive to the word of God. Seeking fancy foodstuffs, or overindulging in food, distracts the Christian from spiritual pursuits that allow him to attain salvation. Like Philo, Clement focuses on moderation and self-control as the physical foundation that creates a proper vessel for seeking knowledge of God. For the properly trained Christian, the metaphorical ingestion of God's word is the source of ultimate pleasure.

Ideas about the proper training of the body continue in the sermons of John Chrysostom, who, even a few hundred years later, continues to preach on the importance of disciplined eating. Indeed, in the sermons of John Chrysostom, vivid images of the consequences of excessive behavior in eating and drinking emphasize even more starkly than Clement the physical and psychological shamefulness of gluttony.

JOHN CHRYSOSTOM

John Chrysostom was born around 347 in Antioch—located in modern-day Turkey—which in the fourth century was one of the most affluent and cosmopolitan cities of the Roman Empire. Its citizens had the reputation for being sophisticated and extravagant.[70] Antioch was also a center for Christianity in the eastern part of the Roman Empire: both Paul and Peter had worked there, and according to Acts 11:26, it was in Antioch that the disciples were first called Christians.[71] Antioch was a picturesque city surrounded by mountains and deserts, which during this time were being increasingly inhabited by hermits and monks who felt called away from worldly decadence to lives of extreme austerity. John, too, felt called to the monastic life, and he lived in the desert before he began his church career.

John's father died soon after he was born, and he was raised by a single mother. His education focused on Greek and Roman philosophy and literature, and he was well-trained in rhetoric, a skill that would later serve him well. He became a priest in 386 and began his journey to becoming one of the greatest preachers in Christian history, hence the moniker "Chrysostom" or "golden mouth."[72] Preaching was a challenge, because his congregation in Antioch was a varied group, made up of rich and poor, men and women, young and old, artisan and laborer, slave and free, baptized and unbaptized.[73] Moreover, tensions between the austere monks and the more worldly Christians in the city, coupled with challenges from small groups of heretical Christians, made for sermons that required doctrinal sophistication and sound scriptural interpretation.[74]

It is clear from his writings that Chrysostom took his role as an instructor of Christian morality seriously. His vision of the perfect Christian life is one of balance, harmony, and self-control that can fend off internal and external forces of chaos and imbalance. To educate his parishioners, he often uses dramatic images and colorful language intended to be both memorable and edifying.[75] He frequently focuses on the spiritual and physical health of his congregation in his sermons, so gluttony, along with wealth and luxury, is often a target of Chrysostom's criticism.

Chrysostom uses a number of rhetorical strategies for discussing the temptations of the flesh in an attempt diminish their appeal. To sympathize with his audience regarding the overwhelming difficulty of warding off gluttonous temptation, Chrysostom uses metaphors that emphasize gluttony's power. His Homily 13 on Philippians, for instance, focuses on the passage in Paul's letter that reads, "for many walk, of whom I told you often, and now tell you even weeping, that they are the enemies of the cross of Christ: whose end is perdition, whose god is the belly, and whose glory is in their shame, who mind earthly things."[76] Chrysostom rails against those who seek ease and luxury, for people who are "lovers of their bodies, are enemies of the Cross."[77] In Chrysostom's sermon, the belly becomes a metaphor for a number of worldly traps, like the desire for the acquisition of property and possessions, or the expenditure of money for pleasure and not for helping the poor. Chrysostom writes that it is our responsibility to be masters of our bellies and not allow our bellies to be masters of us, for when our bellies take control, they are worse than a flooding ocean.

The sea, when it passes its bounds, does not work so many evils, as the belly does to our body, together with our soul. The former overflows all the earth, the latter all the body. Put moderation for a boundary to it, as God has put the sand for the sea. Then if its waves arise, and rage furiously, rebuke it, with the power which is in you.[78]

The image of gluttony as an inundating ocean emphasizes its persuasive power to manipulate behavior. Our job as Christians is to nurture our self-control so that it can be the beach that holds back the tide of gluttony. Indeed, we must avoid any situation where the body drags the soul down to earth, for "you ought to render even your body spiritual."[79]

Again, in his Homily 16 on Acts 7:6–7, Chrysostom appeals to his audience to avoid luxury and gluttony, because gormandizing drenches one's insides like a flooding river. "As at such time we see the fishes floating at top, dead, their eyes first blinding by the muddy slime; so it is with us. For when gormandizing, like a flood of rain, has drenched the inward parts, it puts all in a whirl" and makes our senses, previously healthy, "drift lifeless on the surface," like the dead fishes.[80] Such vivid images of flooding and death suggest the power of gluttony and luxury to overtake body and soul.

In addition to comparing gluttony with a raging ocean and flooding river, Chrysostom also uses the image of the military invasion to illustrate how the soul is besieged by luxury, drinking, and excessive eating. In his sermon on Acts 12:18–19, Chrysostom implores his audience to abstain from luxury.

Let us seek meats to nourish, not things to ruin us; seek meats for food, not occasions of diseases, of diseases both of soul and body; seek food which has comfort, not luxury which is full of discomfort: the one is luxury, the other mischief; the one is pleasure, the other pain; the one is agreeable to nature, the other contrary to nature. For say, if one should give you hemlock juice to drink, would it not be against nature? If one should give you logs and stones, would you not reject them? Of course, for they are against nature. Well, and so is luxury. For just as in a city, under an invasion of enemies when there has been siege and tumult, great is the uproar, so is it in the soul, under invasion of wine and luxury.[81]

Here the soul protests the body's invasion by alcohol and extravagance, for it is overwhelmed by excess. Such excess is unnatural and should be rejected. But the use of the metaphor of excessive eating and drinking as a military attack emphasizes how difficult it is to ward off these unnatural desires for excess and highlights the role of the soul as a weapon that can be used to support and encourage the body and will to be strong.

At the same time that Chrysostom recognizes the temptations of excessive behavior in eating and drinking, he also emphasizes that it is unnatural and irrational for the human being to participate in such excessive behavior. In Homily 27 on Acts 12:18–19, Chrysostom claims that a man who drinks can only be an object of ridicule to his servants and enemies, and an object of pity to his friends. Moreover, excessive drinking couples easily with gluttony. This kind of man is

a wild beast rather than a human being; for to devour much food is proper to panther, and lion, and bear. No wonder (that they do so), for those creatures have not a reasonable soul. And yet even they, if they be gorged with food more than they need, and beyond the measure appointed them by nature, get their whole body ruined by it: how much more we?[82]

Though animals also should not eat to excess, they do eat more because they are irrational. Because humans are rational creatures, we should eat only what is necessary, and not eat too much. God has even helped humans in this endeavor because he has "contracted our stomach into a small compass; therefore has He marked out a small measure of sustenance, that He may instruct us to attend to the soul."[83]

Indeed, Chrysostom is careful not to blame the physical body itself for gluttonous behavior. He confirms this in his Homily 17 on I Corinthians 6:12. In this chapter of I Corinthians, Paul addresses conflicts in the community at Corinth, including immoral sexual acts, like prostitution. Paul emphasizes that we should glorify our bodies for God, not degrade them in immoral sexual acts. In the course of this discussion in I Corinthians 6:12–13, Paul uses a food metaphor to make his point: "'All things are lawful to me,' but not all things are expedient. 'All things are lawful for me,' but I will not be brought under the power of any. 'Meats for the belly, and the belly for meats'; but God will bring to nothing both it and them: but the body is not for fornication, but for the Lord, and the Lord for the body." After referencing the first two sentences of the passage, Chrysostom begins his sermon by stating, "Here he glances at the gluttons. For since he intends to assail the fornicator again, and fornication arises from luxuriousness and want of moderation, he strongly chastises this passion."[84] Chrysostom makes explicit a connection that he sees in this passage between gluttony and lust, suggesting that fornication inevitably arises from excessive eating and luxury. He argues that the issue at hand is not eating and drinking generally, but rather, "it is the passion of greediness and excess in eatables which he [Paul] is censuring."[85]

Moreover, Chrysostom is clear that it is not the body's nature that causes gluttony or fornication; rather, it is the "immoderate license of the mind."[86] Chrysostom's argument in this sermon seeks to convince his audience to believe in the resurrection of the physical body and to understand what features properly belong to the body. He argues against the notion that simply having a physical body leads one to sin, or that a sinful body will not be resurrected. He contends that "the man who does not expect that he shall rise again and give an account of the things which he has done, will not quickly apply himself to virtue," but that belief in the resurrection encourages righteous action. Further, although pain, disease, and "lowness of spirits" belong to the body and are unavoidable, vice is not, for "if the affections of vice were part of the nature of the body they would be universal," but since not everyone commits fornication, vice must not be a necessary feature of bodily existence.[87] We should not blame the body, which can be "an excellent bridle to curb the wanton sallies of the soul," we should impugn "the charioteer who is dragged on, I mean, the man's faculty of reasoning."[88] Bad behavior comes from the "tyranny of gluttonous desire," which stems from the soul or mind, not from the body.[89] Here we see Chrysostom advocate a view of the soul or mind that is contrary to that of Plato and Aristotle, who argued that it was the body's gluttonous desires that threatened to overwhelm the rational mind. For Chrysostom, vice is not a bodily affliction, but, rather, a burden for the soul that must learn to resist temptation.

If it is not enough to realize that gluttonous behavior is unnatural and irrational, Chrysostom appeals to his audience's sense of social respectability to discourage gluttonous behavior. This focus on the propriety of moderate eating emphasizes the shamefulness of gluttony and its immorality for the Christian. Chrysostom repeatedly emphasizes the dishonor in gluttonous acts, highlighting the disgusting effects of overeating—belching, vomiting, excrement, bloating—in an attempt to render the pleasures of overeating unappealing.[90] In his Homily 13 on I Timothy 4:11–14, Chrysostom appeals to widows who have given themselves over to luxurious living. He writes,

Why do you thus gorge your own body with excess, and waste that of the poor with want; why pamper this above measure, and stint that too beyond measure? Consider what comes of food, into what it is changed. Are you not disgusted at its being named? Why then be eager for such accumulations? The increase of luxury is but the multiplication of dung![91]

Here Chrysostom brings into his sermon language that the prim and proper women of his congregation would most likely find distasteful, attempting to provoke their disgust. Instead of retreating from such images, Chrysostom pushes forward, suggesting to his listeners that

the more luxuriously we live, the more noisome are the odors with which we are filled. The body is like a swollen bottle, running out every way. The eructations are such as to pain the head of a bystander. From the heat of fermentation within, vapors are sent forth, as from a furnace, if bystanders are pained, what, think you, is the brain within continually suffering, assailed by these flames?[92]

Too much food causes foul odors that saturate the body and create excessive amounts of excrement. Eating too much or too luxuriously causes the body to become a fetid wasteland.

It is in this context of shame and disgust that Chrysostom raises the issue of the fat body. In one of the few examples that we find of a clear disparaging of the fat body in the ancient world, Chrysostom sees bodily fatness as a representation of the evil of luxurious living. In his Homily 27 on the Acts of the Apostles, Chrysostom makes this connection, referencing the passage in Deuteronomy 32:15, discussed in Chapter 1, where Israel "waxed sleek, grew thick, and kicked," rejecting God for earthy things. In this sermon, Chrysostom attempts to convince his congregants that the true luxuries in life are found in helping others, which brings perpetual pleasure, not in spending money and indulging in the pleasures of the flesh, which brings only momentary pleasure. Chrysostom urges his listeners to "give to the poor; invite Christ, so that even after the table is removed, you may still have this luxury to enjoy."[93] True luxury comes from nurturing the soul, not feeding the belly.

For what evil does not luxury cause? It is contrary to itself: so that I know not how it gets its name: but just as that is called glory, which is (really) infamy, and that riches, which in truth is poverty, so the name of luxury is given to that which in reality is nauseousness. Do we intend ourselves for the shambles, that we so fatten ourselves? Why cater for the worm that it may have a sumptuous larder? Why make more of their humors? Why store up in yourself sources of sweat and rank smelling? Why make yourself useless for everything?[94]

We should not be like animals, fattening ourselves for the slaughter; rather we should refine our bodies and make them like musical strings that "vibrate with full harmony."[95] Chrysostom wants his congregants to think differently about what luxury is, which means an appeal to rationality and compassion.

Indeed, living in the usual state of luxury that encourages overindulgence hides the soul. "Why do you bury the soul alive?" Chrysostom asks, "Why make the wall about it thicker? Why increase the reek and the cloud, with fumes like a mist steaming up from all sides? If none other, let the wrestlers teach you, that the more spare the body the stronger it is: and (then) also the soul is more vigorous."[96] Chrysostom argues here that a fat body hides the soul and makes it flabby, too. Soul and body work together like a charioteer with his horses: if the horses are plump, Chrysostom maintains, the chari-oteer cannot control them and must drag them along. We should feed the soul "with discourse, with frugality," while we feed the body "only so much that it may be healthy, that it may be vigorous, that it may rejoice and not be in pain."[97] Worried about the state of his parishioners' souls, Chrysostom argues that overindulgence that leads to fatness is harmful to both body and soul. In this attitude, Chrysostom comes as close as any ancient author to suggesting that the appearance of one's body reflects an inner state of im-morality.

John Chrysostom's vivid sermons on Christian behavior use a wide range of images and ideas to convince his diverse congregation that overcoming excessive behavior is necessary for living a virtuous Christian life. Like Philo and Clement before him, Chrysostom maintains that living luxuriously and indulging one's desires can lead only to spiritual desolation.

CONCLUSION

In the works of Philo of Alexandria, Clement of Alexandria, and John Chrysostom, we see attempts to engage Greco-Roman philosophical ideas about the dangers of gluttony, and to add to those formulations a layer of moral judgment and shame that have not before been overt. Creating a Christian regimen or Christian identity meant privileging moderation, much in the way that the Greek philosophers privileged moderation. Similarly, ex-cessive pleasure is also seen as a potential danger to both soul and body. What is more intensely emphasized in these early Christian writings are the moral consequences of overindulgence, as gluttonous behavior begins to take on the character of sinfulness and shame, and the fat body begins to be seen—at least in the writings of Chrysostom—as possible evidence of the soul's disgrace.

6

Gluttony Becomes a Deadly Sin

Hence food must be selected that not only tempers the seething
emotions of burning desire and is less likely to inflame them but
that is also easy to prepare, cheap to purchase, and appropriate
for the way of life of the brothers and for their needs.[1]

—John Cassian

At the same time that John Chrysostom is imploring his congregation to shun luxurious living, gluttony is on its way to becoming one of the seven deadly sins. As biblical and Greco-Roman ideas about the morality of gluttony are brought into the burgeoning Christian movement, gluttony and other bad behaviors become particularly undesirable acts for the faithful Christian, and especially for the desert monk. The seven deadly sins as we know them today—pride, envy wrath, sloth, greed, gluttony, and lust—trace their history back to the Egyptian desert, where the monk Evagrius Ponticus (345–399) first formulated a treatise on the eight evil thoughts that commonly tempt the desert ascetic. The monk John Cassian (ca. 360–430), who was ordained by John Chrysostom around 400, brought Evagrius's ideas into the Latin monastic tradition, expanding their definitions for his community. Over time, the eight vices or sins turn into the seven deadly sins when Pope Gregory the Great (540–604) articulates the importance of these sins for lay Christians. As gluttony slowly comes under the analytical scrutiny of Christian theologians, it takes on theological meanings that formalize its causes and effects, thereby helping to define the idea of sin for an early Church struggling to articulate ideas of penance for its adherents. This chapter traces the history of gluttony as a deadly sin, as the idea of eating to excess takes its place in the schema of behaviors inappropriate for the faithful Christian. It follows the development of the seven deadly sins, from their origin in monastic communities to their expansion into lay communities. In both of these Christian communities, gluttony continues to be perceived as a threat to social stability and harmony; it also continues to be associated with irrationality and impurity. But the particularly Christian spin on these ideas shifts their focus: gluttony is linked with irrationality, though in these texts, the focus is on the irrational pursuit of physical pleasures that emphasize bodily and not spiritual interests. While the physical body is to be disciplined, references to the animality of the human body, which were ubiquitous in Greek philosophy, are few. From a Christian perspective, the physical body is also created by God, and though it may pose challenges to spiritual development, it cannot be entirely denigrated, for to do so would also disparage God's creation. Moderation continues to be associated with purity, but here it is spiritual purity that matters most.

In addition, the monastic attitude toward moderation defaults to the side of what would typically be described as abstinence: no more than one meal a day of bread and water, perhaps with a little oil. In this way, gluttony becomes less a marker of what is seen as excessive eating, and more a marker of a particular attitude toward food that can damage the spiritual pursuits of the individual monk and the monastic community. While gluttony itself may not be a sin worthy of eternal damnation, it can set one on that path. Avoiding gluttony means preventing a potential ride down the slippery slope to hell.

In addition to clarification about gluttony's potential damage to the believer's soul, we also find in these writings more ambivalence about the fat body. On the one hand, some writers make connections between gluttony and the fat body, where the fat body stands as evidence for the existence of the soul's passion for gluttony. At the same time, for some writers, the fat body is inconsequential, for the size and shape of the body is not at issue; rather it is the sinfulness of one's behavior with food that matters most. Reviving ideas we first saw in the Hebrew Bible, Christians emphasize that the act of gluttony threatens the constructive relationship between the sinner and God, and it is this that becomes the focus of Christian inquiry.

A BRIEF ACCOUNT OF THE THEOLOGICAL CONFUSIONS REGARDING THE SEVEN DEADLY SINS

The seven deadly sins—gluttony, lust, greed, sloth, wrath, envy, pride—occupy a unique place in the history of Christianity. They exemplify the persistence of popular religious piety, even when the traditional theological foundation for their influence is scanty. For instance, although each of these attitudes and activities is found to be immoral in different places throughout the Bible, they are nowhere in the biblical text found as a list, or called the seven deadly sins. Other lists of sinful behavior, like those found in Romans 1:29–31 or I Corinthians 6:9–10, do not match all of the vices listed in the seven deadly sins: "Do you not know that wrongdoers will not inherit the kingdom of God? Do not be deceived! Fornicators, idolaters, adulterers, male prostitutes, sodomites, thieves, the greedy, drunkards, revilers, robbers—none of these will inherit the kingdom of God." Although several of the activities cited in I Corinthians 6:9–10 align with the seven deadly sins, like greed, fornication (lust), or drunkenness (some forms of gluttony), there is no comprehensive biblical list of the seven sins to avoid. They also have no clear relationship to the Ten Commandments, which would later become a much more commonly used guide for sinful behavior.[2] Given the principle that Christian theology and doctrine should derive from the Bible, the popularity of the seven deadly sins as a constellation of corrupt behaviors proved a challenge to attempts at doctrinal precision in the early Church.[3]

Moreover, if there are seven deadly sins, there should also be virtuous behavior to counter those sins (see Figure 6.1). But there is no list of seven virtues comprehensively listed in the Bible, either, so it was a particular challenge to assign biblical virtues to these sins as correctives. The theological virtues—faith, hope and charity (I Corinthians 13:13)—those virtues necessary for salvation, along with the moral or cardinal virtues—temperance, prudence, courage, and justice (Wisdom of Solomon 8:7)—are found in the Bible, though also not as a single list. Moreover, these seven virtues do not directly align as the vice's opposites. While the theological and cardinal virtues are important guides for Christian behavior, their inability to parallel the seven deadly sins reveals the theological messiness of these vices and exposes the challenge of the seven deadly sins' popularity to theological accuracy.

In addition, although the seven deadly sins are popularly called sins, they do, in fact, not rise to the level of mortal or "deadly" sins. In the biblical book of I John 5:15–17, a distinction is made between a sin that is mortal (or deadly) and a sin that is not: "If you see your brother or sister committing what is not a mortal sin, you will ask, and God will give life to such a one—to those whose sin is not mortal. There is sin that is mortal; I do not say

Vice	Virtue
Lust	Chastity
Gluttony	Temperance or Abstinence
Greed	Charity or Generosity
Sloth	Courage or Fortitude
Wrath	Patience or Meekness
Envy	Kindness or Love
Pride	Humility

Figure 6.1 The seven deadly sins and their corresponding virtues

that you should pray about that. All wrongdoing is sin, but there is sin that is not mortal." Using this passage, Catholic theology defines mortal (or deadly) sins and venial (also known as capital or cardinal) sins. Mortal sins create a rift in the relationship between the human and God because they are done deliberately and willfully. Mortal sins, like murder or blasphemy, are transgressions that, if not repented, lead to the soul's eternal damnation. Venial sins, in contrast, constitute disobedience against God, but not a complete rupture in one's relationship with God. While a venial sin, like gossiping or lying, must also be forgiven, committing a venial sin does not remove one from a state of grace.

Given these definitions, the seven deadly sins, as they are commonly known, are not deadly sins; that is, they are not sins that can lead to damnation. More often, they are understood as capital/cardinal sins or vices, bad habits that inspire sinful behavior. Historically, there has been much confusion about the difference between deadly sins and capital/cardinal sins or vices, so that the seven deadly sins continue to be called deadly even when they are not. Morton Bloomfield attributes this confusion to the development of the sacrament of penance in the Church: he suggests that the vices were a convenient and practical list that helped laypeople understand sinful acts. Moreover, the vices were by that time a standardized list, while the deadly sins were never consistent.[4] What is clear theologically is that, although the behaviors listed in the seven deadly sins are undesirable, they do not lead to a wholesale breach between humans and God as a mortal sin would do. Moreover, it is possible to have a vice, like anger, without committing a sin, and it is possible for a vice to remain even if a sin is forgiven.[5] So, for instance, it is not necessarily sinful to be angry, but if one's anger leads to murder, then the vice of anger has led to sinful behavior that could irrevocably damage one's possibilities for grace.

It is St. Thomas Aquinas (1225–1274), one of the most famous Christian theologians and philosophers, who summarizes many of the important facets of the seven deadly sins. Although he lived at a time long past the scope of this book, his understanding of the difficulties of excessive eating can help set the stage for tracing the history of gluttony's sinful character. According to Aquinas, who writes extensively about the categories of sin in his *Summa Theologiae*, capital vices (from the Latin *caput* or head) are understood as such because they are "directive and in a certain sense the leader of other sins."[6] Aquinas argues that gluttony is a capital sin or vice because it is an immoderate appetite that "departs from the reasonable order of life in which moral good is found" due to an overwhelming desire for the pleasures of food and eating.[7] Aquinas can also conceive of instances in which gluttony could be a mortal sin, but it is much more likely that gluttony is a venial sin:

Now were the inordinateness of desire in gluttony to consist in a direct turning away from our last end it would be a mortal sin; as would be the case were a man so to identify himself with his greed and make it his overriding purpose as to contemn God and be prepared to break his commandments in order to find his pleasures. If, however, his inordinate greed appears to be restricted to the non-ultimate things of his environment, then it is venial sin; as would be the case were his desire for food excessive, yet not to the point of staking his pleasures against a final breach with God's laws.[8]

Any human activity that results in an absolute turning away from God would be a mortal sin; the excessive desire for food is problematic, but it does not usually result in the complete rejection of God. Indeed, Aquinas also argues that because humans need to eat, and because it is difficult to apply "proper discretion and moderation" in eating, "the fault in gluttony is mitigated rather than aggravated."[9] Gluttony may lead to other sins, like pride or lust or greed, but it is impossible to avoid eating, so it is apparently equally impossible for humans to be moderate all the time.[10]

It is this difficulty with regard to eating—humans must eat!—that makes gluttony a particular challenge. Aquinas points out, much like Aristotle, on whose work he bases much of his theology, that only one aspect of eating is subject to reason, and therefore, subject to human control. Like Aristotle, Aquinas recognizes that humans have an irrational or vegetative soul that is not subject to reason; it is this part of the soul that keeps humans alive and requires food. Another part of the soul is subject to reason, and this is the part of the soul that contains our sensory and emotional desires. The desire to be gluttonous is found in a disorder of the sensory and emotional desires, when a person "knowingly exceeds his measure from desire for pleasure."[11] For Aquinas, the key to understanding gluttony is to recognize that a gluttonous person overeats because of a desire for the pleasure that comes from eating, not from eating itself. It is the desire for the excess of pleasure that is the problem. And this desire for pleasure from eating can lead to a desire for pleasure from other activities, too. These other pleasures are primarily lust and greed.

Aquinas's analysis of the seven deadly sins, or, more appropriately, the cardinal vices, highlights behaviors to which all Christians should be attentive, for they can lead to sins considered more damaging to the soul. Because they inspire sin, the cardinal vices thus play an important role in the history of confession and penance in the Church, as Bloomfield suggests. They occupy an important position in penitential manuals, which were developed by the sixth century for priests to use as guides for determining penance during confession.[12] The vices formed a convenient and straightforward list of everyday behaviors to confess and repent, for they highlighted dangerous habits to be avoided. The influence of the seven deadly sins on other aspects of medieval culture can be seen in the numerous treatises on the vices and virtues written throughout the Middle Ages, as well as literary works like Dante's *Inferno* and Spenser's *Faerie Queene*.[13] Chaucer's "Parson's Tale" in the *Canterbury Tales* is a traditional penitential manual crafted into literary form.[14] The cultural influence of the seven deadly sins in the Middle Ages is considerable, and it belies their humble origins, to which we now turn.

EVAGRIUS PONTICUS AND THE EIGHT THOUGHTS

Evagrius was born in 345 in Ibora, Pontus, which is located in modern-day Turkey on the southern coast of the Black Sea.[15] We know little about his youth, but we do know that he was ordained a deacon by his friend Gregory of Nazianzen in 379. Shortly thereafter, Gregory invited him to Constantinople, where he continued his ministry and enjoyed life in the intellectually and culturally stimulating city. When he fell in love with a married woman, the ensuing scandal, along with some portentous dreams, encouraged him to leave town and head for Jerusalem. There he met Melania the Elder, who encouraged him to take up the ascetic life. In 383, he went to Nitria, where he lived for 2 years, and then he moved to Kellia, where he lived for 24 years, until his death in 399. During his time in the desert, Evagrius composed a number of texts that give us insight into the lived experience of the desert monk.

Evagrius's writings focus on monastic practice, especially on the spiritual progression of the monk to a state of inner calm or stillness, or *hesychia*, which required removing oneself from all situations that produce anxiety or worry. Only in stillness can the monk come to know God.[16] Attaining that stillness requires both the knowledge and the management of the self, as it is influenced internally by emotions and externally by the presence of evil in the world.[17] Evagrius's writings are full of psychological descriptions of the eight "passionate thoughts," or *logismoi*, that vex the monk internally.[18] Evagrius also acknowledges the presence of malevolent demons who attempt to destabilize the relationship between humans and God.[19] It is the interplay between these external demons and internal *logismoi* that threatens to tear the monk away from the contemplative life. His focus on defining the *logismoi* so that the monk can recognize them easily, as well as clearly describing the ways that the eight thoughts can be remedied, suggests his commitment to the individual monk's salvation and communal harmony. Although they would primarily be living alone, in individual cells, Evagrius recognizes the importance of dealing with the *logismoi* in both the individual and the communal contexts.

Moreover, because of Evagrius's monastic perspective, gluttony takes on quite a different feeling than it has in other texts we have studied. It is one thing gluttonously to luxuriate in great quantities and varieties of food, as did the participants in "Trimalchio's Feast." It is quite another to define gluttony as the desire for more food than simply bread and water, or the desire to have fellowship with others. Evagrius's view on gluttony reminds us that it is important to understand the context within which gluttony and the fat body are understood, for the definitions change: what is excessive to a wealthy Roman is entirely different from what is excessive to the desert ascetic.

Evagrius's accounts of the eight *logismoi* are found in a number of different texts, "On the Vices Opposed to the Virtues," "On the Eight Thoughts," "The Praktikos, or The Monk: A Treatise on the Practical Life," and "On Thoughts."

Directions on the appropriate diet are also found in "The Foundations of the Monastic Life: A Presentation of the Practice of Stillness" and "To Eulogios. On the Confession of Thoughts and Counsel in Their Regard." When Evagrius addresses the eight thoughts, he usually places them in a particular order—gluttony, lust, greed, anger, sadness, acedia (sloth), vainglory, and pride—which creates a directional movement from physical desires and temptations to more spiritual enticements. (In later accounts of the seven deadly sins, vainglory and pride become one vice—pride—while sadness and sloth come together as melancholy. Pope Gregory adds envy to his list, making seven deadly sins. To keep track of the octads and heptads of sins, mnemonic devices have been employed that create acronyms from the first letters of the Latin words for the vices. Evagrius's system is known as GLATIAVS: Gula, Luxuria, Avaritia, Tristitia, Ira, Acedia, Vana Gloria, and Superbia.)[20]

Evagrius also consistently connects gluttony with lust. In "To Eulogios," he warns that "whenever the demons attempt to dislodge one's thinking with shameful pleasures . . . they introduce the warfare of gluttony, so that once they have fired the stomach beforehand they can the more effortless cast the soul into the pit of lust."[21] We thus see in Evagrius's work the conceptual seed for the concatenation of the sins we will find in Gregory, where one sin inevitably leads to the next, though Evagrius also understands that not everyone has an equal struggle with all of these thoughts.

The most basic version of the eight thoughts is presented in "On the Eight Thoughts," which is written as a series of individual sentences that allow a reader to read as much or as little as desired, and to use single statements for meditation. Sentences are grouped under the topic or the thought being addressed, but they are not put in any particular order, allowing the thought to be examined from a number of different perspectives.[22] This account of the thoughts uses metaphors and biblical associations to assist the beginning monk in understanding the potential pitfalls of the ascetic life, and it only rarely uses the image of demonic forces to emphasize their snares; indeed, Evagrius never invokes the demon of gluttony in this text. Rather, Evagrius seeks both to encourage the monk to proper behavior and to warn him against succumbing to dangerous desires.

The text's interest for the beginning monk can be seen in the emphasis on the first thought, gluttony, which has 35 sentences devoted to it. With the exception of the final thought, pride, which has 32 sentences dedicated to it, no other thought is given so much attention. Here Evagrius emphasizes that if a monk is to move forward along the path to knowledge of God, it is crucial to overcome the very first temptation, that of excessive desire for food.

A number of the sentences in "On the Eight Thoughts" connect gluttony to biblical passages symbolically. There is a reference to gluttony as the first sin: "Desire for food gave birth to disobedience and a sweet taste expelled from paradise," as well as a number of allegorical readings of biblical texts that emphasize the death of the passions and praise abstinence.[23] Jael's murder of Sisera with the tent peg in Judges 4:21 becomes the story of gluttony's execution by abstinence: "A tent peg, passing unnoticed destroyed an

enemy's jawbone; and the principle of abstinence has put passion to death,"
while Amalek, the first nation to attack the Israelites after they flee Egypt, as
recounted in the book of Numbers 24:20, is compared to gluttony, which is
the first of the passions to attack the soul.[24] These biblical connections simultaneously emphasize the pervasiveness of the sins and reveal the lack of
a coherent presentation of the sins in the biblical text.

Gluttony is also likened to a raging fire, an image that emphasizes that
eating too much is about recklessness and danger. Sentences like "wood is
the matter used by fire, and food is the matter used by gluttony," and "a lot
of wood raises a large flame; an abundance of food nourishes desire" underscore the notion that the monk's goal is to extinguish the fire of desire, which
can only be done by not feeding the fire: "a flame grows dim when matter
is wanting; a lack of food extinguishes desire."[25] Eating too much takes one
away from prayer and contemplation, because a full belly both leads to the
desire for sleep and arouses lustful thoughts. As the first sentence in the second set, on fornication, suggests, "Abstinence gives birth to chastity; gluttony is the mother of licentiousness."[26] Gluttony also renders the mind dull
and irrational, smudged like a dirty mirror: "A soiled mirror does not produce
a clear image of the form that falls upon it; when the intellect is blunted by
satiety, it does not receive the knowledge of God."[27]

To remedy the thought of gluttony, Evagrius states that abstinence and
hunger are the only effective ways to keep the body under control. Like Clement and Chrysostom before him, Evagrius invokes the image of the charioteer to explain the benefits of abstinence: "A docile horse, lean in body, never
throws its rider, for the horse that is restrained yields to the bit and is com-
pelled by the hand of the one holding the reins; the body is subdued with
hunger and vigil and does not jump when a thought mounts upon it. Nor
does it snort when it is moved by an impassioned impulse."[28] Hunger leads to
a sharp, trained mind that is ready for prayer, while the glutton's body loses
control over the mind and pays attention only to the body. For Evagrius, even
moderation in eating is not the appropriate response to the physical desire
for food; rather, the good monk abstains from food as much as possible.

This image of the lean, restrained horse is one of the few references that
Evagrius makes to the fat body; only in "On the Eight Thoughts" is fatness
evoked. Evagrius suggests that a "debilitated" body should not be pitied, nor
should it be fattened up "with rich foods" because the fattened body, like
the fattened horse, is more likely to rebel "and wage unrelenting war upon
you, until it takes your soul captive and delivers you as a slave to the passion of fornication."[29] For Evagrius, "passion sprout[s] afresh in a fat body."[30]
Here we see a clear connection between gluttony and fatness, even though
Evagrius's primary concern with gluttony has little to do with the fat body,
and much more to do with articulating the appropriate eating habits for the
monk.

Evagrius further clarifies his ideas about the appropriate diet for a monk
in "The Foundations of the Monastic Life: A Presentation of the Practice of
Stillness." Here, he encourages the monk to "adhere to a frugal and measly

diet, without great quantities and the sorts that easily cause distractions."[31] Like Clement, Evagrius addresses the question of how to deal with food when giving or receiving hospitality. He cautions the monk against thinking that only expensive foods will suffice for proper hospitality, as well, cautioning him to remember that, in having such thoughts, "the adversary is thereby setting a snare for you; he is setting a trap to dislodge you from your stillness."[32] Hospitality within the monastic community is clearly important and suggests Evagrius's concern with maintaining a welcoming community for guests. He reminds the monk that bread, salt, and water are ample offering to the guest, and that if no food is available, "a good disposition" and "a helpful word" will allow the monk "to obtain the reward of hospitality."[33] Evagrius offers the monk alternative strategies for thinking about hospitality, which could come in conflict with his desire for an austere diet. He emphasizes that even thinking about food too much can cause a monk to become flustered and lose his tranquility of mind.

In "The Foundations of the Monastic Life," Evagrius suggests that the suitable monastic diet consists primarily of bread and water. He exhorts the monk to avoid "fine foods" and to avoid foods "favored by worldly people."[34] With the exception of entertaining guests in the monastery, the monk's goal is to avoid invitations to dine with others, to stay in his cell, and to break off relations with outsiders.[35] What is interesting about these exhortations is that they show quite clearly that the act of eating with others, and eating good food, creates community. A relationship with people from outside the monastic community, especially one that includes socializing with fine foods, should be avoided because it distracts the monk from his spiritual focus. In the context of monastic life, gluttony is a temptation that can remove one from spiritual community and encourage worldliness.

Evagrius's definition of gluttony is most clearly expressed in "The Monk: A Treatise on the Practical Life (The Praktikos)" and in "On the Vices Opposed to the Virtues." In "The Praktikos," Evagrius defines the eight thoughts and gives instructions on how to counter them. Evagrius believes that every kind of temptation is found in various forms under the rubric of the eight thoughts. He also understands that not everyone may be particularly bothered by all of the thoughts.

Gluttony is the first thought, and its definition suggests that if a monk cannot get past his thoughts of gluttony, he will not be able to maintain the ascetic life. Here is Evagrius's definition of gluttony in "The Praktikos," in its entirety:

The thought of gluttony suggests to the monk the rapid demise of his asceticism. It describes for him his stomach, his liver and spleen, dropsy and lengthy illness, the scarcity of necessities and the absence of doctors. Frequently it brings him to recall certain of the brethren who have fallen prey to these sufferings. Sometimes it even persuades those who have suffered such maladies to visit those who are practicing abstinence and to tell them of their misfortunes and how they came about as a result of their asceticism.[36]

Robert Sienkewicz points out that this definition of gluttony emphasizes the temptation to stop one's asceticism for fear that eating too little or eating the monastic diet will result in ill health. The austere diet of the monk required getting used to, and if a monk were unable to do so, this failure might lead him to give up his spiritual practice. Indeed, adjusting to the monastic diet would be one of the first hurdles in becoming a monk. Intestinal problems were common in these communities; even Evagrius apparently struggled with health issues related to diet.[37] Additionally, a monk having these difficulties may be tempted to discuss these problems with others, thereby persuading them to leave the ascetic life, as well. In this way, the thought of gluttony is not only harmful to the individual monk, it can distract an entire community.

In "On the Vices Opposed to the Virtues," Evagrius embellishes this definition of gluttony by adding a number of other features to the vice. He suggests that gluttony, too, causes disease, "a groaning of the innards."[38] Gluttony also causes "pollution of the intellect, weakness of the body, wearisome sleep," and "gloomy death."[39] It also tempts one to imagine foods, to be the "picturer of condiments," and to relax one's commitment to fasting.[40] Evagrius again confirms that gluttony is "the mother of fornication," as well.[41]

The remedy for gluttony, according to Evagrius, is not a relaxation of such stringent rules for eating so that he might not focus so intently on his rumbling stomach; rather, he recommends an even more stringent asceticism.

When our soul yearns for a variety of foods, then let it reduce its ration of bread and water so that it may be grateful even for a small morsel. For satiety desires foods of all sorts, while hunger thinks of satiety of bread as beatitude. (Or, "For satiety desires a variety of dishes, but hunger thinks itself happy to get its fill of nothing more than bread.")[42]

Here Evagrius reveals that gluttony is not only about quantity of food, it is also about the variety of food. To counter gluttonous thoughts, one should further reduce one's intake of even the most restricted diet of bread and water, so as to enhance one's gratitude for even the smallest portion of food. Abstinence is a "bridle for the stomach," and a "deliverance from lustful burning."[43] Abstinence also revives the soul and is an "imitation of the resurrection, a life of sanctification."[44] The practice of abstinence apparently also inhibits one from speaking of one's desire for more or different foods with one's fellow monks.

The texts that we have examined so far focus primarily on the beginning monk. In "On Thoughts," Evagrius offers a more advanced perspective on the vices that may continue to tempt the monk. In this text, Evagrius's theology is more detailed and complex. He associates the eight thoughts with different parts of the soul, much like Plato and Aristotle, arguing that the bodily temptations, of which gluttony is the first and most important, belong to the concupiscible soul, which is associated with bodily appetites, while temptations like greed and vainglory more properly belong to the irascible soul, which is associated with the emotions.[45] Evagrius begins "On Thoughts" with a discussion of the three fundamental thoughts, which are gluttony, avarice, and vainglory. The demons of these three thoughts are the first to attack: "to put it briefly," Evagrius claims, "no one can fall into a demon's power, unless he has first been wounded by those in the front line."[46] Gluttony, avarice, and vainglory are the first demons because they correspond to the devil's temptations of Jesus while he was in the desert: the temptation of food, the appeal of having power over the whole world if he would worship the devil, and the challenge to prove his divinity by throwing himself from the highest point of the temple.

Gluttony is the first of the demons to attack the body, for "it is not possible to fall into the hands of the spirit of fornication, unless one has fallen under the influence of gluttony; nor is it possible to trouble the irascible part, unless one is fighting for food, or wealth or esteem."[47] To drive away the demons of gluttony and to discipline the concupiscible part of the soul, a monk must "exhaust" it "with fasts, vigils, and sleeping on the ground."[48] Further, although it is impossible to defeat the demon of gluttony unless one shows "complete disregard for food, riches and esteem" the monk must also be careful not to be too obvious in his rejection of such things, so that the demon of vainglory does not attack the monk for his self-righteousness.[49] Finally, the monk must also be vigilant so that the demon of gluttony not tempt him into extreme asceticism. According to Evagrius, the appropriate diet for the monk is bread, oil, and water, limited to one meal a day, and not eaten to satiety. If a monk chooses "immoderate abstinence," by eating even less than this, he may not be able to attain the appropriate level of abstinence, for his body will be too weak.[50] A weakened body will not allow the monk to reach stillness. As Evagrius shows in "On Thoughts," the demons of gluttony and the other thoughts are devious and cunning, and therefore quite difficult to battle, for they attack on all fronts.

Evagrius's concerns about the challenges of gluttony range from its necessary connection to lustful desires, to issues of communal hospitality, to maintaining appropriate, and not excessive, abstinence. As he highlights all of the dimensions of gluttony, Evagrius reveals his interest in creating a cohesive and harmonious community, where eating neither too much nor too little within the appropriate boundaries of food practices for the monk is encouraged. Evagrius realizes the importance of hospitality within and without the monastic community, while also underscoring the potential damage that mistaking gluttony for hospitality can do.

Evagrius's explanation of the difficulties of gluttony and the other seven thoughts creates a foundation for a more complete and wide-ranging articulation of the seven deadly sins when they move from the Egyptian desert to the Western monastic tradition with John Cassian. Cassian's primary theological influence seems to be Evagrius, even though Cassian never names him specifically as his inspiration.[51] Cassian takes up Evagrius's eight thoughts or spirits, using his understanding of the carnal nature of gluttony, his definition of gluttony as the mother of lust, and his ideas about quantity and quality of food to create an even more thorough understanding of the temptations and remedies for gluttonous desire.

JOHN CASSIAN AND THE SPIRIT OF GLUTTONY

Though we have little information about many aspects of John Cassian's life, we do know that he was born around 360 in what today is Romania.[52] In his youth, he traveled with his friend Germanus to Bethlehem, where he joined a monastery. During his time in the monastery, he also traveled twice to Egypt to learn about Egyptian monasticism, which he found immensely appealing. He stayed in Egypt with Germanus for awhile—some sources say seven years—and then returned briefly to Bethlehem before he returned once more to the Egyptian desert.[53] After his second trip, the duration of which is unknown, he left Egypt and traveled to Constantinople, where he met John Chrysostom.

Though the details are unknown, Cassian's departure from the desert was likely influenced by a theological controversy that also explains his silence on Evagrius. By the time Cassian wrote his monastic guides, Evagrius had been labeled a heretic. Like the early Christian theologian Origen, Evagrius claimed that God is pure spirit, without body, while the Coptic Christians of Egypt claimed that God must have a body since humans are made in God's image. The Coptic view, Anthropomorphism, gained popularity, leading to a rejection of Origen. This Origenist controversy about the nature of God drove a number of people from the desert to Constantinople, where John Chrysostom welcomed them. Chrysostom's association with the monks who favored Origenist views of the nature of God would eventually lead to his exile from Constantinople, as well. Before the controversy intensified, Chrysostom ordained Cassian a deacon.

Cassian left Constantinople during the Origenist controversy and headed to Rome in an attempt to help Chrysostom. What happened during Cassian's time in Rome is not well documented, though it is there that he may have been ordained to the priesthood by Pope Innocent I.[54] He later moved to Marseilles, where he founded two monasteries and wrote two treatises, *The Institutes* and *The Conferences*, both of which are guides to the monastic life and include extensive treatment of the eight principal vices. In his preface to *The Institutes*, which was written between 430 and 429, Cassian declares his intent to explain the rules of the Egyptian monasteries, and, in particular, "the origins and causes and remedies of the principle vices, which they number as eight, according to their traditions."[55] His focus on the vices stems from his interest in "the improvement of our behavior and the attainment of the perfect life," as well as his desire to infuse Western monasticism with the wisdom of the "holy and spiritual fathers" who founded monasteries in the place where the apostles began their ministry.[56] *The Conferences*, composed after *The Institutes*, is written as a series of conversations with the monks in the desert, who explain how best to live a monastic life, including how to overcome the eight principal thoughts, which follows Evagrius's list: gluttony, lust, avarice (greed), anger, sadness, acedia (sloth), vainglory, and pride.

The first four books of *The Institutes* deal with other aspects of monastic life, like appropriate clothing and prayers. Book 5 begins Cassian's discussion of the vices. He explains that his intent is to "take up the struggle against the eight principal vices," by first investigating their natures, "which are so intricate, so hidden, and so obscure," by then attempting to "lay bare their causes," and finally, proposing "cures and remedies for them."[57] The challenge of the vices is that "until they have been revealed they are unknown to everyone, even though we are all hurt by them and they are found in everyone."[58] It is the insidiousness and pervasiveness of the vices that makes them dangerous; revealing them will allow the monks "to be led to a place of refreshment and perfection."[59] Cassian maintains that every monk must struggle with the vices, so it is up to the community to develop a consistent approach to handling them. At the same time, however, Cassian also recognizes that each monk struggles more with some vices than others, or has different needs with regard to the rejection of the vices. Cassian's consistent message is one that balances the individual's needs with those of the healthy monastic community. Each of the vices not only has the potential to lead the individual monk astray, they can also damage the community as a whole.

The discussion of the vices in Book 5 begins with gluttony. Gluttony, or "the desire to gormandize," or eat excessively, is the first of the vices. The vice of gluttony is challenging for the monk for a number of different reasons. First, Cassian recognizes, like Aristotle, that individuals have different minimal requirements for food, based on bodily needs. In addition, he argues that the kind of food one eats, as well as the quantity of food one eats, matters: indulging any kind of bodily pleasure is disadvantageous to the monk because it cuts one off from the possibility of attaining the monastic goal of purity of heart. For Cassian, purity of heart is about many things, but fundamentally it is about fighting temptations and distractions that lead one away from God.[60] Ascetic practice, including overcoming the vices, is one avenue to purity of heart. Here we see in Cassian the continuing historical connection between purity and moderation or asceticism; with Cassian we see purity lifted up as a primary theological goal. We also see Cassian make an even stronger connection between gluttony and lust and the role that excessive eating plays in arousing lustful thoughts. Finally, there is a consistent metaphor that runs throughout Cassian's discussion of the vices, that of the quest of the spiritual athlete, who, like the Olympian, is able to overcome adversity and win the contest.

Cassian's placement of gluttony as the first of the vices follows Evagrius, where the vices proceed from the bodily to the spiritual. Gluttony is also a particular challenge to the monk because one must eat; therefore, one cannot simply stop eating to avoid the temptations of gluttony. Moreover, Cassian recognizes that all bodies are different: some bodies require more food than others, while illness or age may also affect a monk's requirements for

food. Some monks may be satisfied with a bit of dried bread or plain veg-
etables, while others need more or different food. It is clear from Cassian's
discussion, however, that the monk's goal with regard to food is fasting, for
fasting, along with work and little sleep, make up the primary bodily dis-
ciplines for the monk.[61] Fasting in this context is not about eating no food
at all, but eating very little. Cassian argues that it is entirely appropriate for
his monks to see the one daily meal of the Egyptian monks as the model for
adequate food intake.[62]

Whatever the individual monk's basic food needs are, there is a consistent
approach that every monk can take to prevent gluttony, and that is to avoid
"voracious satiety."[63] Cassian explains that "it is not only the quality of food
but also its quantity that dulls the heart's keenness, and when both the mind
and the flesh have been sated the glowing kindling of the wicked vices is set
ablaze."[64] Cassian suggests here that the kind of food one eats satisfies the
mind, while the quantity of food gratifies the body. When both mind and
body are satisfied, gluttony becomes a raging fire, just as it had been for Evagrius. Cassian's concern regarding food is thus not merely about the amount
of food eaten, but also the kind of food one ingests.

Cassian is careful to explain the monk's proper attitude toward food. A
monk who is weak in body and requires more food to sustain himself acts appropriately if he eats more because of his frailty and not because of his desire
for the pleasures of food.[65] The key is not to satisfy the "yearning appetite"
but to eat what is "sufficient to maintain his life."[66] Cassian insists that each
monk figure out for himself "the degree of frugality that his bodily struggle
and combat require."[67] Indeed, he argues that it is better for a monk to eat "a
reasonable and modest daily repast" than to submit to harsh fasts that are
followed by "a period of relaxation and abundance," which he believes will
inevitably lead to gluttony.[68] A steady and consistent approach to food and
eating is most beneficial to the monk seeking to abide by ascetic principles.

The monk who eats properly must also pay attention to other virtues, because abstaining from food cannot, on its own, either lead to or maintain
purity of heart, especially because gluttony will inevitably lead to lust. In this
discussion, Cassian fluctuates between asserting that once a vice has been
overcome, it will never again challenge the monk, and recognizing that all
of the vices need to be overcome multiple times. In other words, Cassian
believes that it is necessary that the monk first overcome the bodily temptation of gluttony, but he is unwilling to claim that gluttonous impulses need
only be overcome once. Therefore, Cassian argues that, in order to overcome
one vice, a person must overcome them all: if all of the "fiery impulses" of the
body are to be extinguished, the other vices must be "cut off at the root."[69]

Despite confusion about whether a vice is ever fully overcome, Cassian is
certain that gluttony is the first vice a monk must defeat. Gluttony's status as
the first vice makes it important as the beginning of the monk's struggle to
attain purity of heart, but it is also a carnal or bodily vice and, as such, is seen
as a smaller or weaker vice than, say, the vice of pride, the final vice, which
is "a most savage beast, fiercer than all those previously mentioned, greatly

trying the perfect and ravaging with its cruel bite those who are nearly estab-lished in the perfection of virtue."[70] If a monk cannot overcome gluttonous urges, he will never be able to stave off lustful temptations. Thus, a monk must pay attention to all of the virtues, and stave off all of the other vices, but it is impossible for this to happen unless he has been successful at overcom-ing the initial vice of gluttony. The monk must fast, read, and participate in vigils in order for the mind to realize that eating is not "a concession to enjoy-ment," but rather "a burden imposed upon it at intervals."[71] As with Clement before him, the only proper attitude toward food for Cassian is that it is nec-essary for the body's survival. Eating should not be about pleasure or desire.

Thus, the first contest for the spiritual athlete, what Cassian calls "our first trial in the Olympic Games" is to trample a "superfluous appetite for food" by "the contemplation of virtue" and to eat what is necessary "with anxious heart," so that we are not "diverted from spiritual pursuits beyond that which compels us to descend to the necessary care of the body, on account of its fragility."[72] This first contest is to "destroy the impulses of the fleshly desires," for only then will the spiritual athlete be able to "be victorious and win a glo-rious crown."[73] Here Cassian reveals his understanding of vice as that which goes beyond necessity and succumbs to desire.[74]

But simply disciplining the body to stave off desire is not sufficient, for the soul "has its own harmful foods by which it is fattened even without ex-cessive eating."[75] The soul feeds on the food of anger, envy, "the desire and wandering of the feckless heart," and any other detraction that leaves it "des-titute of heavenly bread and of solid nourishment."[76] Overcoming the bodily temptations of gluttony is only useful if the soul's food is also pure, so that body and soul together can attain purity of heart. This is also the only place in Cassian's text where an implicit connection is made between fatness and eating to excess, though here he is speaking of the fattening of the heart. Cas-sian implies that a fattened soul is undesirable, for it enjoys the "lethal savor" of other vices.[77] Perhaps a fattened body, too, is undesirable, but nowhere in his discussion of the body's asceticism does he address body size. One may assume that the practice of eating one meal a day of not much food would result in a slim body, but the actual size of the monk's body seems to be of no concern to Cassian.

The simultaneous abstinence of the body and soul leads to Cassian's dis-cussion of different types of gluttony that a monk must avoid. In this sec-tion of the text, Cassian emphasizes that when the practice of the individual monk with regard to food and the quest for purity of heart are aligned, then the entire community of monks will benefit. When individual monks have triumphed over their gluttonous impulses, a more harmonious and hospita-ble community will result.

The first form of gluttony that each monk should avoid is eating before the proper time, or not waiting for the "lawful moment for breaking the fast."[78] This form of gluttony appears to be about eating early or snacking, and it seems a bit odd for these kinds of behaviors to lead to gluttonous downfall. But eating at the wrong time necessitates breaking established communal rules, and Cassian claims that "whatever is eaten that does not fall under regular practice and common usage is polluted by the disease of vanity, boastfulness, and ostentation."[79] Cassian does not thoroughly explain his rationale for the problem with eating at the wrong time in *The Institutes*. He elaborates in *The Conferences* when he suggests that eating at the wrong time leads to a "hatred of the monastery," and with that "grows a dread of the same dwelling place and an inability to endure it."[80] Cassian closely echoes Evagrius here in that gluttonous temptation leads a monk to reject monastic life, but whereas Evagrius claimed that the desire to leave the monastery stemmed from his fear of ill health, Cassian claims that gluttony leads the monk to detest the monastic routine and accommodations. For Cassian, the gluttonous desire to eat whenever a monk wants to leads to a hatred of the monotony of the monk's life, and a desire for worldly distraction. It seems clear that becoming accustomed to one's routine and surroundings would be the first thing that would be required of a new monk. This explains why gluttony is the first vice that must be addressed.

The second form of gluttony is "filling the belly to repletion with any food whatsoever," which means that the monk should "be satisfied with a slender diet."[81] This kind of gluttony is the most obvious, for it is about overeating, succumbing to the pleasures of food and the desire to be sated. This is the form of gluttony that Cassian has dealt with previously, when he suggested that, no matter what a monk ate, he should avoid "voracious satiety." Here, Cassian amends that claim, and suggests that it is best to eat the "cheap and unrefined" bread that is the ordinary diet of the monk.[82] Cassian further clarifies this form of gluttony in *The Conferences*, where he suggests that "burning pricks of lasciviousness and wanton desire are aroused" from eating to fullness.[83]

Cassian's final form of gluttony is that "which is delighted with more refined and delicate foods."[84] This means that the monk should be "content with cheaper foods of whatever sort."[85] Unlike Clement, who understood the desire for delicacy in foods to be about succumbing to the pleasures of taste, Cassian sees this kind of gluttony as the desire for expensive foods or foods that require particular forms of seasoning. This form of gluttony has two implications. The first is that a monk should not ask for unusual or expensive foods, which supports the previous form of gluttony. For Cassian, however, the primary issue with this form of gluttony has to do with the question of hospitality. Here, Cassian echoes Evagrius, who argued that, while it is important for monks to be hospitable to guests, they should not be tempted by an occasion of hospitality to serve fancy food. Cassian adds further detail to this form of gluttonous desire by suggesting that the issue of the kind of food that is served is also relevant to the guest. The monk who is the guest of another and who succumbs to this form of gluttony is "not content to eat the food with the condiment with which it was seasoned by our host but demand with importunate and unbridled boldness that something be poured on it or added to it."[86] The monk who demands different or additional food when he is a guest succumbs both to vainglory and greed, where a monk is not satisfied with what he is offered.

For the monk hosting guests, it is not only important to be satisfied offering the food regularly available, it is equally important for the host to value hospitality over his own practice of fasting. It is always better to "practice the virtue of hospitality and love than to display the strictness of our abstinence and the daily rigor of our chosen orientation."[87] Cassian gives numerous examples of Egyptian monks who emphasize that being hospitable is a commandment that must be carried out, while fasting is "a gift that is voluntarily offered."[88] Cassian ends his discussion of gluttony with numerous examples of monastic hospitality and charity as a way of suggesting that the proper counter to gluttony is not simply fasting, but also giving to others.[89]

Cassian's discussion of gluttony in the context of the monastery articulates a set of moral guidelines that pertain to the proper consumption of food, even though there is no direct condemnation of the fat body. He formulates a perspective on gluttony that aligns it with biblical views by showing how it can damage the spiritual journey of the individual monk. Cassian emphasizes that only by combating the pleasures of the flesh and becoming free from its weaknesses can the monk continue to work towards the goal of purity of heart. At the same time, Cassian shows that, by fulfilling the duty of providing hospitality to others, the monastic community as a whole works to resist gluttony, which is a benefit to the entire community. Thus, Cassian's conception of gluttony emphasizes both the individual and the communal benefits of working against gluttonous temptation to move toward acts of spiritual charity, which can be gained through hospitality to others. In highlighting three forms of gluttony—eating at the wrong time, eating too much, and desiring lavish and expensive food—Cassian not only shows that gluttony must be avoided, he emphasizes that it must be consciously rejected by the monk who wishes to attain purity of heart. By carefully articulating the specific forms of gluttonous behavior, Cassian ensures that the monk becomes aware of the temptations that food can bring.

Cassian's interest in gluttony does not go beyond the walls of the monastery. Yet, his reworking of Evagrius's guidance for monastic life does leave the monastery and become relevant for lay Christians attempting to live morally upright lives as the Church develops the practice of confession and penitence. It is Pope Gregory the Great who interprets the monastic vices for lay Christians, turning Cassian's three forms into five, thereby requiring Christians to be even more attentive to the dangerous pleasures of food.

POPE GREGORY THE GREAT AND THE SEVEN DEADLY SINS AS WE KNOW THEM TODAY

Born around 540 in Rome, Gregory grew up in chaotic, often terrifying times. The western part of the Roman Empire had fallen to the Ostragoths in the late fifth century, but by 554, the eastern portion of the Roman Empire had fought its way west, and Justinian I reestablished imperial control over Italy.[90] Years of chaos since the first barbarian invasions had taken a significant toll on Italy, and renewed imperial government did not immediately lead to order. Theological controversies between different sects of Christianity and Christianity's battle against paganism occupied the Church's attention. When the Lombards and the plague invaded Italy 15 years later, any peace that the country could have hoped for was dashed. Gregory's world was one of death, destruction, political turmoil, and religious confusion.

Gregory's early life in this messy world was as pleasant as could be expected. He was born to a wealthy, aristocratic family, received an excellent classical education in rhetoric and grammar, and was apparently trained in the law with an eye to a career in public life.[91] It is unclear exactly when Gregory made the decision to become a monk, but he did, and he eventually founded seven monasteries, all on land owned by his family. He entered the seventh monastery, St. Andrews, as a monk, probably around 574–575.[92] Gregory enjoyed his life in the monastery but was called to public service for the Church around 578. In 579, Gregory was sent as ambassador by Pope Pelagius II to Constantinople to attempt to bring the sad plight of Rome to the attention of the Emperor. While in Constantinople, he was prompted to write an extensive interpretation of the Book of Job, known as the *Magna Moralia,* which he finished on his return to Rome years later. This massive work is translated in 35 books as *Morals on the Book of Job,* and it is this text that contains Gregory's well-known account of the seven deadly sins. In 586, Gregory was recalled to Rome, and by 590, he was elected Pope Gregory I—known today also as Pope Gregory the Great. Though his skills as an administrator were well-known, he preferred a life focused on spiritual, not worldly matters, even if those worldly matters concerned leadership of the Church in Rome, and he was not particularly happy about becoming Pope.[93] He was still Pope when he died in 604.

Gregory was the first monk to become a pope, and his monastic commitments are seen in his writings. Although written during the time of his public service, the *Morals on the Book of Job* reveals an emphasis on self-control and the need for penitence stressed in the monastery. Indeed, Gregory works with two models of the Christian life in the *Morals:* that of the monk's ascetic life and that of the ascetic who returns to the world, much like he does.[94] To bring the discipline of the monastic "citadel of security" into the lives of lay Christians, Gregory suggests that the "true citadel of virtue" is found in the mind and heart, which must "regulate the impulses of man's carnal nature and weather the vicissitudes of the world outside."[95] In the *Morals,* Gregory accentuates for lay Christians the importance of understanding the nature of sin and performing the appropriate penance for restitution.

The *Morals* is a wide-ranging book, with analysis of the book of Job written in three parts: historical, allegorical or mystical, and moral. Gregory's interpretation of the story of Job's suffering emphasizes the battle between God and the devil, where the devil's wicked ways mirror the righteousness of God's work in the world.[96] Despite these apparently distinct realms of God and the devil, Gregory also affirms God's power to control the universe; therefore, the devil can do nothing without God's permission. God and the devil make a deal, one that allows the devil to become God's "exactor," the one who metes out the punishment that God gives, and tempts humans in order to strengthen their resolve and prove their virtue.[97] Within this perspective, the spiritual and carnal elements of human life are also intermingled so that "carnal 'adversaries,' be they the temptations of the world, service to one's neighbor, or even the wound of sin, can actually restore the humility of the soul."[98] In order to negotiate both the spiritual and carnal sides of human existence, one needs discretion, the ability to discern one's inner motives and desires, and to squelch them in service to the spirit. God and the devil may be waging battle in each individual's soul, but it is up to the individual—with help from God—to put in place the practices of self-examination and self-discipline that will allow the spirit to prevail.[99]

For Gregory, then, the seven deadly sins represent devilish temptations that challenge the Christian to develop and practice discretion and self-control. Gregory's Christian must be constantly vigilant, striving to discern temptation and stave it off. His classic description of the vices for lay Christians is found in Book 31.45.87–90, though he also speaks specifically of gluttony, in the monastic context, in Book 30.18.57–63. For Gregory, the vices are intimately connected, one leading to the other, all leading from pride, which conquers the mind and soul when discretion fails. In the worldly context, pride is both the beginning and end of the vices: it can take over when a person is feeling confident about his ability to conquer sin, and it returns once a person has been able to control them and again feels secure in his virtue. Pride sends the vices to the soul to "lay it waste."[100] Once the vices have taken hold, they follow in quick succession from one another, five spiritual and two carnal. Pride, the root of all sin, engenders vain glory, the temptation to boast about one's successes and "seek the power of an empty name."[101] Vain glory leads inevitably to envy, for if a person sees another admired for his good name, he will envy what he wishes for himself. Once envy has taken hold, it generates anger, because of the perceived injustice of another's good fortune, which festers, leading to melancholy and despair. Depression and sadness lead to avarice, "because when the disturbed heart has lost the satisfaction of joy, it seeks for sources of consolation without, and is more anxious to possess external goods."[102] These are the spiritual vices, those that take over the mind and soul. Once one has succumbed to avarice, the carnal vices, gluttony and lust, are left. Avarice leads to gluttony as one more source of external consolation, and gluttony inevitably and always leads to lust, because the genitals are located below the belly. Therefore, when the belly "is inordinately pampered, the other is doubtless excited to wantonness."[103] Each of the vices stems from the one before it, creating a concatenation that remained influential throughout the Middle Ages.

Gregory not only shortens Cassian and Evagrius's lists by combining sadness and sloth into melancholy, he also reverses the order of the vices for the lay Christian, beginning with the spiritual and ending with the carnal, unlike his predecessors who began with gluttony. Straw points out that, for

Gregory, the failure of discretion leads a sinner to devolve from a spiritual to a carnal place, from lofty spiritual pursuits into the muck of food and sex.[104] Richard Newhauser speculates that the reversal in order would have made more sense to a lay audience, who might more easily "comprehend the need for obedience to authority, secular as well as divine, than to grasp the importance of suppressing natural appetites, such as the desire for food."[105] Indeed, Gregory, like Evagrius and Cassian before him, understands the ambiguities of the conflict between the need for sustenance and the desire for food. For the lay Christian, he also sees the need for sexual activity to produce children, and the need to avoid lustful desires. When discussing the vices for the lay Christian, Gregory acknowledges that eating and sex are entangled in a web of necessity and desire that cannot be entirely overcome by those who live in the world.

For the monk, however, gluttony remains the first temptation to be overcome. Here Gregory follows Cassian, and also appears to acknowledge that the monk's spiritual battle requires a different focus than that of the lay Christian. In Book 30, Gregory explores the dimensions of gluttony. He argues that, for those who have "scorned the multitude of the city" and entered into the "narrow gate" of monastic life, the temptations of the flesh must first be conquered.[106] He acknowledges the difficulty of this for the monk as he does for the lay Christian; after all, monks and lay people alike must eat to live. But for the monk, the spiritual battle cannot begin until the appetite of gluttony is defeated, "because if we overthrow not those evils which are nearer to us, we doubtless proceed in vain to attack those which are further off."[107] To neglect the taming of the appetite means certain failure in spiritual battle, for "war is in vain waged in the plain against outward foes, if a treacherous citizen is restrained within the very walls of the city."[108] Gluttony must be vanquished in order for the true spiritual battle to be won. In making distinctions between the spiritual battles of the monk and the lay Christian, Gregory suggests that the monk's battle is intensified, for the concentrated focus on one's spiritual life requires a greater emphasis on the suppression of all but the most minimal bodily desires, and a nominal submission to bodily requirements.

Hence, the monk must be even more careful to discern all of the possible ways that he can be lured into gluttony. Gregory expands on Cassian's three forms of gluttony, adding another two temptations. Gluttony tempts by "anticipating the seasons of want," enticing the monk to eat before he should.[109] Like Cassian, Gregory understands snacking between meals—eating too early—to be a gluttonous act. If a monk should not care to eat between meals, gluttony can strike in the desire for "daintier food," food that is more refined or tasty.[110] The desire for daintier food could also address the finicky eater, who is unwilling to eat what is put in front of him. A monk must also be aware of the desire for food to be prepared in a particular way. If these three forms of gluttony do not tempt, then there is the desire simply to eat more than one needs, to exceed "the measure of moderate refreshment."[111]

Finally, gluttony is seen when monks do none of these things except eat too quickly or greedily what is available to eat. These five ways are characterized later by Thomas Aquinas as "hastily, sumptuously, daintily, too much, greedily," and this formulation continues throughout the Middle Ages. In Geoffrey Chaucer's *Canterbury Tales,* these sins are labeled by the Parson as the "fyve fyngres of the develes hand, by whiche he draweth folk to synne."[112] In Gregory's case, these five forms of gluttony suggest a kind of attention to, or interest in, food that takes one away from the proper Christian life.

While the order in which a monk or a layperson confronts the vices may differ, the way that the vices are conquered is the same for both. It is here that Gregory emphasizes the responsibility of the sinner to counter the temptations of the vices. In this, Gregory shifts from the external idea of temptation we see with Evagrius, or the sometimes uncontrollable desires we see with Cassian: for Gregory, overcoming the vices lies within the sinner, who must use discretion to discern where feeding the body's needs ends and succumbing to fleshly desires begins. Gregory emphasizes that the key to understanding the vices is the recognition that they often appear in disguise, as "a kind of reason."[113] Gregory explains, "Gluttony is also wont to exhort the conquered heart, as if with reason, when it says, God has created all things clean, in order to be eaten and he who refuses to fill himself with food, what else does he do but gainsay the gift that has been granted him."[114] This false reasoning disguises the true spiritual harm in gluttony, which, for Gregory, is our inability to see through the temptations of the devil to make the proper distinctions between what is required and what is desired. It is not the food itself that makes one a glutton, it is succumbing to desire for that food and not accepting the responsibility for having done so that makes gluttony a sin. The good Christian, "the soldier of God," sees the battle coming, realizes the temptations, and is prepared to resist them.[115]

Gregory never speaks of the fat body; for him, the problem with gluttony is not the body's appearance, but rather, the body's need to balance necessity and desire. Gregory affirms, as did Evagrius and Cassian, that too much abstinence can be harmful and not have the desired effect of continence: "And sometimes, while we endeavor to oppose our desires too immoderately, we increase the miseries of necessity. For it is necessary for a man to maintain the citadel of continence as to destroy, not the flesh, but the vices of the flesh."[116] Balance is the key to overcoming the temptations of the flesh. Yet, Gregory's emphasis on the Christian's responsibility to discern what is necessary and what is desire opens the door for moral condemnation for those who appear to be unable to do so, which could lead to moral disapproval of the fat body as evidence of discretion's failure. Gregory suggests that the body and soul align in action and intention, for

our vices become proud upon the same food, on which our virtues are nourished and live. And when a virtue is nourished, the strength of our vices is frequently increased. But when unbounded abstinence weakens the power of vices, our virtue also faints and pants. Whence it is necessary for our inward man to preside, as a kind of impartial arbiter between itself, and him whom it hears without: in order that its outward man may both be always able to serve at its appointed ministry, and never proudly oppose it with unshackled neck; nor be moved if it whispers any suggestion, provided it always tramples it down with the heel of authority stamped upon it. And thus, whilst we allow our vices, when checked, to struggle against us, and yet prohibit their engaging with us on equal terms, it comes to pass that neither our vices prevail against our virtue, nor does our virtue again settle down to rest with entire extinction of our vices.[117]

When virtue struggles truly against the vices, the inward man (soul) and outward man (body) are aligned in the struggle against all forms of gluttonous behavior.

Gregory's understanding of the vices and their remedies takes place in the context of a Christian community—whether monastic or lay—which strives to carry out the word of God. An individual's conquest of the vices takes place under the gaze of others, who strive similarly and assist in overcoming the vice that is both the beginning and end of the vices: pride. Gregory writes,

But we know that he, who, when he acts rightly, omits looking at the merits of his betters, extinguishes the eye of his heart, by the darkness of pride. But, on the other hand, he who carefully weighs the good qualities of others, enlightens his own deeds, by a powerful ray of humility; because when he sees the things he has done himself, done by others also without, he keeps down that swelling of pride, which strives to break forth within from singularity.[118]

Only in community can we manage to keep the powerful vice of pride at bay, as we notice the good deeds of those around us.

For Gregory, the vices may tempt and seduce, but the good Christian can conquer their power by developing the skill of discretion. His interest in the Christian community outside of the monastery shifts his focus from ideas of the soul's purity or a definition of abstinence toward a rational approach to balancing necessity and desire. Gregory emphasizes the Christian's responsibility for determining this balance by not becoming excessively focused on bodily desires. As in Evagrius and Cassian, Gregory understands gluttony to be an interest in food that goes beyond one's bodily needs and moves into the place of excessive desire. Unlike Evagrius and Cassian, however, the challenge of the vices for Gregory is that they occur in the context of worldly duties and commitments.

CONCLUSION

As the idea of gluttony moves from a monastic setting in the Egyptian desert to Spain, and on to Rome, the demon of gluttony who whispers in the ear of the monk relocates inward, becoming an internalized temptation of the soul that the lay Christian must overcome with discretion. As one among many vices that tempt the Christian away from proper attention to God, gluttony becomes defined by a broad range of food behaviors and attitudes, only one of which—eating excessively—has any possible connection to the fat body. Indeed, the early medieval world's attention to the cardinal vices suggests the importance of balancing one's worldly self with spiritual matters in order to create the perfect setting for spiritual growth and development. Too much attention to any worldly matter could mean spiritual disaster for any Christian hoping for salvation.

Epilogue

> Gluttony is what the belly loves and it wastes both body and
> soul, and a man's good. It pleases much the fiend, and greatly
> grieves God. And we find in the gospel that our Lord Jesus gave
> fiends leave to enter into hogs. And they grew crazy and drowned
> themselves in the sea; for those who are like hogs in gluttony, the
> fiends have power to dwell in them and to drown them in the sea
> of hell.[1]
>
> —*Jacob's Well*

The anonymous author of the early 15th-century collection of sermons
called *Jacob's Well* clearly delighted in using vivid images and language to
convey moral messages to his audience. The book's title comes from John
4:6 and refers to the well where Jesus spoke to the Samaritan woman. The
text reads the well as an allegory for the sinful body of man, a morass of de-
bauched sludge and ooze that must be cleansed in order that it can be filled
with the refreshing waters of God's grace.[2] The collection is one of many penitential manuals created during the Middle Ages to assist priests in meting
out the proper punishments for confessed sins and to instruct lay Christians
on the fine points of sinful behavior so that they would know what to confess. Like many penitential manuals, *Jacob's Well* is not particularly original,
and it combines stories and sources from many previous manuals and texts,
including Gregory's *Morals on the Book of Job*.[3] But as we look beyond the
ancient world, texts like *Jacob's Well* demonstrate a remarkable consistency
in ideas about gluttony and the fat body, even as these ideas expand out into
the broader community. Here we find gluttony associated with irrationality, disease, animality, femininity, and death, while it continues also to be
thought of as a threat to the stability of a Christian community.

The glutton is like a bear, in two ways. One is this; he has such an inclination for meat
that he evermore licks after it, with his tongue. So the glutton loves delicacies, so that
his tongue always delights to speak of them. Another is this; the bear delights much in
honey, and therefore he goes to a hive, to a swarm of bees, and licks away the honey

that they have worked hard for; so the glutton delights so much in delicacies that he is not ashamed to devour and waste what many others have worked hard for.[4]

The bear-glutton talks incessantly about food and eats more than his share, even when others have worked hard for it. Talking too much about food adds an additional dimension to the challenges of gluttony that we did not see in the ancient world. Nonetheless, this type of behavior wastes communal goodwill as the glutton allows his selfish and animalistic desires for food to take precedence over the feelings of others.

The glutton also fails to fulfill his religious duties. He is a hypocrite, for he either pretends to fast on required days for fasting but eats in secret, or he fasts too much to appear more spiritual.[5] This is one of the failings of the "second ooze of gluttony," eating too much. The "first ooze of gluttony" is about eating at the wrong time. With this kind of gluttony, the glutton eats and drinks too late at night, misses going to church, and tempts others from a righteous life with gaming and fun.

This sin displeases God, for God bids you to fast, and thy belly says "nay"; God bids you to get up and go to church, and your belly says it is full and must take a rest, for the church is not a hare; where men leave it they may find it. And when you get up, God bids you to pray; your belly says "what shall we eat today?" where shall we have any good food or good drink? God bids you to weep for your sins; your belly says, "I am heavy as lead. I am sick tonight for excess of food and drink last evening. My head aches. I shall not be well at ease until I have drunk again." Thus you make your belly your God. This sin draws you to the tavern, to dice playing, to lechery, to ribaldry, to slander, to rest and ease and to other sins.[6]

Here, eating at the wrong time is not about snacking between meals, as it was for the monks, yet such eating leads the glutton and his associates to immoral living and avoidance of spiritual growth and development.

Gluttony also leads to death, because it leads to all kinds of sinful behavior. Eating too much, eating expensive food, enjoying the pleasures of food, eating too quickly or voraciously, and eating at the wrong time: these are the five ways that gluttony's ooze infests the Christian, and all of these kinds of gluttony create habits in the sinner that lead to death.

Gluttony is represented in Proverbs [30:15]. There it is written that a waterleach or a tick that is sucking blood, it has daughters that say, "bring, bring." The sucker is your belly. His two daughters are gluttony and drunkenness. Gluttony cries ever after excess of food, drunkenness cries ever after excess of drink. And a waterleach or a tick has never enough, until it bursts; so your belly has never enough but cries ever, "give me more" until it ends with death.[7]

Death comes to the man who cannot avoid gluttony, but here again, as we have seen throughout this book, gluttony is associated with femininity. As the daughter of the bloated tick, gluttony urges the man to eat until he dies. In the end, *Jacob's Well* determines that gluttons and drunkards will be excluded from heaven; this should be incentive enough for the Christian to cast the ooze of gluttony from his body so that he can, with the "sweetness of abstinence," enter into the kingdom of heaven.[8]

The author of *Jacob's Well* mentions the fat body only once, in the context of eating when one is supposed to be fasting, in order to appear "fair and fat."[9] As in the ancient texts examined throughout this book, being fat is not of significant concern in the discussion of gluttony; appearing fair and fat appears to be a positive thing, except when others assume that you are fasting.

At least up to the 15th century, then, gluttony has only a meager relationship to the fat body. Ken Albala traces "the modern anxiety over obesity" to the 17th century, "when fat was fashionable."[10] New ideas about body chemistry and physiology at that time led medical professionals to begin to question whether being fat was unhealthy, thereby creating "a nascent fear of fat."[11] As time went on, the bond between gluttony and fatness solidified, underscoring our current assumption that the glutton is, inevitably, fat.

Yet, as this book has demonstrated, such a connection between gluttony and the fat body need not be perceived to be a historical or conceptual inevitability. Indeed, gluttony and the fat body have been historically and conceptually disconnected for many more years than they have been linked. Eating to excess is only one aspect among the many varieties of gluttonous behavior, and the fat body's meaning remains doggedly ambivalent: a negative sign of overindulgence and worldliness or a positive sign of wealth and prosperity. Perhaps, then, it is time to rethink—or at the very least, examine carefully—contemporary assumptions regarding the inevitable link between them. As this foray into the ancient world has shown, an examination of the history of gluttony is like sitting down to a feast of ideas, rife with intriguing and remarkable dishes, bursting with tantalizing flavors. It is a feast that may—or may not—make us fat.

Notes

INTRODUCTION

1. Jeremy Iggers, "Innocence Lost: Our Complicated Relationship with Food," *The Utne Reader* 60 (December 1993): 54.

2. William Ian Miller, "Gluttony," *Representations,* no. 60 (Autumn 1997): 93.

3. Anne Scott Beller, *Fat and Thin: A Natural History of Obesity* (New York: Farrar, Straus and Giroux, 1977), 5.

4. Susan Bordo, *Unbearable Weight: Feminism, Western Culture, and the Body* (Berkeley: University of California Press, 1993), 206.

5. Caroline Malone, "God or Goddess: The Temple Art of Ancient Malta," in *Ancient Goddesses: The Myths and the Evidence*, ed. Lucy Goodison and Christine Morris (Madison: University of Wisconsin Press, 1998), 155.

6. Helen Christopoulou-Aletra and Niki Papavramidou, "Methods Used by the Hippocratic Physicians for Weight Reduction," *World Journal of Surgery* 28, no. 5 (2004): 516, 513.

7. Robert J. Kuczmarski and Katherine M. Flegal, "Criteria for Definition of Overweight in Transition: Background and Recommendations for the United States," *The American Journal of Clinical Nutrition* 72, no. 5 (November 1, 2000): 1078.

8. John Cassian, *The Conferences*, trans. Boniface Ramsey, Ancient Christian Writers no. 57 (New York: Paulist Press, 1997), 186.

9. Ibid., 183, 185.

10. Aldhelm, *Aldhelm, the Prose Works*, trans. Michael Lapidge and Michael W. Herren (Cambridge, U.K.: D. S. Brewer, 1979), 67.

11. This description was crafted in an e-mail exchange with fat activist Marilyn Wann, author of *FAT!SO?: Because You Don't Have to Apologize for Your Size* (Berkeley, CA: Ten Speed Press, 1998), May 12–19, 2009.

12. Richard Kearney, *Modern Movements in European Philosophy* (Manchester: Manchester University Press, 1986), 241ff.

13. Ibid., 252, 283.

14. Claude Lévi-Strauss, "The Structural Study of Myth," *The Journal of American Folklore* 68, no. 270 (October 1955): esp. 437–41.

15. William G Doty, *Mythography: The Study of Myths and Rituals* (University, AL: University of Alabama Press, 1986), 282–83.

16. Michel Foucault, *The Use of Pleasure,* trans. Robert Hurley, vol. 2 of *The History of Sexuality* (New York: Pantheon Books, 1978), 10.

17. Ibid., 2:44.

18. Ibid.
19. Ibid., 2:45.
20. Ibid., 2:119.
21. Ibid., 2:129.
22. Ibid., 2:120.
23. Ibid., 2:118.

CHAPTER 1

1. Nobuyoshi Kiuchi, *Leviticus*, vol. 3, Apollos Old Testament Commentary (Downers Grove, IL: InterVarsity Press, 2007), 61.

2. Gordon J. Wenham, *The Book of Leviticus*, vol. 3, The New International Commentary on the Old Testament (Grand Rapids, MI: W.B. Eerdmans, 1979), 52.

3. *The New Oxford Annotated Bible with the Apocrypha, Third Edition, New Revised Standard Version*, ed. Michael D. Coogan (New York: Oxford University Press, 2001), commentary on Leviticus 2:1–6, 144.

4. Wenham, *The Book of Leviticus*, 74.

5. Baruch J. Schwartz, "The Prohibitions Concerning the 'Eating' of Blood in Leviticus 17," in *Priesthood and Cult in Ancient Israel*, ed. Gary A. Anderson and Saul M. Olyan, *Journal for the Study of the Old Testament Supplement Series 125* (Sheffield, U.K.: Journal for the Study of the Old Testament Press, 1991), 34–66.

6. Jean Soler, "The Semiotics of Food in the Bible," in *Food and Culture: A Reader*, ed. Carole Counihan and Penny van Esterik (New York: Routledge, 1997), 57.

7. Jacob Milgrom, *Leviticus: A Book of Ritual and Ethics: A Continental Commentary* (Minneapolis, MN: Fortress Press, 2004), 13.

8. Milgrom, *Leviticus*, 29; Baruch A Levine, *Leviticus = Va-Yikra. The Traditional Hebrew Text with the New JPS Translation*, 1st ed., The JPS Torah Commentary (Philadelphia: Jewish Publication Society, 1989), 16n3.

9. Bernard Jacob Bamberger, "Commentary on Leviticus," in *The Torah: A Modern Commentary* (New York: Union of American Hebrew Congregations, 1981), 767.

10. *The New Oxford Annotated Bible*, Note on Leviticus 3:9, 149.

11. *The New Interpreter's Bible, Volume 1: General and Old Testament Articles; Genesis; Exodus; Leviticus* (Nashville: Abingdon Press, 1994), 1025.

12. Wenham, *The Book of Leviticus*, 81.

13. Kiuchi, *Leviticus*, 79.

14. Ibid.

15. Ibid.

16. Ibid., 83.

17. Milgrom, *Leviticus*, 29; Wenham, *The Book of Leviticus*, 3:80; Martin Noth, *Leviticus; a Commentary*, Old Testament Library (Philadelphia: Westminster Press, 1965), 64.

18. Jacob Milgrom, *Leviticus 1–16: A New Translation with Introduction and Commentary*, vol. 3, Anchor Bible Commentaries (New York: Doubleday, 1991), 207; Kiuchi, *Leviticus*, 79.

19. Levine, *Leviticus*, 16.

20. Derek Tidball, *The Message of Leviticus: Free to Be Holy* (IVP Academic, 2005), 60.

21. Ibid.

22. Erhard Gerstenberger, *Leviticus: A Commentary*, The Old Testament Library (Louisville, KY: Westminister John Knox Press, 1996), 48.

23. J. R. Porter, *Leviticus*, Cambridge Bible Commentaries on the Old Testament (Cambridge: Cambridge University Press, 1976), 31.

24. *The New Interpreter's Bible,* 1026.

25. Mary Douglas, *Leviticus as Literature* (Oxford: Oxford University Press, 1999), 73.

26. Ibid.

27. Ibid., 66–67.

28. Mary Douglas, *Purity and Danger: An Analysis of Concepts of Pollution and Taboo; with a new preface by the author,* Routledge Classics (London: Routledge & Kegan Paul, 1966; Routledge, 2007), xiii. Citations are to the Routledge Classics edition.

29. Douglas, *Leviticus as Literature,* 75.

30. Ibid., 81.

31. Ibid., 79.

32. Jeffrey H Tigay, *Deuteronomy = [Devarim]: The Traditional Hebrew Text with the New JPS Translation,* The JPS Torah Commentary (Philadelphia: Jewish Publication Society, 1996), 295–96.

33. Philo, "On the Special Laws, Book 4," in *Philo, Vol. 8: On the Special Laws, Book 4. On the Virtues. On Rewards and Punishments,* trans. F. H. Colson, Loeb Classical Library 341 (Cambridge: Harvard University Press, 1939), 4.24.

34. Howard Eilberg-Schwartz, *The Savage in Judaism: An Anthropology of Israelite Religion and Ancient Judaism* (Bloomington: Indiana University Press, 1990), 194.

35. Hesiod, *Theogony and Works and Days,* trans. M. L. West, Oxford World Classics (New York: Oxford University Press, 2009), 535–57; Gerstenberger, *Leviticus,* 61.

36. Eilberg-Schwartz, *The Savage in Judaism,* 179–82.

37. *The New Oxford Annotated Bible,* Note on Judges 3:12, 359.

38. E. John Hamlin, *At Risk in the Promised Land: A Commentary on the Book of Judges,* International Theological Commentary (Grand Rapids, MI: W.B. Eerdmans, 1990), 70; Barry G. Webb, *The Book of the Judges: An Integrated Reading,* Journal for the Study of the Old Testament Supplement Series 46 (Sheffield, U.K.: Journal for the Study of the Old Testament Press, 1987), 129.

39. Douglas, *Purity and Danger,* 44.

40. Ibid., 142.

41. Eilberg-Schwartz, *The Savage in Judaism,* 183.

42. Ibid., 186.

43. Ibid., 187.

44. *The New Oxford Annotated Bible,* Note on Judges 3:12, 360.

45. Eilberg-Schwartz, *The Savage in Judaism,* 191.

46. Elizabeth Bellefontaine, "Deuteronomy 21:18–21: Reviewing the Case of the Rebellious Son," *Journal for the Study of the Old Testament* 4, no. 13 (1979): 19; Tigay, *Deuteronomy,* 197.

47. Tigay, *Deuteronomy,* 197.

48. Bellefontaine, "Deuteronomy 21," 21.

49. Robert J. Karris, *Luke: Artist and Theologian: Luke's Passion Account As Literature* (Mahwah, NJ: Paulist Press, 1985), 70.

50. Ibid., 47.

51. Joseph A Fitzmyer, *The Gospel According to Luke I–IX: Introduction, Translation, and Notes,* 1st ed., Anchor Bible Commentary 28 (Garden City, NY: Doubleday, 1981), 469, 581, 591.

52. Ibid., 596–97.

53. Robert Horton Gundry, *Matthew, a Commentary on His Literary and Theological Art* (Grand Rapids, MI: W.B. Eerdmans, 1982), 213.

54. Leon Morris, *The Gospel According to Matthew,* Pillar New Testament Commentary (Grand Rapids, MI: W.B. Eerdmans, 1992), 285.

55. Ibid., 286.

56. Fitzmyer, *The Gospel According to Luke,* 681; Howard Clark Kee, "Jesus: A Glutton and a Drunkard," *New Testament Studies* 42, no. 3 (1996): 391.

57. Kee, "Jesus," 391.

58. Ibid.

59. Ibid.

60. Karl Olav Sandnes, *Belly and Body in the Pauline Epistles* (Cambridge, U.K.: Cambridge University Press, 2002), 57.

61. Ibid., Chap. 8–10.

62. Ibid., 165.

63. Helmut Koester, "The Purpose of the Polemic of a Pauline Fragment (Philippians 3)," *New Testament Studies* 8, no. 4 (1962): 317–32; Peter Thomas O'Brien, *The Epistle to the Philippians: A Commentary on the Greek Text* (Grand Rapids, MI: Eerdmans, 1991), 455.

64. Sandnes, *Belly and Body,* 8.

65. Ibid., 134.

66. Ibid., 8, 169.

CHAPTER 2

1. Plato, *Timaeus,* trans. Donald J. Zeyl (Indianapolis, IN: Hackett Publishing, 2000), 72e.

2. Aristotle, *Nicomachean Ethics,* trans. Martin Ostwald, Library of Liberal Arts (Upper Saddle River, NJ: Prentice Hall, 1962), 1118b.

3. Alfred North Whitehead, *Process and Reality: An Essay in Cosmology,* ed. David Ray Griffin and Donald W Sherburne, corrected ed., Gifford lectures 1927–28 (New York: Free Press, 1978), 39.

4. Donald J. Zeyl, Introduction to the *Timaeus,* by Plato (Indianapolis, IN: Hackett Publishing, 2000), xiv.

5. Carlos Steel, "The Moral Purpose of the Human Body: A Reading of "Timaeus" 69–72," *Phronesis* 46, no. 2 (May 2001): 106–7.

6. Plato, *Timaeus,* 32e.

7. Plato, *Plato's Cosmology; the Timaeus of Plato,* trans. with a running commentary by Francis Macdonald Cornford (New York: Harcourt Brace, 1937), 291.

8. Daniel C. Russell, *Plato on Pleasure and the Good Life* (Oxford: Clarendon Press, 2005), 12–13; Chapter 7.

9. Zeyl, Introduction the *Timaeus,* xvi-xx; Russell, *Plato on Pleasure and the Good Life.*

10. Zeyl, Introduction to the *Timaeus,* xxxiv. This description is indebted to Zeyl's clear and concise summary of the dialogue.

11. Ibid.

12. Ibid., lxxviii.

13. Plato, *Timaeus,* 69c.

14. Russell, *Plato on Pleasure and the Good Life,* 231.

15. Plato, *Timaeus,* 69d.

16. Zeyl, Introduction to the *Timaeus,* lxxix.

17. Plato, *Timaeus,* 69d; Plato, *Plato's Cosmology,* commentary by Cornfeld, 282.

18. Plato, *Timaeus,* 42b.

19. Mary Douglas, *Purity and Danger: An Analysis of the Concepts of Pollution and Taboo; with a new preface by the author,* Routledge Classics (London: Routledge & Kegan Paul, 1966; Routledge, 2007) 3.

20. Ibid., 4.

21. Plato, *Timaeus,* 69e.

22. Ibid., 70a.

23. Ibid., 69c–70b.
24. Ibid., 70e.
25. Ibid., 71a.
26. Ibid., 71b.
27. Ibid., 72e.
28. Ibid.
29. Ibid., 73a.
30. Russell, *Plato on Pleasure and the Good Life,* 232.
31. Plato, *Timaeus,* 73a.
32. G. E. R. Lloyd, "The Hot and the Cold, the Dry and the Wet in Greek Philosophy," *The Journal of Hellenic Studies* 84 (1964): 93n2.
33. Plato, *Timaeus,* 82a.
34. Ibid., 82b.
35. Ibid., 86b.
36. Ibid.
37. Ibid., 86c.
38. Ibid., 86d.
39. Ibid., 87c.
40. Ibid., 87d.
41. Ibid.
42. Ibid., 88a.
43. Ibid., 88b.
44. Donald Zeyl, e-mail message from translator, August 18, 2006.
45. Plato, *Timaeus,* 88b.
46. Ibid., 90c.
47. Ibid., 90d.
48. Ibid.
49. Ibid., 88c.
50. Ibid., 82a (my emphasis).
51. Ibid., 82b (my emphasis).
52. Ibid., 89d.
53. Ibid., 90a.
54. Russell, *Plato on Pleasure and the Good Life,* 236–37.
55. Plato, *Timaeus,* 90b.
56. Ibid.
57. Ibid., 90c.
58. Ibid., 90d.
59. Ibid., 89e.
60. See Christine Garside Allen, "Plato on Women," *Feminist Studies* 2, no. 2/3 (January 1, 1975): 131–38, and Page DuBois, *Sowing the Body: Psychoanalysis and Ancient Representations of Women* (Chicago: University of Chicago Press, 1988).
61. Plato, *Timaeus,* 91b.
62. Ibid., 69d.
63. Aristotle, *Nicomachean Ethics,* xxii, 1098a.
64. Martin Ostwald, Introduction to the *Nichomachean Ethics,* by Aristotle (Upper Saddle River, NJ: Prentice Hall, 1962), xxiii.
65. Ibid.
66. Aristotle, *Nicomachean Ethics,* 1107a.
67. Ibid., 1102a, 1102b.
68. Ibid., 1102b.
69. Ibid.
70. Ibid., 1103a.

71. Ibid., 1102b.
72. Ibid., 1103a.
73. Ibid.
74. Ibid., 1104b.
75. Ibid.
76. Ibid.
77. Ibid., 1104a.
78. Ibid.
79. Ibid.
80. Ibid., 1106a, 1106b.
81. Ibid., 1106b.
82. Ibid., 1107a.
83. Ibid., 1117b.
84. Ibid.
85. Ibid., 1118a.
86. Ibid.
87. Ibid.
88. Ibid., 1118b.
89. Ibid.
90. Ibid.
91. Ibid.
92. Ibid., 1119a.
93. Ibid.
94. Ibid.
95. Charles M. Young, "Aristotle on Temperance," *The Philosophical Review* 97, no. 4 (October 1988): 532.
96. Aristotle, *Nicomachean Ethics,* 1118b.
97. Ibid., 1119a.
98. Ibid.
99. Young, "Aristotle on Temperance," 535.
100. Aristotle, *Nicomachean Ethics,* 1119a.
101. Ibid.
102. Ibid., 1118a.
103. Ibid., 1118a, 1118b.
104. Ibid., 1119a.
105. Ibid., 1119b.
106. Ibid., 1151a.
107. Ibid.
108. Ibid.
109. Ibid.
110. Ibid., 1151b.
111. Ibid., 1152a.
112. Ibid., 1151b.
113. Ibid., 1104a.

CHAPTER 3

1. Aristotle, *Prior Analytics and Posterior Analytics,* trans. A. J Jenkinson (Digireads.com, 2006), 2:27.
2. Helen King, ed., *Health in Antiquity* (London: Routledge, 2005), 2.
3. Ibid., 2–3.

4. Hippocrates, "Ancient Medicine," in *Hippocrates, Volume 1: Ancient Medicine. Airs, Waters, Places. Epidemics 1 and 3. The Oath. Precepts. Nutriment,* trans. W.H.S. Jones, Loeb Classical Library 147 (Cambridge, MA: Harvard University Press, 1923), 3.

5. Hesiod, *Theogony and Works and Days,* trans. M. L. West (New York: Oxford University Press, 2009), 53–105.

6. King, *Health in Antiquity,* 8.

7. G. A. Bray, "Obesity: Historical Development of Scientific and Cultural Ideas," *International Journal of Obesity* 14, no. 11 (November 1990): 909.

8. Helena Christopoulou-Aletra and Niki Papavramidou, "Methods Used by the Hippocratic Physicians for Weight Reduction," *World Journal of Surgery* 28 (2004): 513.

9. Sander L. Gilman, *Fat Boys: A Slim Book* (Lincoln: University of Nebraska Press, 2004), 35.

10. Lawrence Conrad, ed., *The Western Medical Tradition: 800 BC to AD 1800* (Cambridge: Cambridge University Press, 1995), 21ff; Helen King, *Greek and Roman Medicine,* Classical World Series (London: Bristol Classical Press, 2001), 9.

11. King, *Greek and Roman Medicine,* 13; Hippocrates, "Regimen 1," in *Hippocrates, Vol. 4: Nature of Man. Regimen in Health. Humours. Aphorisms. Regimen 1–3. Dreams. Heracleitus: On the Universe,* trans. W.H.S. Jones, Loeb Classical Library 150 (Cambridge, MA: Harvard University Press, 1931), 4.

12. Hippocrates, "Nature of Man," in *Hippocrates, Vol. 4: Nature of Man. Regimen in Health. Humours. Aphorisms. Regimen 1–3. Dreams. Heracleitus: On the Universe,* trans. W.H.S. Jones, Loeb Classical Library 150 (Cambridge, MA: Harvard University Press, 1931), 4; Hippocrates, "Prorrhetic 2," in *Hippocrates, Vol. 8: Places in Man. Glands. Fleshes. Prorhetic 1–2. Physician. Use of Liquids. Ulcers. Haemorrhoids and Fistulas,* trans. Paul Potter, Loeb Classical Library 482 (Cambridge, MA: Harvard University Press, 1995), 23.

13. Hippocrates, "Humours," in *Hippocrates, Vol. 4: Nature of Man. Regimen in Health. Humours. Aphorisms. Regimen 1–3. Dreams. Heracleitus: On the Universe,* trans. W.H.S. Jones, Loeb Classical Library 150 (Cambridge, MA: Harvard University Press, 1931), 16.

14. Hippocrates, "Nature of Man," 7.

15. Ibid.

16. Hippocrates, "Airs, Waters, Places," in *Hippocrates, Vol. 1: Ancient Medicine. Airs, Waters, Places. Epidemics 1 and 3. The Oath. Precepts. Nutriment,* trans. W.H.S. Jones, Loeb Classical Library 147 (Cambridge, MA: Harvard University Press, 1923), 16.

17. Ibid., 24.

18. Ibid.

19. Ibid.

20. Ibid., 23.

21. Ibid., 24.

22. Hippocrates, "Regimen 1," 2.

23. Ibid.

24. Ibid.

25. Ibid.

26. Hippocrates, "Breaths," in *Hippocrates, Volume 2: Prognostic. Regimen in Acute Diseases. The Sacred Disease. The Art. Breaths. Law. Decorum. Physician (Ch. 1). Dentition,* trans. W.H.S. Jones, Loeb Classical Library 148 (Boston: Harvard University Press, 1923), 1.

27. Hippocrates, "Regimen in Health," in *Hippocrates, Vol. 4: Nature of Man. Regimen in Health. Humours. Aphorisms. Regimen 1–3. Dreams. Heracleitus: On the Universe,* trans. W.H.S. Jones, Loeb Classical Library 150 (Cambridge, MA: Harvard University Press, 1931), 2.

28. Christopoulou-Aletra and Papavramidou, "Methods Used by the Hippocratic Physicians for Weight Reduction," 513–517.

29. Hippocrates, "Prorrhetic 2," 23.

30. Hippocrates, "Regimen in Health," 4.

31. Hippocrates, "Regimen 2," in *Hippocrates, Vol. 4: Nature of Man. Regimen in Health. Humours. Aphorisms. Regimen 1–3. Dreams. Heracleitus: On the Universe,* trans. W.H.S. Jones, Loeb Classical Library 150 (Cambridge, MA: Harvard University Press, 1931), 63.

32. Hippocrates, "Regimen 1," 7.

33. Hippocrates, "Regimen 3," in *Hippocrates, Vol. 4: Nature of Man. Regimen in Health. Humours. Aphorisms. Regimen 1–3. Dreams. Heracleitus: On the Universe,* trans. W.H.S. Jones, Loeb Classical Library 150 (Cambridge, MA: Harvard University Press, 1931), 67.

34. Hippocrates, "Regimen 1," 35 n2.

35. Ibid.

36. Ibid.

37. Ibid.

38. Ibid.

39. Ibid.

40. Hippocrates, "Regimen 3," 85.

41. Hippocrates, "Aphorisms," in *Hippocrates, Volume 4: Nature of Man. Regimen in Health. Humours. Aphorisms. Regimen 1–3. Dreams. Heracleitus: On the Universe,* trans. W.H.S. Jones, Loeb Classical Library 150 (Cambridge, MA: Harvard University Press, 1931), 5.47.

42. Hippocrates, "Prorrhetic 2," 24. The translation of *pachus* as "obese" in Potter's translation of the "Prorrhetic II" is overstated. As noted in the introduction, *pachus* implies stout, heavy, strong, solid.

43. Ibid.

44. Ibid.

45. Hippocrates, "Airs, Waters, Places," 20.

46. Ibid., 21.

47. Ibid.

48. Ibid., 3.

49. Ibid., 4.

50. Ibid., 7.

51. Ibid., 5.

52. Hippocrates, "Aphorisms," 2.44.

53. Edwin Burton Levine, *Hippocrates,* Twaynes' World Authors Series 165 (New York: Twayne Publishers, 1971), 85.

54. Hippocrates, "Regimen 3," 72–73.

55. Ibid., 73.

56. Hippocrates, "Affections," in *Hippocrates, Vol. 5: Affections. Diseases 1. Diseases 2,* trans. Paul Potter, Loeb Classical Library 472 (Cambridge, MA: Harvard University Press, 1988), 50.

57. Hippocrates, "Ancient Medicine," 9.

58. Elizabeth Cornelia Evans, *Physiognomics in the Ancient World,* Transactions of the American Philosophical Society 59, pt. 5 (Philadelphia: American Philosophical Society, 1969), 6.

59. Ibid.

60. Aristotle, *Aristotle, Volume 14, Minor Works: On Colours. On Things Heard. Physiognomics. On Plants. On Marvellous Things Heard. Mechanical Problems. On Indivisible Lines. The Situations and Names of Winds. On Melissus, Xenophanes, Gor-*

gias, trans. W. S. Hett, Loeb Classical Library 307 (Cambridge, MA: Harvard University Press, 1936), viii.

61. Evans, *Physiognomics in the Ancient World,* 7; G. R Boys-Stones, "Physiognomy and Ancient Psychological Theory," in *Seeing the Face, Seeing the Soul: Polemon's Physiognomy from Classical Antiquity to Medieval Islam,* ed. Simon Swain (Oxford: Oxford University Press, 2007), 56.

62. Simon Swain, trans., "The Physiognomy Attributed to Aristotle," in *Seeing the Face, Seeing the Soul: Polemon's Physiognomy from Classical Antiquity to Medieval Islam,* ed. Simon Swain (Oxford: Oxford University Press, 2007), 805a.

63. Ibid.

64. Ibid., 805b.

65. Ibid., 805a.

66. Ibid.

67. Ibid., 805b.

68. Ibid., 806a.

69. Ibid.

70. Ibid., 807a.

71. Ibid., 807b.

72. Ibid., 809a.

73. Ibid.

74. Ibid.

75. Ibid., 809b.

76. Ibid.

77. Maud W Gleason, *Making Men: Sophists and Self-Presentation in Ancient Rome* (Princeton, NJ: Princeton University Press, 1995), 28.

78. Ibid., 55, 28.

79. Ibid., 28.

80. Swain, "The Physiognomy Attributed to Aristotle," 808a.

81. Ibid., 810b.

82. Ibid., 813b.

83. Ibid.

84. Ibid., 808b.

85. Ibid., 810b.

86. Robert Hoyland, trans., "The Leiden Polemon," in *Seeing the Face, Seeing the Soul: Polemon's Physiognomy from Classical Antiquity to Medieval Islam,* ed. Simon Swain (Oxford: Oxford University Press, 2007), 405.

87. Ibid.

88. Ian Repath, trans., "Anonymus Latinus, Book of Physiognomy," in *Seeing the Face, Seeing the Soul: Polemon's Physiognomy from Classical Antiquity to Medieval Islam,* ed. Simon Swain (Oxford: Oxford University Press, 2007), 599.

89. Karl Olav Sandnes, *Belly and Body in the Pauline Epistles* (Cambridge: Cambridge University Press, 2002), 31.

90. Hillel Schwartz, *Never Satisfied: A Cultural History of Diets, Fantasies, and Fat* (New York: Free Press, 1986), 42.

91. Swain, "The Physiognomy Attributed to Aristotle," 814b.

CHAPTER 4

1. Homer, *The Odyssey of Homer,* trans. Alan Mandelbaum (Berkeley: University of California Press, 1990), 1.373.

2. Ibid., 9.96.

3. Ibid., 7.217ff.

4. Athenaeus, *The Learned Banqueters, Vol. 4, Books 8–10.420e,* trans. S. Douglas Olson, Loeb Classical Library 235 (Cambridge. MA: Harvard University Press, 2008), 10.412b.

5. Athenaeus, *The Learned Banqueters, Vol. 4,* 10.412b.

6. Homer, *The Odyssey of Homer,* 8.136, 5.169, 5.204.

7. John Wilkins, *The Boastful Chef: The Discourse of Food in Ancient Greek Comedy* (Oxford: Oxford University Press, 2000), 27.

8. Homer, *The Odyssey,* trans. Robert Fagles and Bernard Knox (New York: Penguin Classic, 1997), 11.691.

9. Ibid., 11.698.

10. Timothy Gantz, *Early Greek Myth: A Guide to Literary and Artistic Sources,* vol. 1 (Baltimore, MD: Johns Hopkins University Press, 1996), 380.

11. Karl Galinsky, *The Herakles Theme: The Adaptations of the Hero in Literature from Homer to the Twentieth Century* (Totowa, NJ: Rowman and Littlefield, 1972), 4.

12. Thalia Papadopoulou, *Heracles and Euripidean Tragedy,* Cambridge Classical Studies 50 (Cambridge: Cambridge University Press, 2005), 7.

13. Arthur Wallace Pickard-Cambridge, *Dithyramb, Tragedy and Comedy,* 2nd ed. rev. T.B.L. Webster (Oxford: Clarendon Press, 1962), 233.

14. Athenaeus, *The Learned Banqueters, Vol. 4,* 10.411b.

15. J. M. Edmonds, ed., *The Fragments of Attic Comedy after Meineke, Bergk, and Kock; Augmented, Newly Edited with Their Contexts, Annotated, and Completely Translated into English Verse by John Maxwell Edmonds.* 3 vols. (Leiden: E. J. Brill, 1957), 2:411.

16. Ibid., 2:439.

17. Aristophanes, *The Birds,* trans. William Arrowsmith (Ann Arbor: University of Michigan Press, 1961), 14.

18. Galinsky, *The Herakles Theme,* 86.

19. Aristophanes, *The Birds,* 96.

20. Ibid., 98.

21. Ibid., 99.

22. Ibid., 104.

23. William Arrowsmith, Richmond Alexander Lattimore, and Douglass Parker, trans., "Introduction to Aristophanes' "The Frogs," in *Four Plays by Aristophanes* (New York: Penguin Books, 1994), 474.

24. Wilkins, *The Boastful Chef,* 91.

25. Aristophanes, "The Frogs," in *Four Plays by Aristophanes,* trans. William Arrowsmith, Richmond Alexander Lattimore, and Douglass Parker (New York: Meridian, 1994), 485.

26. Ibid., 487.

27. Ibid., 482.

28. Ibid., 519.

29. Ibid., 522.

30. Ibid., 533.

31. Ibid., 580.

32. Nicole Loraux, "Herakles: The Super-Male and the Feminine," in *Before Sexuality: The Construction of Erotic Experience in the Ancient Greek World,* ed. David M. Halperin, John J. Winkler, and Froma I. Zeitlin (Princeton, NJ: Princeton University Press, 1990), 30.

33. Ibid., 31.

34. Athenaeus, *The Learned Banqueters,* Vol. 4, 10.412b.

35. Jeremy McInerney, *The Cattle of the Sun: Cows and Culture in the World of the Ancient Greeks* (Princeton, NJ: Princeton University Press, 2010), 12.

36. Mark William Padilla, *The Myths of Herakles in Ancient Greece: Survey and Profile* (Lanham, MD: University Press of America, 1998), 22.

37. McInerney, *The Cattle of the Sun,* 14.

38. J. R. Green and Eric Handley, *Images of the Greek Theatre* (Austin: University of Texas Press, 1995), 60–61.

39. Philip B Corbett, *Petronius* (New York: Twayne Publishers, 1970), 13.

40. Ibid., 14.

41. J. P. Sullivan, *The Satyricon of Petronius: A Literary Study* (London: Faber, 1968), 82, 89.

42. Froma I. Zeitlin, "Petronius as Paradox: Anarchy and Artistic Integrity," *Transactions and Proceedings of the American Philological Association* 102 (1971): 635.

43. Ibid., 682.

44. Ibid., 683.

45. Emily Gowers, *The Loaded Table: Representations of Food in Roman Literature* (Oxford: Clarendon Press, 1993), 121ff.

46. Petronius, *The Satyricon,* trans. William Arrowsmith (New York: Penguin Books, 1994), 39.

47. Ibid.

48. Ibid., 40.

49. Ibid., 41.

50. Ibid., 42.

51. Ibid., 44.

52. Ibid., 47, 49, 60, 66, 67.

53. Ibid., 75.

54. Ibid., 45.

55. Ibid.

56. Ibid., 49.

57. Ibid., 57.

58. Ibid., 58.

59. Ibid., 38, 51.

60. Ibid., 66.

61. Ibid., 50.

62. Ibid.

63. Ibid., 51.

64. Ibid., 75.

65. Ibid., 55.

66. Ibid., 45.

67. Ibid., 78.

68. Ibid., 38, 77.

69. Ibid., 84.

70. Ibid., 76.

71. David Braund, "Learning, Luxury and Empire: *Athenaeus' Roman Patron,*" in *Athenaeus and His World: Reading Greek Culture in the Roman Empire,* ed. David Braund and John Wilkins (Exeter, UK: University of Exeter Press, 2000), 19.

72. John Wilkins, "Dialogue and Comedy: The Structure of the *Deipnosophistae,*" in *Athenaeus and His World: Reading Greek Culture in the Roman Empire,* ed. David Braund and John Wilkins (Exeter, UK: University of Exeter Press, 2000), 24.

73. Ibid., 26.

74. Ibid., 24. My description of the text's structure is indebted to Wilkins's clear and careful delineation of the "structural devices" of Athenaeus's text.

75. Athenaeus, *The Learned Banqueters, Vol. 1, Books 1–3.106e,* trans. S. Douglas Olson, Loeb Classical Library 204 (Cambridge, MA: Harvard University Press, 2006), 1.1e.

76. Ibid., 3.96f.

77. Ibid. 3.97a-c

78. Ibid., 3.97c.

79. Ibid., 3.100b.

80. Ibid., 3.100b-101e.

81. Athenaeus, *The Learned Banqueters, Vol. 2, Books 3.106e-5,* trans. S. Douglas Olson, Loeb Classical Library 208 (Cambridge, MA: Harvard University Press, 2006), 3.125c; for an excellent analysis of the dinner parasite in Athenaeus, see Tim Whitmarsh, "The Politics and Poetics of Parasitism: *Athenaeus on Parasites and Flatterers,*" in *Athenaeus and His World: Reading Greek Culture in the Roman Empire,* ed. David Braund and John Wilkins (Exeter, UK: University of Exeter Press, 2000), 304–15.

82. Athenaeus, *The Learned Banqueters, Vol. 4,* 9.385a.

83. Athenaeus, *The Learned Banqueters, Vol. 3, Books 5–7,* trans. S. Douglas Olson, Loeb Classical Library 224 (Cambridge, MA: Harvard University Press, 2008), 6.270c.

84. Athenaeus, *The Learned Banqueters, Vol. 2,* 3.108f.

85. Ibid., 4.156a.

86. Athenaeus, *The Learned Banqueters, Vol. 4,* 10.411b.

87. Ibid., 10.412c.

88. Ibid., 10.412d.

89. Ibid., 10.412f.

90. Ibid., 10.413b.

91. Ibid., 10.413c.

92. Ibid., 10.413c-d.

93. Ibid., 10.413c.

94. Ibid., 10.415f.

95. Ibid., 10.415d.

96. Ibid., 10.416b.

97. Ibid., 10.417c.

98. Ibid., 10.418a.

99. Ibid., 10.418d.

100. Ibid., 10.417d.

101. Athenaeus, *The Learned Banqueters, Vol. 5, Books 10.420e-11,* trans. S. Douglas Olson, Loeb Classical Library 274 (Cambridge, MA: Harvard University Press, 2009), 10.420e-421c.

102. Ibid., 10.422a-b.

103. Athenaeus, *The Learned Banqueters, Vol. 4,* 10.419d.

104. Ibid., 10.420d.

105. Athenaeus, *The Learned Banqueters, Vol. 6, Books 12–13.594b,* trans. S. Douglas Olson, Loeb Classical Library 327 (Cambridge, MA: Harvard University Press, 2010), 12.549a.

106. Ibid.

107. Ibid., 12.549c.

108. Ibid., 12.549d.

109. Ibid., 12.551a.

110. Ibid., 12.551d-f.

111. Dorothy Thompson, "Athenaeus in his Egyptian Context," in *Athenaeus and His World: Reading Greek Culture in the Roman Empire,* ed. David Braund and John Wilkins (Exeter, UK: University of Exeter Press, 2000), 83.

112. Ibid.

CHAPTER 5

1. Philo, "On the Special Laws, Book 1," in *Philo, Vol. 7: On the Decalogue. On the Special Laws, Books 1–3,* trans. F. H. Colson, Loeb Classical Library 320 (Cambridge, MA: Harvard University Press, 1937), 35.174.

2. Clement, *Christ, the Educator (The Paidagogos),* trans. Simon P. Wood, Fathers of the Church, A New Translation 23 (Washington, DC: Catholic University of America Press, 1954), 95.

3. Homer, *The Odyssey of Homer,* trans. Alan Mandelbaum (Berkeley: University of California Press, 1990), 9.96.

4. Samuel Sandmel, *Philo of Alexandria: An Introduction* (New York: Oxford University Press, 1979), 6.

5. Ibid., 15.

6. Ibid., 14.

7. James N. Rhodes, "Diet and Desire: The Logic of the Dietary Laws According to Philo," *Ephemerides Theologicae Lovanienses* 79, no. 1 (2003): 123.

8. Philo, "On the Special Laws, Book 4," in *Philo, Vol. 8: On the Special Laws, Book 4. On the Virtues. On Rewards and Punishments,* trans. F. H. Colson, Loeb Classical Library 341 (Cambridge, MA: Harvard University Press, 1939), 14.80.

9. Ibid., 14.81.

10. Ibid., 14.82.

11. Ibid., 14.83.

12. Ibid., 15.84.

13. Ibid., 15.92.

14. Ibid., 15.94.

15. Ibid., 16.99.

16. Ibid., 17.100.

17. Philo, "Special Laws, Book 1," 145–47.

18. Philo, "Special Laws, Book 1," 29.148; Plato, *Timaeus,* 70e.

19. Philo, "Special Laws, Book 1," 29.150.

20. Philo, "Special Laws, Book 4," 17.100.

21. Ibid., 17.102.

22. Ibid., 23.122.

23. Ibid., 24.124.

24. *Blue Letter Bible.* "Dictionary and Word Search for Na'amah (Strong's 5279)." *Blue Letter Bible. 1996–2011,* http://www.blueletterbible.org/lang/lexicon/lexicon. cfm?Strongs=H05279&t=KJV (accessed March 6, 2007).

25. Philo, "On the Posterity and Exile of Cain," in *Philo: Vol. 2: On the Cherubim. On Abel and the Sacrifices Offered by Him and by Cain. That the Worse is Wont to Attack the Better. On the Posterity of Cain and His Exile. On the Giants,* trans. F. H. Colson and G. H. Whitaker, Loeb Classical Library 227 (Cambridge, MA: Harvard University Press, 1929), 35.120.

26. Philo, "Exile of Cain," 35.122–123; Richard Hecht, "Patterns of Exegesis in Philo's Interpretation of Leviticus," *Studia Philonica* 6 (1979): 102.

27. Philo, "Exile of Cain," 35.123.

28. Ibid.

29. Philo, "On the Creation," in *Philo, Vol. 1: On the Creation. Allegorical Interpretation of Genesis 2 and 3,* trans. F. H. Colson and G. H. Whitaker, Loeb Classical Library 226 (Cambridge, MA: Harvard University Press, 1929), 56.157.

30. Ibid., 56.158.

31. Ibid., 59.165.

32. Ibid.

33. Ibid.

34. Ibid.

35. Ibid., 56.158.

36. Clement, *Christ, the Educator,* vi.

37. David T. Runia, "Philo of Alexandria and the Beginnings of Christian Thought," *Studia Philonica Annual* 7 (1995): 151.

38. Peter Brown, *The Body and Society: Men, Women, and Sexual Renunciation in Early Christianity,* Lectures on the History of Religions new ser., no. 13 (New York: Columbia University Press, 1988), 126.

39. Eric Francis Osborn, *Clement of Alexandria* (Cambridge: Cambridge University Press, 2005), 5.

40. John Ferguson, *Clement of Alexandria* (New York: Twayne Publishers, 1974), 68.

41. Clement of Alexandria, *Christ, the Educator,* 4.

42. Ibid., 93.

43. Veronika Grimm, *From Feasting to Fasting, the Evolution of a Sin: Attitudes to Food in Late Antiquity* (London: Routledge, 1996), 112.

44. Clement, *Christ, the Educator,* 93.

45. Ibid., 94.

46. Ibid.

47. Ibid.

48. Ibid.

49. Ibid.

50. Ibid., 101.

51. Ibid.

52. Ibid., 102.

53. Ibid., 94.

54. Ibid.

55. Ibid., 95.

56. Ibid.

57. Ibid.

58. Ibid., 98.

59. Ibid.

60. Ibid.

61. Ibid., 94.

62. Ibid.

63. Grimm, *From Feasting to Fasting,* 45–46.

64. Clement, *Christ, the Educator,* 100.

65. Ibid., 101.

66. Ibid., 103.

67. Ibid., 106.

68. Ibid.

69. Ibid., 101.

70. J.N.D. Kelly, *Golden Mouth: The Story of John Chrysostom—Ascetic, Preacher, Bishop* (Ithaca, NY: Cornell University Press, 1995), 3.

71. Ibid., 1–2.

72. Chrysostom Baur, "St. John Chrysostom," in *The Catholic Encyclopedia,* vol. 8 (Robert Appleton Co.), http://www.newadvent.org/cathen/08452b.htm (accessed August 31, 2010).

73. Jaclyn L. Maxwell, *Christianization and Communication in Late Antiquity: John Chrysostom and his Congregation in Antioch* (Cambridge: Cambridge University Press, 2006), 65.

74. Kelly, *Golden Mouth,* 52.

75. Maxwell, *Christianization and Communication in Late Antiquity,* 91.

76. John Chrysostom, "Homily 13 on Philippians," in *Nicene and Post-Nicene Fathers,* ed. Philip Schaff and Kevin Knight, trans. John Broadus, vol. 13, First (Buffalo, NY: Christian Literature Publishing Co., 1889), http://www.newadvent.org/fathers/230213.htm (accessed September 2, 2010); Chrysostom's version of Phil. 3:18–20 is quoted at the beginning of this sermon.

77. Ibid.

78. Ibid.

79. Ibid.

80. John Chrysostom, "Homily 16 on the Acts of the Apostles," in *Nicene and Post-Nicene Fathers,* ed. Philip Schaff and Kevin Knight, trans. J Walker, J. Sheppard, and H. Brown, first series, vol. 11 (Buffalo, NY: Christian Literature Publishing Co., 1889), http://www.newadvent.org/fathers/210116.htm (accessed September 2, 2010).

81. John Chrysostom, "Homily 27 on the Acts of the Apostles," in *Nicene and Post-Nicene Fathers,* ed. Philip Schaff and Kevin Knight, trans. J Walker, J. Sheppard, and H. Brown, vol. 11, First (Buffalo, NY: Christian Literature Publishing Co., 1889), http://www.newadvent.org/fathers/210127.htm (accessed September 2, 2010).

82. Ibid.

83. Ibid.

84. John Chrysostom, "Homily 17 on First Corinthians," in *Nicene and Post-Nicene Fathers,* ed. Philip Schaff and Kevin Knight, trans. Talbot W. Chambers, first series, vol. 12 (Buffalo, NY: Christian Literature Publishing Co., 1889), http://www.newadvent.org/fathers/220117.htm (accessed September 2, 2010).

85. Ibid.

86. Ibid.

87. Ibid.

88. Ibid.

89. Ibid.

90. Teresa M Shaw, *The Burden of the Flesh: Fasting and Sexuality in Early Christianity* (Minneapolis, MN: Fortress Press, 1998), 133.

91. John Chrysostom, "Homily 13 on First Timothy," in *Nicene and Post-Nicene Fathers,* ed. Philip Schaff and Kevin Knight, trans. Philip Schaff, first series, vol. 13 (Buffalo, NY: Christian Literature Publishing Co., 1889), http://www.newadvent.org/fathers/230613.htm (accessed September 2, 2010).

92. Ibid.

93. John Chrysostom, "Homily 27 on the Acts of the Apostles."

94. Ibid.

95. Ibid.

96. Ibid.

97. Ibid.

CHAPTER 6

1. John Cassian, *The Institutes,* Ancient Christian Writers no. 58, (New York: Newman Press, 2000), 5:23.

2. John Bossy, "Moral Arithmetic: Seven Sins into Ten Commandments," in *Conscience and Casuistry in Early Modern Europe,* ed. Edmund Leites (Cambridge: Cambridge University Press; Paris: Editions de la Maison des sciences de l'homme, 1988), 214–34.

3. See Siegfried Wenzel, "The Seven Deadly Sins: Some Problems of Research," *Speculum* 43, no. 1 (January 1968): 1–22.

4. Morton W Bloomfield, *The Seven Deadly Sins; an Introduction to the History of a Religious Concept, with Special Reference to Medieval English Literature* (East Lansing: Michigan State College Press, 1952), 43.

5. Joseph Delany, "Vice," in *The Catholic Encyclopedia*, vol. 15 (New York: Robert Appleton Co., 1912), http://www.newadvent.org/cathen/15403c.htm (accessed September 23, 2010).

6. St. Thomas Aquinas, *Summa Theologiae. Latin Text and English Translation, Introductions, Notes, Appendices, and Glossaries*, vol. 26 (Cambridge and New York: Blackfriars and McGraw Hill, 1964), Ia2ae. 84.3.

7. St. Thomas Aquinas, *Summa Theologiae. Latin Text and English Translation, Introductions, Notes, Appendices, and Glossaries*, vol. 43 (Cambridge and New York: Blackfriars and McGraw Hill, 1964), 2a2ae. 148,1.

8. Ibid., 43:2a2ae. 148.2.

9. Ibid., 43:43:2a2ae. 148.3.

10. Ibid., 43:2a2ae. 148.4.

11. Ibid., 43:2a2ae. 148.1.

12. Bloomfield, *The Seven Deadly Sins*, 97–99.

13. See Richard Newhauser, *The Treatise on Vices and Virtues in Latin and the Vernacular*, Typologie des sources du Moyen Age occidental fasc. 68 (Turnhout, Belgium: Brepols, 1993), which includes an extensive bibliography of such texts.

14. Bloomfield, *The Seven Deadly Sins*, 191.

15. John Eudes Bamberger, "Introduction to Evagrius of Pontus, *The Praktikos*," in *The Praktikos. Chapters on Prayer*, Cistercian studies series no. 4 (Spencer, MA: Cistercian Publications, 1970), xxxv–xliii.

16. Robert E. Sinkewicz, "Introduction," in *Evagrius of Ponticus, The Greek Ascetic Corpus*, trans. Sienkewicz (Oxford: Oxford University Press, 2006), xxi.

17. Columba Stewart, "Evagrius Ponticus and the 'Eight Generic Logismoi'," in *In the Garden of Evil: the Vices and Culture in the Middle Ages*, ed. Richard Newhauser, Papers in Mediaeval Studies 18 (Toronto, ON: Pontifical Institute of Mediaeval Studies, 2005), 5.

18. Bamberger, "Introduction to Evagrius," lxviii.

19. Stewart, "Evagrius Ponticus and the 'Eight Generic Logismoi'," 5.

20. Newhauser, *The Treatise on Vices and Virtues*, 181.

21. Evagrius of Pontus, "To Eulogios. On the Confession of Thoughts and Counsel in Their Regard," in *The Greek Ascetic Corpus*, trans. Robert E. Sinkewicz (Oxford: Oxford University Press, 2006), 38.

22. Bamberger, "Introduction to Evagrius," lxix–lxx.

23. Evagrius of Pontus, "On the Eight Thoughts," in *The Greek Ascetic Corpus*, trans. Robert E. Sinkewicz (Oxford: Oxford University Press, 2006), 74.

24. Ibid., 74, 73.

25. Ibid., 73.

26. Ibid., 76.

27. Ibid., 74.

28. Ibid.

29. Ibid., 75.

30. Ibid.

31. Evagrius of Pontus, "The Foundations of the Monastic Life: A Presentation on the Practice of Stillness," in *The Greek Ascetic Corpus*, trans. Robert E. Sienkewicz (Oxford: Oxford University Press, 2006), 5.

32. Ibid.

33. Ibid.

34. Ibid., 8.

35. Ibid.

36. Evagrius of Pontus, "The Monk: A Treatise on the Practical Life (The Praktikos)," in *The Greek Ascetic Corpus*, trans. Robert E. Sinkewicz (Oxford: Oxford University Press, 2006), 98.

37. Ibid., 250n17.

38. Evagrius of Pontus, "On the Vices as Opposed to the Virtues," in *The Greek Ascetic Corpus,* trans. Robert E. Sinkewicz (Oxford: Oxford University Press, 2006), 62.

39. Ibid.

40. Ibid.

41. Ibid.

42. Evagrius of Pontus, "Praktikos," 101; alternative translation in Bamberger, *The Praktikos,* 21.

43. Evagrius of Pontus, "On the Vices," 62.

44. Ibid.

45. Robert E. Sinkewicz, "Introduction to 'On Thoughts'," in *The Greek Ascetic Corpus,* trans. Sienkewicz (Oxford: Oxford University Press, 2006), 138.

46. Evagrius of Pontus, "On Thoughts," in *The Greek Ascetic Corpus,* trans. Robert E. Sinkewicz (Oxford: Oxford University Press, 2006), 153.

47. Ibid.

48. Ibid., 154.

49. Ibid., 153–54.

50. Ibid., 177–88.

51. Columba Stewart, *Cassian the Monk,* Oxford Studies in Historical Theology (New York: Oxford University Press, 1998), 11.

52. Boniface Ramsey, "Introduction to John Cassian: The Institutes," in *The Institutes,* Ancient Christian Writers no. 58 (New York: Newman Press, 2000), 3.

53. Owen Chadwick, *John Cassian,* 2nd ed. (Cambridge: Cambridge University Press, 1958), 16.

54. Chadwick, *John Cassian,* 32–33; Stewart, *Cassian the Monk,* 14.

55. Cassian, *The Institutes,* Preface.7.

56. Ibid., Preface.8.

57. Ibid., 5.1.

58. Ibid., 5.2.

59. Ibid.

60. Stewart, *Cassian the Monk,* 42–48, offers an in-depth discussion of Cassian's understanding of purity.

61. Ibid., 72.

62. Ibid.

63. Cassian, *The Institutes,* 5.5.

64. Ibid.

65. Ibid., 5.7.

66. Ibid.

67. Ibid., 5.9.

68. Ibid.

69. Ibid., 5.11.

70. Ibid., 12.1.

71. Ibid., 5.14.

72. Ibid.

73. Ibid., 5.16.

74. Carole Straw, "Gregory, Cassian and the Cardinal Vices," in *In the Garden of Evil: The Vices and Culture in the Middle Ages,* ed. Richard Newhauser, Papers in Mediaeval Studies 18 (Toronto, ON: Pontifical Institute of Mediaeval Studies, 2005), 40.

75. Cassian, *The Institutes,* 5.21.

76. Ibid.

77. Ibid.

78. Ibid., 5.23.

79. Ibid.

80. John Cassian, *The Conferences*, trans. Boniface Ramsey, Ancient Christian Writers no. 57 (New York: Paulist Press, 1997), 5.11.

81. Cassian, *The Institutes*, 5.23.

82. Ibid.

83. Cassian, *The Conferences*, 5.11.

84. Cassian, *The Institutes*, 5.23.

85. Ibid.

86. Cassian, *The Conferences*, 5.11.

87. Cassian, *The Institutes*, 5.23.

88. Ibid., 5.24.

89. Lauren Pristas, "The Unity of Composition in Book V of Cassian's De Institutis," in *Studia Patristica, vol. 25*, ed. E. A. Livingstone (Leuven, Belgium: Peeters Publishers, 1993), 442–43.

90. Jeffrey Richards, *Consul of God: The Life and Times of Gregory the Great* (London: Routledge & Kegan Paul, 1980), 4.

91. Ibid., 26.

92. Ibid., 32.

93. Ibid., 42.

94. Carole Ellen Straw, *Gregory the Great: Perfection in Imperfection*, Transformation of the Classical Heritage 14 (Berkeley: University of California Press, 1988), 45.

95. Ibid., 25.

96. Ibid., 61.

97. Ibid., 62–63.

98. Straw, "Gregory, Cassian and the Cardinal Vices," 48.

99. Ibid., 54–55.

100. Gregory the Great, *Morals on the Book of Job*, trans. John Henry Parker and J. Rivington (Oxford: Oxford University Press, 1844), 31.45.87.

101. Ibid., 31.45.89.

102. Ibid.

103. Ibid.

104. Straw, "Gregory, Cassian and the Cardinal Vices," 47.

105. Newhauser, *The Treatise on Vices and Virtues*, 188.

106. Gregory the Great, *Morals on the Book of Job*, 30.17.56.

107. Ibid., 30.17.58.

108. Ibid.

109. Ibid., 30.18.60.

110. Ibid.

111. Ibid.

112. Geoffrey Chaucer, "The Parson's Tale," in *The Riverside Chaucer*, ed. Larry Dean Benson, 3rd ed. (Boston: Houghton Mifflin, 1987), 10.1.815–830.

113. Gregory the Great, *Morals on the Book of Job*, 31.45.90.

114. Ibid.

115. Ibid.

116. Ibid., 30.18.63.

117. Ibid.

118. Ibid., 31.53.107.

EPILOGUE

1. Arthur Brandeis, ed., *Jacob's Well, an English Treatise on the Cleansing of Man's Conscience* (London: Pub. for the Early English Text Society, by K. Paul, Trench, Trübner & Co., Ltd, 1900), 141. All translations of the Middle English text are my own.

2. Arthur Brandeis, "Preface to *Jacob's Well*," in *Jacob's Well, an English Treatise on the Cleansing of Man's Conscience* (London: Pub. for the Early English Text Society, by K. Paul, Trench, Trübner & Co., Ltd, 1900), vi.

3. Ibid.

4. *Jacob's Well,* 142.

5. Ibid., 142–43.

6. Ibid., 141.

7. Ibid., 145.

8. Ibid., 147.

9. Ibid., 143.

10. Ken Albala, "Weight Loss in the Age of Reason," in *Cultures of the Abdomen: Diet Digestion and Fat in the Modern World,* ed. Christopher Forth and Ana Carden-Coyne (New York: Palgrave Macmillan, 2005), 169.

11. Ibid., 169–71.

Further Reading

INTRODUCTION

Albala, Ken. "Weight Loss in the Age of Reason." In *Cultures of the Abdomen: Diet, Digestion, and Fat in the Modern World,* edited by Christopher Forth and Ana Carden-Coyne. New York: Palgrave Macmillan, 2005, 169–183. Food scholar Albala discusses the shift in perspective on gluttony from the ancient world to the modern world in this article.

Beck, Margaret. "Female Figurines in the European Upper Paleolithic: Politics and Bias in Archaeological Interpretation." In *Reading the Body: Representations and Remains in the Archaeological Record,* edited by Alison E. Rautman, 202–14. Philadelphia: University of Pennsylvania Press, 2000. A helpful overview of scholarship relating to ancient female figurines.

Beller, Anne Scott. *Fat and Thin: A Natural History of Obesity.* New York: Farrar, Straus and Giroux, 1977. Good analysis of evidence pertaining to the history of the fat body.

Bordo, Susan. *Unbearable Weight: Feminism, Western Culture, and the Body.* Berkeley: University of California Press, 1993. Classic feminist reading of the politics of the female body in the contemporary world.

Campos, Paul. *The Obesity Myth: Why America's Obsession with Weight Is Hazardous to Your Health.* New York: Penguin Books, 2004. Full of data pertaining to the history of the "obesity epidemic," this book explores the politics and economics of being fat in the United States.

Foucault, Michel. *The Use of Pleasure.* Translated by Robert Hurley. Vol. 2. 1st ed. *The History of Sexuality.* New York: Pantheon Books, 1978. Foucault's work on the history of sexuality has set the parameters of sexuality studies.

Gimbutas, Marija. *The Language of the Goddess.* New York: HarperCollins, 1991. Classic work on the idea of prehistoric goddess worship.

Guthrie, R. Dale. *The Nature of Paleolithic Art.* Chicago: University of Chicago Press, 2005. Guthrie discusses possible biological and sociological aspects of ancient fat figurines.

LeBesco, Kathleen. *Revolting Bodies?: The Struggle to Redefine Fat Identity.* Amherst: University of Massachusetts Press, 2004. One of the first books to articulate the need for examining the meaning of the fat body in the contemporary world. LeBesco also discusses the feminist and fat studies politics of ancient fat figurines.

Malone, Caroline, Anthony Bonanno, Tancred Gouder, Simon Stoddart, and David Trump. "The Death Cults of Prehistoric Malta." *Scientific American Special:*

Mysteries of the Ancient Ones, 2005. Great assessment of archaeological find-
ings in Malta that are beginning to yield ancient evidence of the meaning of
fat bodies.

Miller, William Ian. "Gluttony." *Representations*, no. 60 (Autumn 1997): 92–112. An excellent, sweeping overview of the history and meaning of gluttony.

Oliver, J. Eric. "The Politics of Pathology: How Obesity Became an Epidemic Disease."
Perspectives in Biology and Medicine 49, no. 4 (2006): 611–27. This article summarizes the medical and political history of the "obesity epidemic."

Popenoe, Rebecca. *Feeding Desire: Fatness, Beauty and Sexuality among a Saharan
People.* New York: Routledge, 2003. Excellent anthropological study of the role of
the fat body in an African tribal culture.

Robins, Gay. *The Art of Ancient Egypt.* Cambridge, MA Harvard University Press, 1997.
Discussion of the Egyptian god Hapy.

Rothblum, Esther, and Sondra Solovay, eds. *The Fat Studies Reader.* New York: New
York University Press, 2009. The first collection of articles that addresses the field
of Fat Studies.

Tringham, Ruth, and Margaret Conkey. "Rethinking Figurines: A Critical View from
Archaeology of Gimbutas, the 'Goddess' and Popular Culture." In *Ancient Goddesses: The Myths and the Evidence,* edited by Lucy Goodison and Christine Morris. Madison: University of Wisconsin Press, 1999. A critical analysis of Gimbutas's
view of ancient fat female figurines.

CHAPTER 1

Abingdon Press. *The New Interpreter's Bible, Volume 1: General and Old Testament
Articles; Genesis; Exodus; Leviticus.* 12 vols. Nashville, TN: Abingdon Press, 1994.
Excellent series of biblical commentary.

Bellefontaine, Elizabeth. "Deuteronomy 21:18–21: Reviewing the Case of the Rebellious Son." *Journal for the Study of the Old Testament* 4, no. 13 (1979): 13–31. Well-
argued article about the rebellious son in Deuteronomy.

Douglas, Mary. *Leviticus as Literature.* Oxford: Oxford University Press, 1999. Thought-
ful and provocative anthropological analysis of the book of Leviticus.

Douglas, Mary. *Purity and Danger: An Analysis of Concepts of Pollution and Taboo;
with a new preface by the author.* Routledge Classics. London: Routledge & Kegan
Paul, 1966; London: Routledge, 2007. Classic and influential examination of the
cultural construction of order and chaos, purity and dirt.

Eilberg-Schwartz, Howard. *The Savage in Judaism: An Anthropology of Israelite Religion and Ancient Judaism.* Bloomington: Indiana University Press, 1990. Useful
exploration of ancient Jewish culture, using Douglas's ideas.

Karris, Robert J. *Luke: Artist and Theologian: Luke's Passion Account As Literature.*
Mahwah, NJ: Paulist Press, 1985. Many of Karris's books, including this one, focus
on food practices in the New Testament.

Sandnes, Karl Olav. *Belly and Body in the Pauline Epistles.* Cambridge: Cambridge
University Press, 2002. Wide-ranging account of the symbolism of the belly in
the ancient world.

CHAPTER 2

Allen, Christine Garside. "Plato on Women." *Feminist Studies* 2, no. 2/3 (January 1,
1975): 131–38. An excellent article on Plato's varying views of women in the *Republic* and the *Timaeus.*

Lloyd, G.E.R. "The Hot and the Cold, the Dry and the Wet in Greek Philosophy." *The Journal of Hellenic Studies* 84 (1964): 92–106. Lucid account of the wide variety of humoral theories in Greek thought.

Russell, Daniel C. *Plato on Pleasure and the Good Life.* Oxford: Clarendon Press, 2005. Fascinating philosophical study on Plato's ideas regarding pleasure.

Steel, Carlos. "The Moral Purpose of the Human Body: A Reading of 'Timaeus' 69–72." *Phronesis* 46, no. 2 (May 2001): 105–28. One of a few good articles to examine the role of the physical body in Plato's thought.

Young, Charles M. "Aristotle on Temperance." *The Philosophical Review* 97, no. 4 (October 1988): 521–42. Clear account of Aristotle's understanding of pleasure and excess.

CHAPTER 3

Evans, Elizabeth Cornelia. *Physiognomics in the Ancient World.* Transactions of the American Philosophical Society 59, pt. 5. Philadelphia: American Philosophical Society, 1969. A thorough study of ancient physiognomy.

Gilman, Sander L. *Fat Boys: A Slim Book.* Lincoln: University of Nebraska Press, 2004. This book focuses on the idea of the fat male body in Western literature. All of Gilman's books on the fat body are worth reading.

King, Helen. *Greek and Roman Medicine.* Classical World Series. London: Bristol Classical Press, 2001.

King, Helen, ed. *Health in Antiquity.* London: Routledge, 2005. King's books provide excellent insight into Greek and Roman medicine.

Schwartz, Hillel. *Never Satisfied: A Cultural History of Diets, Fantasies, and Fat.* New York: Free Press, 1986. For a more contemporary look at the history of the fat body, Schwartz's book is worth reading.

Swain, Simon, ed. *Seeing the Face, Seeing the Soul: Polemon's Physiognomy from Classical Antiquity to Medieval Islam.* Oxford: Oxford University Press, 2007. A comprehensive set of translations and commentaries on ancient physiognomic texts.

CHAPTER 4

Braund, David, and John Wilkins, eds. *Athenaeus and His World: Reading Greek Culture in the Roman Empire.* Exeter, UK: University of Exeter Press, 2000. The only extensive collection of essays on Athenaeus's work.

Corbett, Philip B. *Petronius.* New York: Twayne Publishers, 1970. A solid introduction to Petronius.

Galinsky, Karl. *The Herakles Theme: The Adaptations of the Hero in Literature from Homer to the Twentieth Century.* Totowa, NJ: Rowman and Littlefield, 1972. Slightly dated but still excellent work on Herakles.

Gantz, Timothy. *Early Greek Myth: A Guide to Literary and Artistic Sources.* 2 vols. Baltimore, MD: Johns Hopkins University Press, 1996. A comprehensive guide to the sources of Greek myth.

Gowers, Emily. *The Loaded Table: Representations of Food in Roman Literature.* Oxford: Clarendon Press, 1993. Excellent analysis of the role of food in Roman literature.

Loraux, Nicole. "Herakles: The Super-Male and the Feminine." In *Before Sexuality: The Construction of Erotic Experience in the Ancient Greek World,* edited by David M. Halperin, John J. Winkler, and Froma I. Zeitlin. Princeton, NJ: Princeton University Press, 1990. An excellent essay in a first-rate collection of essays on sexuality, gender, and eroticism in the ancient Greek world.

Padilla, Mark William. *The Myths of Herakles in Ancient Greece: Survey and Profile.* Lanham, MD: University Press of America, 1998. A good bibliographic study of Herakles's myths.

Wilkins, John. *The Boastful Chef: The Discourse of Food in Ancient Greek Comedy.* Oxford: Oxford University Press, 2000. A comprehensive analysis of food in Greek comedy.

CHAPTER 5

Brown, Peter. *The Body and Society: Men, Women, and Sexual Renunciation in Early Christianity.* Lectures on the History of Religions, new ser., no. 13. New York: Columbia University Press, 1988. Excellent study on the way early Christians understood the body and bodily practices.

Grimm, Veronika. *From Feasting to Fasting, the Evolution of a Sin: Attitudes to Food in Late Antiquity.* London: Routledge, 1996. Superb study of food practices in late antiquity, focusing primarily on fasting and asceticism.

Kelly, J.N.D. *Golden Mouth: The Story of John Chrysostom—Ascetic, Preacher, Bishop.* Ithaca, NY: Cornell University Press, 1995. Detailed examination of John Chrysostom's life and work.

Osborn, Eric Francis. *Clement of Alexandria.* Cambridge: Cambridge University Press, 2005. Comprehensive study of Clement's life and work.

Runia, David T. "Philo of Alexandria and the Beginnings of Christian Thought." *Studia Philonica Annual* 7 (1995): 143–60. Excellent summary of Philo's relationship to Christian thought. Runia's books and articles on Philo are top-notch.

Shaw, Teresa M. *The Burden of the Flesh: Fasting and Sexuality in Early Christianity.* Minneapolis, MN: Fortress Press, 1998. Thorough analysis of the relationship between fasting and sexuality in early Christianity. Includes an excellent chapter on Chrysostom and gluttony.

CHAPTER 6

Bloomfield, Morton W. *The Seven Deadly Sins; an Introduction to the History of a Religious Concept, with Special Reference to Medieval English Literature.* East Lansing: Michigan State College Press, 1952. Still important book about the origins of the seven deadly sins and their importance throughout the Middle Ages.

Bossy, John. "Moral Arithmetic: Seven Sins into Ten Commandments." In *Conscience and Casuistry in Early Modern Europe,* edited by Edmund Leites, 214–34. Cambridge: Cambridge University Press, 1988. Fascinating article on the historical circumstances that led to the move away from the seven deadly sins toward an emphasis on the Ten Commandments in Christianity.

Newhauser, Richard, ed. *In the Garden of Evil: The Vices and Culture in the Middle Ages.* Papers in Mediaeval Studies 18. Toronto, ON: Pontifical Institute of Mediaeval Studies, 2005. Excellent collection of essays on the idea of the vices in the Middle Ages.

Wenzel, Siegfried. "The Seven Deadly Sins: Some Problems of Research." *Speculum* 43, no. 1 (January 1968): 1–22. Important—and still relevant—article about the seven deadly sins.

Index

About the Author

SUSAN E. HILL is an associate professor of religion at the University of Northern Iowa in Cedar Falls, Iowa. Dr. Hill has published articles on pedagogy, the art of translation, and the intersections between religious ideas and literary expression in the works of George Eliot and Willa Cather.